S0-AJN-402

THE SELF-PUBLISHING MANUAL

HOW TO WRITE, PRINT AND SELL
YOUR OWN BOOK

By Dan Poynter

THE SELF-PUBLISHING MANUAL

HOW TO WRITE, PRINT AND SELL
YOUR OWN BOOK

By Dan Poynter

Published by:

Parachuting Publications
Post Office Box 4232
Santa Barbara, CA 93103, U.S.A.

All rights reserved. No part of this book may be reproduced or transmitted in any form or by any means, electronic or mechanical, including photocopying, recording or by any information storage and retrieval system without written permission from the author, except for the inclusion of brief quotations in a review.

Books by the author

PARACHUTING MANUAL WITH LOG, *a basic training text.*
THE PARACHUTE MANUAL, *a technical treatise on the parachute.*
I/E COURSE, *a home study course for parachuting Instructor/Examiner candidates.*
HANG GLIDING MANUAL WITH LOG, *a basic training text.*
HANG GLIDING, *the basic handbook of skysurfing.*
MANNED KITING, *the basic handbook of tow launched hang gliding.*
HANDBUCH DES DRACHENFLIEGERS.
PARACHUTE RIGGING COURSE, *a course of study for the FAA senior rigger certificate.*
PARACHUTING, *the skydivers' handbook.*
FRISBEE PLAYERS' HANDBOOK.
MANUAL BASICO DE PARACAIDISMO.
FRISBEE *(Japanese Edition)*
THE SELF-PUBLISHING MANUAL. *How to write, print and sell your own book.*

Copyright © 1979 by Daniel F. Poynter
First Printing 1979
Second Printing 1980 Revised
Printed in the United States of America

Library of Congress Cataloging in Publication Data.
Poynter, Daniel F., 1938 -

The Self-Publishing Manual
How to Write, Print and Sell Your Own Book
Bibliography: p. Includes index.
1,   Publishers and publishing ---
      Handbooks, manuals, etc.
2,   Authorship -- Handbooks,
      manuals, etc. I. Title.
Z285.5.P69   658.8'09'070573   79-712
ISBN 0-915516-22-5 Hardcover
ISBN 0-915516-21-7 Paperback

ABOUT THE AUTHOR

Dan Poynter fell into publishing. He spent eight years researching a labor of love. Unable to interest a publisher or a bank in his manuscript, he went direct to a printer and "self-published." The book sold, the money poured in, he became an "instant expert." Fame and fortune were suddenly his; he was in demand.

In 1973, he became interested in a new aviation sport, couldn't find a book on the subject and sat down and wrote one. After four months of writing and intense research which took him from coast to coast, he delivered the manuscript to the printer. So far, it has sold over 125,000 copies; a "best seller!"

Continuing to write, he has produced twelve books and some have been translated into Spanish, French, Japanese, Russian, Romanian and German. Concentrating on aviation sports, Dan has become one of the most successful of the author/publishers. In fact, considering his volume, he is probably the world's largest one-person publishing company. In addition to his other work, he serves as a marketing consultant to the mail order and publishing industries. He operates this writing publishing empire from his hill-top estate overlooking the Pacific just up the coast from Santa Barbara, California.

Over the years, Dan has developed a system of writing which makes it all so easy and fun. He has been able to knock out several of his manuscripts in less than two weeks each. His books are loaded with facts and figures and contain detailed inside information. They are always up-to-date as he prints small quantities so they may be periodically revised.

As a one man show, an author/publisher who handles all the writing, publishing, and promotion himself, Dan is in the best position to advise a first time self-publishing author who is on a limited budget. He has sold over a quarter million books including several best sellers for over one and a half million dollars in sales. Many of his books sell at the rate of a steady 10,000 copies per year, every year.

Dan was prompted to write this book because so many of his friends, noting his success, approached him to publish their manuscripts. To Dan, writing has become easy because he has developed a system. Now he is revealing to you the secrets of writing, printing and selling your book . . . the good life of self-publishing.

ACKNOWLEDGMENT

Many people helped to make this manual possible. Some were inspirational and some provided valuable information while others supplied needed editorial talent. I am deeply indebted to: Lachlan MacDonald, Marilyn & Tom Ross, John Huenefeld, Virginia Wiley, Judyl Mudfoot, Jim Maynard, Dennis Stricker, Jim Wildman, Kathy Thompson, Peggy Blanchard, Len Fulton, Ellen Ferber, Michèle Gratton, Dennis Roeder, Maryann Murphy, Sasha Newborn, Albert Nussbaum, Jill LeVan, Judy Magee Dugan and Gary Bencar. My special thanks to Jan Venolia, author of "Write Right!", for editorial proofing.

I sincerely thank all these fine people and I know they are proud of the part they have played in the development of the self-publishing movement as well as their contribution to this work.

TABLE OF CONTENTS

This is a manual for the small publisher and the writer/self-publisher. Do not feel obligated to read this reference book from page one, it certainly wasn't written that way. You will probably want to read Chapter one for its introduction to self-publishing and the publishing industry and then Chapter two to learn how easy it is to research, write and illustrate your book. From there, you may wish to skip around. Use the list in the Table of Contents to help locate areas of particular interest.

This manual is your constant reference source for material on the writing, printing, publishing, marketing and distribution of books. Whether you have already published a book or would like to write and publish one soon, you will find this manual invaluable.

CHAPTER ONE

YOU, AN AUTHOR/PUBLISHER

YOUR SHORTCUT TO FAME AND FORTUNE

Everyone wants to "write a book." Most have the ability, some have the drive and few have the organization. Therefore, the greatest need is for a simple system, a "road map." The basic organizational plan in this book will not only provide direction, it will promote drive and expose ability no one thought existed.

Magazines devoted to men, business and sales are littered with full page ads featuring people with fabulous opportunity offers. Usually these people discovered a successful system of business in sales, real estate or mail order and, for a price, they are willing to let the reader in on their secret. To distribute this information, they have written a book. Upon close inspection, one often finds that the author is making more money from the book than he did at his revealed original enterprise. The irony is that the purchaser gets the wrong information; what he needs is a book on how to write a book.

Writing a book is easy! If you can voice an opinion and think logically, you can write a book. If you can *say* it, you can *write* it. The trick is to break a mammoth project down into little, bite-sized chunks. Most people have to work for a living and, therefore, can spend only a few minutes of each day on their book. Consequently, they can't keep the whole manuscript in their head. Being overwhelmed and confused, it is easy to quit the project. The solution is to break up the manuscript into many small easy-to-attack sections. Then concentrate on one at a time and do a good job on it.

Since poetry and fiction are very difficult to sell and, even when sold, have a short sales life, we will concern ourselves with nonfiction. Nonfiction doesn't require any great literary style, it is simply the sale of researched, reorganized, up-dated and, most important, repackaged information. Some of the recommendations here may be applied to fiction just as the chapters on publishing, promotion and the mail order business may be taken separately and used elsewhere. However, all are written toward and for the reader who wishes to become an author or an author/publisher of useful information.

People want to know "how-to" and "where-to" and they will pay well to find it. The information industry, the production and distribution of ideas and information as opposed to goods and services, now amounts to over one-half of the gross national product. There is money in it. To see how this market is being tapped by books, check the best seller lists in the back of *Publishers Weekly* noting especially the "Trade Paperback" section.

Your best sources for this saleable information are from your own experience plus research. Write what you know. Whether you already have a completed manuscript, have a great idea for one or need help in locating a suitable subject, this book will point the way.

> *"The No. 1 reason any professional writes is to pay the bills. This isn't the Lawn Tennis Association, where you play just for the thrill of it"* — Jimmy Breslin.

The prestige enjoyed by the published author is unparalleled in our society. A book can bring recognition, wealth and an acceleration in one's career. People have always held books in high regard, possibly because in past centuries they were very expensive and were, therefore, purchased only by the rich. Even a hundred years ago, many people could not read or write. To be an author then was to be an "educated" person.

Many enterprising people are using books to establish themselves in "the ultimate business." Usually starting with a series of non-paying magazine articles, they develop a name and make themselves visible. Then they expand the series of articles into a book. Now with their credibility established, they operate seminars in their field of expertise, command high speaking fees and issue a high-priced business advice newsletter. From there, they teach a course in the local junior college and become a consultant advising large corporations and commenting on legal briefs for lawyers. They find they are in great demand. People want their information or simply want them around. Clubs and corporations fly them in because it is cheaper than sending all their people to the expert.

This "dream product" is the packaging and marketing of information. Starting with a field you know, then researching it further and reducing it to paper will establish you as an expert. Then your expert standing can be pyramided with interviews, articles, T.V. appearances, talks at local clubs, etc. and most of this is done to promote your book sales. In turn, all this publicity not only sells books but opens more doors and produces more invitations leading to more opportunities to prove your expert status and make you more money. People seek experts whose opinions, advice and ideas are quoted in the media. Becoming an expert does not require a great education or a college degree. You can become one on a small particular area if you are willing to go to the library, read up on it and write down the important elements.

A book is like a new product design, similar to an invention but usually much, much better. A patent on a device or process runs only 17 years whereas, since the 1978 change in the law, a copyright runs for the author's life plus 50 years. Patents cost hundreds, usually thousands of dollars to secure and normally require a lot of legal help. By contrast, a copyright may be filed by the author with a simple form and $10; there is no waiting period. Once you write a book, it is yours, you have a monopoly and there is no direct competition.

The next secret is to cut out the middlemen by by-passing the commercial publishers to produce and sell the book yourself. You can take the author's royalty, the publisher's profit, the distributor's markup, the retailer's piece of the action, all of it because you are all of them. Now, in addition to achieving the wealth and prestige of a published author, you have propelled yourself into your own lucrative business: a publishing house. This shortcut not only makes more money (why share it?) it saves you the time and trouble required to sell your manuscript to a publisher. You know the subject and market better than some distant corporation anyway.

This doesn't mean purchasing a printing press to actually put the ink on the paper yourself. Some people feel this is the best part and enjoy the actual printing process but most would prefer to write and publish leaving the production to a printer.

In addition to the writing and publishing of your book, you will want to investigate its distribution. Today, more books are sold through the mail than through book stores. In fact, books are the leading mail order product. One-third of all these books are in the "how-to" category. Mail order is considered one of the best ways for the beginner with no previous business experience to start a venture of his own. Selling books by mail is a good, solid day-to-day business opportunity.

> *"People can be divided into three groups: those who make things happen, those who watch things happen and those who wonder what happened"* — John W. Newbern

Mail order is not only the simplest way to distribute books, it is an ideal way to build a second income and even build a fortune. You don't have to give up your job, there is little overhead, there are tax breaks, you work for yourself and it can be operated anywhere: you need only be near a Post Office. No one knows about your age, education, race or sex; your opportunities are indeed equal.

Mail order marketing is like fishing. You throw out a line by promoting your products and you find out almost immediately if you've made a sale. Everyday is like Christmas; opening envelopes and finding cheques is great fun.

Initially, you will warehouse your books in a closet and will slip them into padded bags for mailing. It is really quite easy and starting out is not expensive or time consuming.

Your writing/publishing/mail order company is actually combining three profitable fields and concentrating on only the best parts of each. A business of your own is the great American dream and it is still an attainable possibility. In your own business, you make the decisions to meet only those challenges you find interesting. This is not "goofing off," it is making more effective use of your time; "working smarter, not harder." After all, there are only 24 hours in a day and only one day at a time to each person. You have to concentrate on the good areas if you are to prosper.

Running your own enterprise will provide you with many satisfying advantages. You should earn more money because you are working for yourself rather than splitting your efforts with someone else. You have job security and never have to worry about a surprise pink slip. If you keep your regular job and "moonlight" your own enterprise as recreation, it will always be there as a fall back position should you need it. You start at the top, not the bottom, in your own company and you work at your own pace and schedule. You'll meet interesting people because as an author and publishing executive, they will seek you out.

You can work when and where you wish; you don't have to go to where the job is. You can work 'til dawn, sleep 'til noon, rush off to Hawaii without asking permission: this is flexibility not available to the clock punchers. Now, here is some background on the book publishing industry.

"PUBLISH" means to prepare and issue printed material for public distribution or sale or "to place before the public." It doesn't have to be beautiful, it doesn't even have to sell, it needs only to be issued. Saleability will depend upon the content and the packaging.

A "PUBLISHER" is the one who puts up the money, the one who takes the risk. He has the book printed and then distributes it hoping to make back more money than he has gambled. He may be a big New York firm or a first-time author but he is always the investor.

A "BOOK" by international standards is a publication with at least 49 pages not counting the covers. The U.S. Post Office will accept publications with 24 or more pages for "book rate" postage. Books should not be confused with pamphlets which have less than 49 pages, or periodicals. Magazines and newspapers are published regularly and usually carry advertising.

THE BOOK PUBLISHING INDUSTRY in the U.S. consists of nearly 6,000 firms by R.R. Bowker's count and they do not include the printers who are capable of manufacturing bound books. About 100 publishers are considered to be the big firms and most are located in New York City. Altogether, some 30,000 to 50,000 people are employed in book publishing in the U.S. Sales amount to nearly $5 billion per year for the some 40,000 new titles (33,000 brand new books and 10,000 new editions) and a half-million older "backlisted" titles offered. Even though nearly 40% of the titles are reprints of older books, the volume still amounts to about 100 brand new titles each day for every day the bookstores are open.

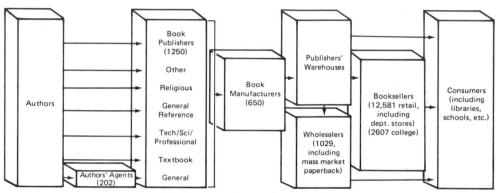

How books get from writer to reader.

CHOICE. An author who wishes to get into print has many choices. He may approach a large New York publisher or a smaller "alternative" publisher. He may work with an agent or deal with a "vanity" press. If he decides to self-publish, he may go to a book printer, a regular printer who can manufacture books or get his own press. If he chooses to go his own route, he will be one of the many tiny presses. As he expands his list of titles, he may graduate to the ranks of the alternative or small publisher. With drive and desire, he could, one day, even become a major conventional publisher. Now let's take a look at the choices.

THE BIG PUBLISHING FIRMS concentrate on books which anticipate audiences in the millions. Many houses have recently been absorbed by much larger soap and oil companies and are very sophisticated in their marketing. A look at the economics of big publishing will help us to better understand their motivations. It has been estimated that some 350,000 book length manuscripts are written each year but that only 40,000 go into print. Reading manuscripts takes an enormous amount of editorial time and a very high percentage are poorly written or do not fit the publisher's line; they are a waste of his time.

The bookstores don't have the space to display all of the 40,000 new titles published each year so they concentrate on the ones that move the best. Consequently, most pub-

"There's a vitality, a kind of frontier edge, to California publishing. It's an attitude toward life, something very fertile but very unpredictable. A little publishing house may surface with one or two books — how-to, self-help, pop psychology — and start a national trend" — Patricia Holt, western correspondent for *Publishers Weekly*.

lishers figure that even after selecting the best manuscripts and pouring in the promotion money, only three books of ten will sell well, four will break even and three will be losers.

Ever wonder why all the books in the store have very recent copyright dates? They are seldom more than a year old because the store turns them over so fast. Shelf space is expensive and in short supply. The books either sell or they go back. If one book doesn't move, it is replaced by another.

Most initial print runs are for 5,000 books. Then they remain "in print" (available for sale) for a year or so. If they sell out quickly, they are reprinted and the publisher dumps in more promotion money. If they don't catch on, they are pulled off the market and "remaindered" (sold off very cheap) to make room for new titles. The publisher has a business to run; there is overhead to consider and bills must be paid. The financial demands cause him to be terribly objective about his line. To many of them, in fact, a book is a book. If they already cover a subject, they won't be interested in a new one. They already serve that interest and don't care that yours might be better. Many big publishers are not interested in whether it is a good book, all they want to know is it will sell. Therefore, they concentrate on authors with good track records or Hollywood and political personalities who can move a book with their name. Only occasionally will they accept a well-written manuscript by an unknown and then it must be on a topic with a ready and massive audience. A published writer has a much better chance of selling than an unpublished one, regardless of the quality of the work. Large publishers usually must sell close to 10,000 copies in hardcover to break even. They hope to make their money on subsidiary rights for the paperback edition, book clubs, movie rights, etc. They spend several thousand dollars on promotion and often more than $50,000 on a blockbuster. This makes it tough on the small publisher with less volume who must compete on the basis of sales and can't afford large scale promotion.

Publishers, like most businesses, seem to follow the "80-20" principle. That is, they spend 80% of their effort on the top 20% of their books. The remaining 20% of the time goes to the bottom 80% of their line. Most books have to sell themselves to induce the publisher to dump in more money. There is a story about one author who sent her relatives around to bookstores to buy up every copy of her new book. The sudden spurt in sales excited the publisher who increased the ad budget. The increase in promotion produced greater sales and her book became a success.

The author will get a royalty of 5% to 15% usually on a sliding scale and the economics here are not encouraging. For example, a print run of 5,000 copies of a book selling for $6 will sell for $30,000 and 10% of this is $3,000. That isn't enough money to pay for all the time spent at the typewriter. The chances of selling more than 5,000 copies is highly remote because after a year or two, the publisher takes the book out of print.

If your manuscript is a blockbuster with potential sales in the millions, you may need a big publisher and they certainly want you. They will take care of all the printing and distributing and you can have your royalty cheques sent to you in Bimini. If it is a nonfiction book, they will ask you to furnish sales leads and, in any case, you will be expected to go on tour. You will wind up doing most of the promotion yourself while losing control over the program. When sales drop off, you will probably ask to buy the book and the remaining stock back from the publisher so you can pursue the marketing yourself. At this time you may also discover to your dismay that your contract provides that you must submit your next two manuscripts to this same publisher.

The big publishing houses provide a needed service but for many first-time authors they are unapproachable. Once in, the author doesn't get the best deal and getting out may be very difficult. To begin with, the publisher may sit on the manuscript for many months prior to rejecting it. Then if he does accept it, he will chop it up editorially and change the title; you lose artistic control of your book. The publisher's experts will change everything in the name of enhancing commercial appeal.

13

This might all be acceptable if the big commerical publishers were great financial sucesses. They aren't, or at least, they haven't been so far. One publishing house even admits it would have made more money last year if it had vacated its New York office and rented out the floor space.

The publishing industry attracts lovely creative people who find their rewards in its nonmaterial aspects. They come from tax-supported academic or library communities; they have never been marketing oriented. In fact, the editorial function in most publishing houses jealously guards its independence so it won't be "corrupted" by the marketing department. This leads them into the greatest trap in publishing: producing titles which "should be published" and they don't sell. The publishing houses call them "prestige" books and justify their production as a public service. Even the books which sell well are usually underpriced making their whole line a losing proposition.

Many of the people working in the big firms know this is wrong (or that losing money is wrong) and they are frustrated by it. But no matter how many seminars they attend or books they read, they can't emerge from their rut.

In the big firms, salaries are too low to attract highly motivated marketing people. Without better marketing, the companies can't afford to pay more. It is a vicious circle and only recently has there been an effort to reverse it.

The big soap and oil companies are moving in and have bought up many of the well known publishing houses. While they are introducing new, sophisticated marketing techniques, they tend to concentrate their efforts on the best selling books only. This leaves the first time author with an even smaller chance of getting into print. Submitting your manuscript to them is a waste of time, both yours and theirs.

But there is a brighter side for the small publisher who understands what the public wants to read. Since the old line big publishers don't pursue marketing and the new big ones concentrate on the top selling books only, there is a lot of room left for the smaller publishing house and self-publisher.

Be careful if you hang around with people from the book industry. Learn but don't let their ways rub off. Study the big New York publishing firms but don't copy them. You can do a lot better.

THE ALTERNATIVE PUBLISHERS or "small presses" are the smaller firms which specialize to serve certain minority interests such as specialized technical fields, particular geographic regions or their own personal interests. Many emerged from the antiestablishment movement of the sixties and their entry into publishing was made possible by the coincidental introduction of newer, simpler, cheaper (offset) printing methods. Some are very small while others are fairly large but most are specialized. Many people in the industry are attracted to the flexibility offered by small publishing. When their firm grows too large, they break off to form a new small firm. There are over 2000 small presses and because of their relatively low overhead, they can produce their books much cheaper (perhaps 1/10th the cost) than the big publishers.

However, while they may be closer to their market, they don't necessarily promote a title any harder than a big publisher. Most will agree that they are usually nice to deal with and provide good personal attention but they are faced with many of the same economic problems as the rest of the industry and don't always have the resources to combat them. To find a small press, consult Dustbook's *International Directory of Little Magazines and Small Presses.*

"Alternative publishing epitomizes the American Ideals of independence and initiative, of humane scale and free speech" — Richard Kostelanetz in *Publishers Weekly.*

14

THE "TINY PRESS" has been defined as those publishers who normally make press runs of 500 books or less. Often these are fiction, poetry or very specialized material.

CO-OP PUBLISHING HOUSES have been formed in many areas. Usually three to ten people join together to share the work of editing, design, layout, typesetting, compilation and financing. Often they contribute more labor than money to the publishing venture. A good article on this subject appeared in the August, 1978 edition of *Writer's Digest* magazine. For a list of co-op publishers, see the Appendix.

VANITY OR SUBSIDY PUBLISHERS produce some 6,000 titles each year. They offer regular publishing services, but the author invests the money. Under this arrangement, the author pays the full publishing (more than just printing bill) costs, receives 40% of the retail price of the books sold and 80% of the subsidiary rights, if sold. According to *The Wall Street Journal*, the cost is between $2,000 and $15,000 to get into print. Others say you can figure roughly on $25 per page. The vanity publisher claims he will furnish all the regular publishing services including promotion and distribution. All this might not be so bad if they had a good track record for delivery. But according to *Writer's Digest*, vanity published books rarely return one-quarter of the author's investment.

The point is that they often don't deliver the promotion they promised. It doesn't get done at all, and the author wonders why his book isn't selling.

The ads reading "To the author. . ." or "Manuscripts wanted by. . ." easily catch the eye of the writer with a book length manuscript. Vanity presses almost always accept a manuscript for publication and usually with a glowing review letter. They don't make any promises regarding sales and usually the book sells fewer than 100 copies. The vanity publisher doesn't have to sell any books because the author has already paid him for his work. He is interested in manufacturing the book, not in editing, promotion, sales or distribution.

Since binding is expensive, he often binds only a few hundred; the rest of the sheets remain unbound unless needed.

The "advertising" promised in the contract normally turns out to be only a "tombstone" ad listing many titles in the *New York Times*. Results are rare indeed.

The review copies sent to columnists usually go straight into the circular file. The reviewer's time is valuable and he doesn't like vanity presses because he knows that so little attention was paid to the editing of the book. Further, he realizes that there will be little promotional effort and that the book won't be in the stores.

Only a local bookstore might be persuaded to carry an author's vanity press book. The rest know there won't be any public demand for it.

The vanity publisher can get your book into print if this is all you want and they won't cut it all to pieces but, even then, they aren't the least expensive way to go. It would make more sense to contact a book printer or even a regular local printer who has the equipment to print books.

Before considering a vanity publisher, send for *Does it pay to pay to have it published* (Writer's Digest, 9933 Alliance Road, Cincinnati, OH 45242). From everything you read, it appears that no one likes vanity publishers. Some have been in trouble with the Federal Trade Commission (FTC) and at least one has been sued by a client author. But then, many tyro authors don't like any publishers at all. Reasoning that they must do most of the work anyway, they opt for self-publishing.

"Vanity publishing is to legitimate publishing as loansharking is to banking" — Martin J. Baron

OTHER PUBLISHING CHOICES. Textbook publishers offer the author a royalty based on the net amount received by the publisher. University presses don't pay well because they accept manuscripts on the basis of merit, not sales potential. Contract books are those written for a company on a subject of their choice. For example, a mail order house might need a book on a particular subject to round out its line. Sponsored books are commissioned by a company. They are usually about the company and, in addition to their regular sale, may be used as a promotional tool.

LITERARY AGENTS provide publishers with a valuable service by screening out the bad manuscripts and most new material comes to big publishers through them. The agent has to serve the publisher well for if he submits a poor manuscript, the publisher will never give him another appointment. Therefore, agents like sure bets too, and are reluctant to even consider an unpublished writer. When they do, their fee is often higher than their normal commission of 10%.

For the author, they will make manuscript suggestions, negotiate the contract and try to sell the book to one of their many contacts. If your manuscript is a winner, it is wise to have professional management. If you deal with an agent, it is best to contract with one in New York; he will have closer contacts and can deal in person.

On the fringe, there are a number of "agents" who charge a "reading fee" and then pay students to read and critique the manuscript. They make their money on these fees, not from placing the manuscripts. For a list of reputable agents, write The Authors Guild, 234 W. 44th St., NYC, NY 10036.

SELF-PUBLISHING is where you bypass all the middlemen and deal directly with the printer and then handle your own marketing and distribution. You maintain complete control over your product. You have to invest your time as well as your money but the rewards are greater; you get it all.

Self-publishing is not new. In fact, it has solid early American roots; it is almost a tradition. Many authors have elected to go their own way after being turned down by regular publishers and many others have decided to go their own way from the beginning. Well-known self-publishers include Mark Twain, Zane Grey, Upton Sinclair, Carl Sandburg, James Joyce, D.H. Lawrence, Ezra Pound, Edgar Rice Burroughs, Stephen Crane, Mary Baker Eddy, George Bernard Shaw, Edgar Allen Poe, Rudyard Kipling, Henry David Thoreau, Walt Whitman and many, many more. These people were self-publishers though today the vanity presses claim they were "subsidy" published. Today's success stories are usually in the nonfiction how-to books.

There are some 5,500 of these very small author/publisher firms, many of them in California. Some are growing and some are withering, but practically all are hanging on. They are proving that a self-published book is not inferior to one marketed by a big New York firm. Some are very successful and some are making a lot of money.

Self-publishing is not difficult. In fact, it may even be easier than dealing with a publisher. The job of the publishing manager is not to perform every task, but to see that everything gets done. The self-publisher deals directly with his printer and handles as many of the editing, proofing, promotion, and distribution tasks as he can. What he can't do, he farms out. Therefore, self-publishing may take on many forms depending on the author's interests, assets and abilities. It allows you to concentrate on those areas you find most challenging.

> "Subsidy publishing is closer to trade publishing than it is to self-publishing" — Freda Morris.

Properly planned, there is little monetary risk in self-publishing. If you follow the plan, the only variable is the subject of the book. Poetry and fiction are difficult to sell but most nonfiction topics sell easily. In fact, many authors do it themselves because this method provides the best return on their labor in the long run. Because the big publisher only tries a book for a year or two and then lets sales dictate its fate: reprint or remainder, the first year is most important. The self-publisher, on the other hand, uses the first year to build a solid market for a future of sustained sales. While a big publisher may sell only 5,000 copies total, the self-publisher can usually count on 5,000 or more each year, year after year.

A self-published book has a better chance of success because it is under the control of someone who cares — the author. A book is a product of one's self. An analogy may be drawn with giving birth. The author naturally feels that his book is terrific and that it would sell better if only his publisher would dump in more promotion money. He is very protective about his book (ever try to tell a mother her child is ugly?). The publisher answers that he is not anxious to dump more money into a book that isn't selling. So, if the author self-publishes, he gains a better understanding for the arguments on both sides. It is his money and his choice.

Many self-publishers find that once they have proven their books with good sales, they are approached by the big publishing houses with offers to print a new edition. Some use self-publishing to break into the big time. Others keep on self-publishing, keeping the work and the money to themselves.

BOOK PRINTERS are those print shops which specialize in the manufacture of books. They are not regular publishers or vanity presses, they are simply specialty printers with book machinery. Many of them advertise in magazines like *Writer's Digest*, and every self-publisher should compare their quote with that of the local printers. Incidentally, some of them have an interesting sales tool: a book on how to self-publish. Of course, they strongly recommend their own press. Some of the others are running seminars for the same purpose: to make contact with potential clients.

The chapters which follow describe in detail an alternative route to traditional publishing. They will enable you to get your name into print at minimum cost. There is no reason why you shouldn't gain great fame and considerable financial reward.

This book could be your "second chance." It will show you the way to wealth and prestige you never thought possible. Even if you just want the satisfaction of being published and are not interested in, or do not require, the extra income, this book will lead the way.

Obviously your success cannot be guaranteed but many people are doing very well in the writing/publishing business. This isn't a pipe dream, there is work involved. While you are working for yourself, at your own pace, it is still work. You won't get rich overnight. Building a sound business venture takes several years.

The secret is to invest your labor. Your time is more precious than gold. There is a finite quantity; you have only 24 hours of it each day. You may use your time in several ways: you may throw it away, sell it or invest it. You can waste your valuable time in front of the television set; it is easy to "lose." Most people punch in at the clock, go to work and get a cheque. They trade their labor for money on a one-for-one basis. If you don't punch in, you don't get paid. How much better it is to spend your time on a book which will sell and generate income while you are away doing something else. Your labor becomes an investment which pays dividends for years while you are playing or working on another investment.

Dan's first book took eight years to produce. He worked on this labor of love without guidance or direction. The huge, steady selling manual became the base for his publishing company. His second book was a study guide for an obscure rating; it sold better than expected.

In 1973, he became interested in the new sport of hang gliding. Unable to find any information at the library, he wrote the first book on it. He foresaw a trend and cashed in on it: it has sold 125,000 copies and is still going strong. Total writing time: two months.

By this time, he had developed a writing formula. His fourth book took less than 30 days from conception and decision until he delivered the manuscript to the printer. And most of this time was used in waiting for answers to his many letters requesting information. The first draft took only five days.

From there he concentrated on several high-priced, low-cost course pamphlets, turning out most within a week. His ninth book took all of two weeks to first-draft and it was typed "clean." Very few editing changes had to be made to the original copy and he even used different type styles in his IBM Selectric typewriter to indicate those he wanted in the book.

Writing a book is easy if you know the formula. Now Dan will reveal his system to you.

CHAPTER TWO

WRITING YOUR BOOK

HOW TO GENERATE SALEABLE MATERIAL

Where are your talents and what do you want to do? Do you enjoy writing or do you want to be a published author without the "pain" of writing? Analyze yourself. Do you want to write, print or sell books, any combination or even all three? Here we will cover all three to help you make an educated choice. We will discuss both sides of publishing: as seen by the author and as seen by the publisher.

Now, to obtain the written copy you have the choice of obtaining it from others or writing it yourself. In this chapter, we will discuss the many possibilities. Not all of them will be right for you but only one has to be. If one "clicks," you are on your way. This discussion of both sides of publishing will provide you with the whole picture. First we'll cover obtaining material from others and then we'll show you how to write it yourself.

Many of the big name book houses approach publishing from a hard-nosed marketing position. They know what they've been able to sell in the past and they stay in their field of expertise often by assigning writers to produce more of these "commissioned books." Once you have decided on an area of concentration, you too may approach others to write for you by paying cash outright or using modest royalty advances as an inducement. Flat fees are often around $2,500, half on assignment and half on acceptance. They are often wrapped up in less than sixty days by moonlighting advertising copywriters. One advantage of this approach is that you aren't deluged with manuscripts, many of which are outside your area of interest. By encouraging others to work on your ideas, you'll keep your editorial strategy on course.

Another source of material is the traditional one of author submissions. Letting them know your editorial interest area will slow the flow of inappropriate material.

Of course, you can always wait for manuscripts in your interest area to come to you but you'll save time and a lot of useless copy reading by issuing one-paragraph outlines of books you need to round out your list. Most publishers will not waste their time reading an unsolicited manuscript; they are interested only in outlines of the proposed book and biography of the author. They want to be sure they can use the material and that the author knows what he is writing about before investing their valuable time in manuscript reading.

If you are concentrating on a certain interest area and are selling books to a certain market, you are also in contact with those people best qualified to generate new material for you. And once you publish something they like, they'll come to you. Many people

"I guess every normal writer has a desire to give birth to a book someday — to become, in fact, an author. Books are . . . a chance at immortality" — Margaret Bennett in *Publishers Weekly*.

have always wanted to be an author and they'll seek you out once they recognize your success.

If you have a book you want to do yourself but recognize that you lack the required expertise, consider co-authorship. Find an expert in the field to write part of it and then each of you can edit the other's material. This has many advantages including smaller royalties, the endorsement of an expert, credibility and you have someone else to send on the promotional tour.

Many author-publishers have gone the easy route by simply editing the material of others. Deeply interested in an area, they have thoroughly researched a subject only to find that many fine experts have already written good material on several aspects of it. The collection of these articles, one per chapter, formed a book. Contact each author for permission to use his material and ask him to go over a photocopy to update it with any new information or changed views. This makes your chapter better than the original article. If the chapter must be shortened, ask the author to do it. This is faster and easier than doing it yourself and then negotiating your changes with him. If, for example, you are deeply involved in the sport of parachuting, you might contact the national association and their magazine about gathering like articles which have appeared over the years and republishing them in a series of booklets. Booklet Number One might consist of all the articles on student training. Your primary market would be the members of the association. You would sell them through the organization's "store" and via mail order by advertising in their magazine. Thus, the association is providing both the material and the customers. As an editor, you simply repackage the information.

NEGOTIATING AND CONTRACTING WITH AUTHORS. The object of an author-publisher contract is to clarify thinking and positions by laying all the details out on the table and arriving at a mutually beneficial agreement. There will never be a second book if one side takes unfair advantage of the other; it pays to keep the future in mind. Small publishers should not offer less than the industry norm unless they're satisfied with just one book per author, and there is no need to offer more. Most likely, if the author had a chance with a big publishing concern, he wouldn't even be talking to you. Then again, he may be working on one of your ideas. Each contract will be a little different but you can start with a standard one. For some published references on book contracts, write The Authors Guild, 234-P West 44th St., NYC, NY 10036.

First-time authors will be eager to become published and may not be terribly concerned about the contract. It is imperative that its negotiation and signing be taken care of first. Ask the author whether it is generally acceptable. If he has made any other commitments, such as for some subsidiary rights, this information must be added into the contract. Include a schedule and a clause allowing you to cancel if he fails to meet it; keep the pressure on him to perform. Unless you have a narrow field of interest or the author has very strong feelings about a particular area, you will want a contract which includes all possible rights. Once you have published the basic book, you will want to entertain the possibilities of translations to other languages or co-publishing in other English-speaking markets (however, unless the market is quite large, it will be more economical to ship your own print run in "direct sacks of prints"). Then there are book club adoptions, film rights, magazine excerpts, newspaper serializations and the mass market paperback rights. Your promotion will rub off on all areas so take advantage of it by taking complete control of the manuscript. Remember that people who write contracts slant them their way. The author's royalty will depend on the proposed selling price,

> *"The writer does the most who gives his reader the most knowledge and takes from him the least time"* — Sydney Smith.

print run and the amount slated for promotion. The author will want to check the publisher's track record; how long do his books normally stay in print?

ADVANCES AGAINST ROYALTIES. The advance both seals the deal, an important legal consideration, and puts pressure on the author to perform. It makes him feel accepted as an author and has great psychological value. The advance doesn't have to be large to work as an incentive. They generally range from $100 to $5,000 and small publishers often keep it low. A good rule of thumb is to offer an advance equal to the projected first year royalties. One way to create an incentive, or at least make the author feel morally obligated, is to make progress payments. One-third may be paid on signing the contract, one-third when he submits the first draft and one-third when he completes the proof reading. Ordinarily, advances are non-refundable; the author keeps them even if he fails to deliver. This is another good reason to protect your money with progress payments. The advance is also your gamble. The author keeps it even if the book fails to sell and generate enough royalties to cover the advance. Some authors with little faith in their work will, therefore, request large advances.

ROYALTIES and their possible division must be considered. Does the author own all the material or did he contract out some of the writing or illustrations? The publisher and the author have to decide whether other contributors should get a percentage of the book or be paid a flat fee. Obviously flat fees are simpler and occasionally cheaper. An illustrator creating a major portion of the book should get royalties while someone doing basic research, typing or contributing a drawing should be paid a set fee. Everyone must understand clearly what's in it for him. If you require a few drawings, go to a graphic artist and have them drawn to order. Then pay the bill and be done with it. The artist deserves royalties no more than the man who painted your car prior to your selling it. Normally, the author supplies, and is responsible for, all illustrations (but this is negotiable). Royalty reports are a time-consuming chore which may be avoided if you pay a flat rate for material received.

THE ROYALTY FORMULA, traditionally, has been to pay the author 10% of the list (cover) price for each hardcover book sold through regular channels such as book wholesalers, book stores and libraries. Remember that after discounting the book to dealers, this amounts to 15-20% of the publisher's budget. Mass Market (pocket sized) paperback reprints and those books sold in special negotiations at greater than 50% discount or in mail order promotion where advertising costs are very high pay 5-7½%. But the book market is changing now with many books being published in soft cover only. These aren't the "pocket books" but are, rather, the more expensive "quality paperbacks." Often their authors command 7%-10%. Recently some small publishers have attempted to force the author to assume some of the risk by offering a flat 15% of the **NET PROFIT** on books marketed through normal trade channels and 10% for mail orders. Percentages of the net rarely work out to the author's advantage as it is too easy for the publisher to pad the expenses. Further, the accounting required is incredible and this is another expense to be considered. A percentage of the **NET SALES** is preferable, however. Net sales are easy to calculate and difficult to pad.

Sometimes authors are offered a sliding royalty scale opting for a small amount initially and a greater percentage if the book is successful.

Most contracts call for the author and publisher to split the subsidiary rights (films, book clubs, etc.) 50-50. Many of the big publishers barely break even on the book itself and hope to make their money on the subsidiary rights. Book clubs often want a lower price on their print run to make their deal look better; the author and publisher should not project their royalties based on the price of the original book.

TRANSLATIONS offer another source of material and are a royalty consideration. A good translator is a highly skilled artist who issues a product which doesn't read like a word-for-word translation. He will spend hours searching for the single right word or phrase to convey the original meaning. He must not only be bilingual, he must be a good writer, too. There may be some 1200 literary translators in the U.S. but few are very good. The going rate is $30 or less per 1,000 words so few can make a living at it. Citing their creative input, translators are now requesting royalties but few have been successful so far. The English language rights to foreign language books are rarely expensive so this is another interesting source of material.

COPYRIGHT CLEARANCES are the responsibilty of the author and this should be spelled out in the contract. The author knows his sources better than the publisher and should be responsible for obtaining permission and paying the fees for extracted material, articles, photos or drawings. This includes the right to translate foreign material. See the discussion in Chapter five.

PROOFS are valuable to both the publisher and the author. Authors want to see the blue-line proof before the book goes on the press, and their review is valuable to the publisher as they can avoid major defects. But any changes at this point are very expensive so authors must be limited to correcting typographical errors only. Major changes in the text are "author's alterations" and must be made at the author's expense by deducting from his royalties.

PROMOTION is the responsibility of both the author and the publisher, though they play much different roles. Most contracts are very general on this point, recognizing that if the book sells and the publisher is doing well, he'll be more agreeable to expanding the promotion budget. The author must agree to devote his time to these promotions in author tours, T.V. talk shows, autograph parties, etc.

TERM AND CONTINUITY OF THE CONTRACT. The agreement may be for a stated period or for the copyright life of the book. It should be made binding on those who succeed both sides: the heirs of the author and the new purchaser of the publishing firm. Most contracts give the rights back to the author if the publisher goes bankrupt.

NEXT WORK OPTIONS are often written into contracts with first book authors. They give the publisher the right to take the next couple of books from the author on the same terms as the original. The clause is written into the original contract when the new author is eager to sell. It is often doubtful that he would agree to such an arrangement at a later date, once he sees the editing done to his manuscript and the lack of promotion provided by the publisher.

As a result, many authors rebel at this roping technique that creates friction between them and the publisher. Sometimes, they send in obvious trash to fulfill their end of the hated contract.

FURTHER CLAUSES include arbitration agreements in case of dispute, a paragraph saying the contract is being entered into on the basis of "good faith" and a statement that this is the only agreement, that neither party is bound by any other discussion during the negotiations.

The help of a lawyer is advised especially in drawing up the first contract. It may then be used as a general model for subsequent agreements. A well written contract which is fully understood by both sides will avoid many later problems assuring a long and satisfying author-publisher relationship.

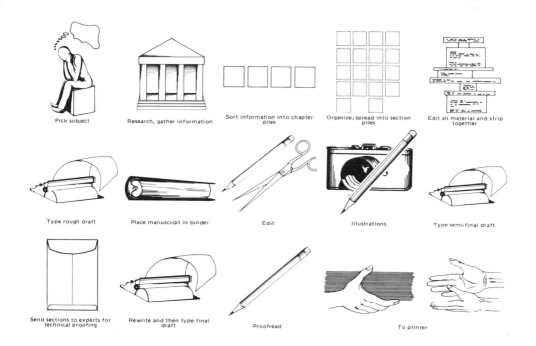

Pick subject · Research, gather information · Sort information into chapter piles · Organize; spread into section piles · Edit all material and strip together · Type rough draft · Place manuscript in binder · Edit · Illustrations · Type semi-final draft · Send sections to experts for technical proofing · Rewrite and then type final draft · Proofread · To printer

The flow of your manuscript.

WRITE IT YOURSELF. Creating your own material is easy if you have a system; all it takes is organization and discipline. Following the system outlined below, creating copy becomes challenging fun and it allows you to easily see the progress you are making which is encouraging. While this method may be of some help in writing fiction, it has been developed specifically for non-fiction.

While writing a book is not difficult, it is not for the lazy. Like AA or a diet, you will have to change your lifestyle. This means waking up one morning and making a decision: to do it now. To get into the system and develop good habits will provide you with a sense of purpose and a feeling of accomplishment. Once you've selected a topic, only the decision to go stands between you and the finished book.

TIME or lack of it is the most frequently heard excuse. But somehow we always find the time for those things most important to us. We just put them first. Often we can fit in an hour of writing time each day by completing our other chores faster. One way is to get up one hour earlier each day. This is perfect scheduling as the house is quiet, the telephone doesn't ring and most writers find the early morning to be their most creative and productive time. Once you gather momentum in your project, you'll find arising early will be easy; you won't even miss that hour of sleep. You must put this hour first and not let anything interfere with it.

Set up a writing area in a spare room or a corner of the living room. Keep all your writing materials and research tools there. Your creative writing time is precious, don't waste it trying to get started. Then use the area at least once a day even if you can't think of anything to write. Sit down and create words.

PICKING A SUBJECT is the first step. It should be on a subject in which you are interested and where you are an expert or would like to become an expert. You have spent years working at, specializing in and learning something and there are thousands of people out there willing to pay good money to get the inside information on it. Write what you know! If you select your hobby, there are a number of advantages. You know what has been written in the past, you have the contacts for gathering more information and your further participation in it will become tax deductible.

Poetry doesn't sell and few people will purchase your autobiography. Protest subjects usually have built-in audience limitations. You must decide whether you wish to write, publish or make money.

Women provide a growing market which is taking on new importance. Many have entered the world of business with a lack of applicable education or experience. Once out of the kitchen and into the office, they are also faced with a shortage of time. They need information and their employment provides them with the money to pay for it. Books aimed at women have great sales potential.

The subject of a book, not the name of the author or the comments of a reviewer, is what sells it. Every new national craze requires how-to books. According to *Newsweek* there are over 1,300 books on fitness and health currently in print. Don't be discouraged if it has already been covered. That just proves there is a demand for it. Using your own experience and the latest information, you can do it better. The subjects with the best sales potential are how-to's, money, health, self-improvement, hobbies, sex and psychological well being. Find a need and fill it.

One specialized book that has been selling for years is Kershner's *The Student Pilot's Flight Manual* which has gone through the press 26 times for 485,000 copies. Anticipate reader interest and pick a subject which will sell on its own even if the buyer has never heard of the book.

You don't have to be an expert — yet. If you are new to a subject, you should produce a better book than an old hand because you are better able to understand and relate to the reader-novice. You know what his reactions are, what he is thinking. Once you are finished writing, you will be an expert.

RESEARCH is simply reading, making notes and rearranging the gathered information. The importance of the use of the library cannot be over-emphasized. All research must begin there and most of the required information will be found within its walls. The first project will be to determine whether the subject has already been beaten to death. If not, then on to the book.

Ask the reference librarian for Bowker's *Books in Print* which lists all books currently available by subject, title and author. Make a list of those you would like to review. Research the library's card file to see which books may be obtained there. The others you may purchase at your local bookstore or by writing direct to the publisher; addresses are listed in the back of *Books in Print*. And remember that this is probably not the only library in town, try the local college, too; it will have different books. Research the *Readers' Guide to Periodical Literature* which lists magazine articles on the subject. There are thousands of associations and many have their own special interest magazine. Be a detective. When you run out of leads, ask the librarian. Libraries carry hundreds of indexes, listings and source books. Gather everything ever written on your subject. Load yourself up with so much material you'll have to decide on what to leave out. Overdo it and you'll be proud of the result, secure in the knowledge that you have covered it completely.

> *"Every conceivable piece of information imaginable is available somewhere in your local library. There are indexes and references on everything. Ask the reference librarian for help."*

Check out those books and magazines you can. On those restricted to the reference room, make notes of small bits of information and use the photocopy machine to record longer pieces. Where you wish to use photos and drawings of material with expired copyrights, use a plain paper photocopier such as Xerox or IBM for the drawings and use a camera to reshoot the photos (more on this later). But even where the copyright has not expired, make a photocopy of valuable illustrations to guide you in your research. Photocopy checked-out books and magazines at the local copy center with a plain paper copier which is cheaper, cleaner and easier to read than the wet process models used in many libraries. After exhausting the library of its information, there are many other sources. Write for *Selected U.S. Government Publications* to the Superintendent of Documents, USGPO, P.O. Box 1821, Washington, DC 20402. This is a monthly catalogue of government publications. Many of them are also available at U.S. Government bookstores in the larger cities. Check the white pages. Then, there are interviews with the experts you uncover in your research. You may write or call them. Now that you are researching, you are a member of the media and will be able to attend a lot of related events free. Use your new business card to get a press pass, media packet and preferential treatment.

ORGANIZING YOUR MATERIAL comes next. To determine your market and target it properly, approach your book in this order: first, write an advertisement for it; second, pick a title; and last, write the book. Define the scope of the book. Find a market and aim the book at the market. Most non-fiction books are written without a specific market in mind and since they don't provide what the potential buyers want, they don't sell. Don't ignore other markets though. If you have an instruction book aimed at students of flying schools and the bookstores pick it up, so much the better. But this is the frosting, not the cake. The more areas the book may be fitted into, the better its chances of success. Slant the book as required.

IN THE "PILOT" SYSTEM OF ORGANIZATION start by drawing up a preliminary table of contents. Then take all your research material and "pile it" as required. Decide on your chapter titles and, using scissors, tape and staples, sort all this copied material into the applicable chapter piles. During your library research, you must have written down a number of interesting observations, many of your own experiences. Add your own notes to the piles.

The piles.

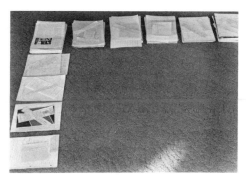

The spread.

Now spread out the individual chapters. This should completely fill the living room. Pick an interesting pile, any one, not necessarily the first, and go through it, underlining important points and writing in your additional comments. Write out longer thoughts on a tablet and file them in order in the pile.

25

This floor spread will enable you to see the whole interrelated project lending excitement and encouragement — a great incentive. Move the piles around to insure a good, logical flow of thought and to avoid duplication of copy. Discard bad and duplicate material.

This use of other information is not plagiarizing, it is simply to organize your thoughts and to insure that you won't leave out any important points. However, you will be entertained as you compare what different authors say about the same item. The similarities are often remarkably coincidental, sometimes to the point of including the same words and phraseology.

As you read what others say on a particular point, your memory will be jogged. You will have additional points, a clearer explanation or an illustrative story. Where you disagree with another author, you can always say "some people believe. . ." and then tell it your way. You have the advantage of the most recent information since you came last.

Carry paper and pen with you at all times, expecially when driving, running or engaging in any solo activity. This is the time to think, create, compose; this is when there is no one around to break your train of thought. Some authors keep a pad in their car and compose while commuting. When you are confined, captive, isolated, you have nothing else to do but write. Some people like to work with a small pocket tape recorder, but remember that someone must transcribe this noise onto paper. It all depends on what you are used to, how you perform best. If you often dictate letters and have a secretary to transcribe your tapes, this may be the most comfortable and most efficient method for you.

Write it down when you think of it or you will lose it. Keep on thinking and keep on note-taking. Add your thoughts and major pieces to the piles. As you go along, draw up a list of questions as they come to mind so that you will remember to follow them up for an answer.

The taped strips of notes.

STRIP your notes by cutting, sorting and taping. Paste the strips together with Magic Transparent Tape. If your photocopies were made on a plain paper copier, you'll be able to write on the tape and the paper when adding notes.

Type on 3-hole punched mimeo paper; it is good and inexpensive. The holes even help you to see when the bottom of the page is coming in the typewriter; it comes quickly when you are double spacing. Don't use erasable paper, the ink comes off on the hands. Type, don't handwrite. You'll need a typed copy of your draft to better visualize it and this will save you one complete step.

WRITING from the pasted strips may be done, as above, with either a tape recorder or a typewriter. With practice you will learn to think, create and compose at the machine. Many law schools allow their students to take their exams by typewriter and they do it in spite of the racket in the typing room. Type it out or dictate it rough the first time. Write as you speak, relax and be clear. Make notes where you are considering illustrations. Type the manuscript double spaced as you would the final copy. Initiate good habits.

Don't be concerned with what goes down on paper the first time around. The important thing is to get it down. Often these first impressions are the best; they're complete, natural and believable. Later you'll go through the draft, making corrections, additions and deletions. Major changes will require rewriting while minor ones only some

26

proofing marks. Sentences and paragraphs will be added through cutting and pasting-in the new material. Set up in a loose leaf-form; it will be easy to add to the manuscript with a little cutting, pasting and page additions.

Read the whole pasted-up section to grasp the overall theme. Then boil it down and use your own words. Think about the section and how you might explain the basic message better. Can't you say it better with fewer words? Don't just write from the strips sentence-by-sentence, that approaches plagiarism. For organization, list the main points and rearrange the pieces. If you are having trouble with a section, arrange it as best you can and then sleep on it. If you still can't bring it all together with a few well-chosen sentences, you may have to call another expert for his or her explanation.

As you type up the rough first draft and later as you review it, you'll decide whole paragraphs are misplaced and belong elsewhere. Using three-hole punched paper and a binder, it is an easy matter to cut, move and paste material.

If you lack a certain piece of information, a number or fact, leave a blank space, put a note in the margin and go on. Don't lose momentum. Similarly, if you find yourself repeating material, make a note in the margin so you may compare it with the other material later.

Remember, this is not plagiarism but solid, thorough research and an efficient system made possible by Xerox. There is nothing new in the universe. Practically every nonfiction book is simply a repackaging of existing material.

Type one complete section at a time if possible. One chapter at a time is better and the whole book straight through is the best way to go. Most beginning authors must work and are able to devote only a short period each day to their writing. But, the more time you can put into each piece of the book, the better, as there will be greater continuity, less duplication and clearer organization. If you can only do a small section at a time, try arranging the pieces in the evening, reviewing them in the early morning, thinking about them while commuting, etc. and then come home to type it all up.

On the other hand, if you can, take two weeks off from work, shut out all distractions and become totally involved in the manuscript. Don't pick up the mail or answer the telephone. Eat when hungry, sleep when tired and forget the clock except as a gauge of your pace. Keep up the pressure and keep on typing. Pace yourself at, say, one chapter per day. You shouldn't have to force yourself to write but it will take organization and discipline.

After a couple of books, you'll find yourself making very few changes in your original draft. In fact, using an IBM Correcting Selectric typewriter, you will even change the type balls to indicate to the printer which type faces you want for body type, bold face, italics and captions.

Don't throw out your materials once your draft is typed. Put them in a cardboard carton. Keep a source record, as you write, for all the material you may be called upon later to identify. This is especially important with photographs and artwork.

WRITING STYLE. Before writing a magazine article, always read one or more editions of the magazine thoroughly to absorb the style. It helps one to subconsciously adapt to their way of writing. The same technique may be used in writing a book by reading a couple of chapters of a book by a writer you admire.

Writing is a communication art. You should not try to impress. Write as you speak, avoiding big words where small ones will do. Most people regularly use only 800-1,000 of the some 26,000 English words available to them. Use simple sentences and be precise in

"It's not creative plagiarism when you're writing non-fiction. In fact, it's not plagiarism at all. They call it research" — Lawrence Block.

your selection of words. Vary sentence and paragraph length and favor the shorter ones. Try to leave yourself out of the copy: avoid the word "I."

Use action nouns and verbs. Help the reader draw a mental picture by introducing sight, sound, smell, touch and taste to your copy. Be precise by avoiding superlatives and overuse of adverbs and adjectives. Study newspaper writing and place the words you wish to emphasize at the beginning of the sentence. The important sentence should start the paragraph and the main paragraph should head up the chapter.

Relax, talk on paper, be yourself. Explain each section in your own words as you would trying to help a friend who is new to the subject. Use contractions in your writing as you do in your speech and you'll (there's one) get your message across more easily. "Which" and "that" can usually be left out to the benefit of the sentence. Keep it short. You are paying for the words so edit out the junk.

Writing is hard work; it's an intellectual and emotional workout. Some authors enjoy the discipline it requires but more have a greater appreciation for the reward of results.

As a published author you have the responsibility of being a recognized expert. Be accurate; you will be quoted. Use proper terms; don't start a new language. Steer away from highly technical language; you'll only turn off your reader. For example, a few years ago, hang gliding was a hot new subject. It was the rebirth of aviation using a wing made in the sail industry and whose participants were kids off the streets. The elements of flying and parts of the glider could have come from the aviation community, the sail industry or popular jargon could have been used. Obviously aviation terms were in order. This was impressed upon the early book and magazine writers; aviation terms were used almost exclusively and this aided the introduction of hang gliding into the community of sport aviation. One technique of educating your readers to the correct terms is to use the proper term and then follow it with the more popular word in parentheses.

Be a professional and give the reader his money's worth. Your material will be used by others in coming years and you will be quoted. If you are accurate and correct now, you won't be embarrassed later by the written legend you've created.

Anticipate trends to keep your work up to date. Use metric and non-sexist terms wherever possible. Cookbooks may not be ready to switch to metric and books on printing will deal with 17x22 presses and 6x9 books for a long time, but many measurements may be avoided by using comparisons. For example, instead of telling a parachutist to prepare for landing at "30 feet," say "at tree top height." The comparison is clearer anyway.

LAYOUT THE BINDER. Now that you are generating copy, you need a place to store it. Find a large 3", three-ring binder and add divider cards corresponding to the chapters you've selected. Insert the rough typed pages as you complete them. They should be numbered by chapter and page. For example, "6-14" would be page 14 in Chapter 6. As the piles come off the floor, cross the desk and flow through the typewriter into the binder, you will gain a great feeling of accomplishment.

Author and publisher (in this case you are both) should decide whether secondary matter is of value or just window dressing. An index, appendix, bibliography or directory may add to the usefulness of the book or it may just cost more than it is worth to include. It depends on the subject and your treatment of it. But all these items should be decided upon early, so a running list may be maintained as you do your research. Remember, some books are composed of nothing but lists.

> *"I just sat down and started all by myself . . . it never occurred to me that I couldn't do it as well as anyone else"* – Barbara Tuchman.

You will be further encouraged by setting up the preliminary pages of the book. Soon you will have a partial manuscript, the book will be taking shape and you will have something tangible to carry around. This makes you feel proud and gives you the flexibility to proof and improve your manuscript away from home. Carry it around and work on it whenever you can. If the book is a short one, you may even use the binder to collect your material and this will allow you to avoid the piles of notes. Write your name and address in the front with a note that it is a valuable manuscript. You don't want to misplace your future book.

It is wise to photocopy your manuscript periodically so that it may be stored in another location. You may lose a lot of important things in a fire but to have the fruit of your creativity destroyed would be a disaster.

PARTS OF A BOOK. Most books are divided into three main parts: preliminary pages or "front matter," the text and the end pages. We will discuss them in order so you can add a sheet for each to the binder with as much information as you have so far. It is not necessary to have all the pages mentioned or even to place them in any given order, but it is recommended that convention be followed unless you have a good, specific reason to stray. Set up these sections as best you can so the book will take shape. You will make additions and revisions to it later.

There are two pages to each sheet or leaf of paper. The "verso" pages are on the left-hand side and are even numbered while the "recto" pages are opposite.

THE FRONT MATTER is that material placed at the beginning of the book.

END PAPERS may be plain or printed, usually of heavier paper, and are glued to the inside front and back covers of a hardbound (casebound) book. They hold the book together.

THE BASTARD TITLE or half title is usually the first printed page of a book and is more often found in hardbound books than in paperbacks. It contains only the title and it is a right-hand page.

THE FRONTISPIECE is a photograph found on the reverse of the bastard title page. Often this page is left blank instead or it is used more economically to list other books by the same author or as part of the title page which follows.

THE TITLE PAGE is on the right-hand side and lists the full title of the book with its subtitle if it has one. It may also include the name of the author or editor, the publisher, whether this is an original or revised edition and the date.

THE COPYRIGHT PAGE or "title page verso" is on the reverse of the title page and is the most important. Proofread it a dozen times! Here you print the copyright notice, indicate the printing history (number of printings and revisions), list the Library of Congress Catalogue number, the ISBN, the Library of Congress Cataloguing in Publication Data, name and address of the publisher (you) and "printed in the United States of America" (to avoid export complications).

Anyone who knows books will turn to the copyright page first when picking up a book. Next to the cover, this page is the most important in selling a book so make it look

---

"Today, as always, if a talented author remains unpublished and unnoticed, the fault is the author's" — Bill Henderson

good. See Chapter 5 regarding copyright, ISBN's, etc. and list all your numbers. You want to look like a big time publisher, not a basement print shop.

Each time you revise the book, it is worthwhile to restrip and reshoot the copyright page in order to add "Second Printing, revised, 1980," as this lets the potential purchaser know the book is up to date. The big publishers don't make any changes and print a string of numbers on the copyright page instead. You'll note: " 1 2 3 4 5 6 7 8 9 10" which indicates to the trained eye that this is the first edition. On reprinting it, they will opaque out the "1" on the photographic negative.

THE DEDICATION PAGE usually contains a short statement, if one is made at all, but some authors like to praise their friend(s) in great detail. It isn't likely that anyone other than the person mentioned will care about the dedication. This right-hand page was used historically by writers to acknowledge their patrons: the person or institution that supported them during the writing.

THE EPIGRAPH PAGE contains a pertinent quotation which sets the tone of the book. Using a separate page for it is usually a waste of space.

THE TABLE OF CONTENTS should start on the right-hand side. It will include the chapter number, chapter title and beginning page number. You can leave these page numbers blank for now. They will be filled in by the printer when the book is layed out. Use the Table of Contents as a promotional piece for the book. Make it as detailed as possible and then reproduce it in your brochures. Remember, when buying technical, professional or how-to books, most people turn immediately to the Table of Contents to check the coverage.

A LIST OF ILLUSTRATIONS is in order if the book is heavily illustrated or if it is a picture type book. Usually this is a waste of space. The same goes for a list of tables, especially if they are tied directly to the text.

THE FOREWORD is positioned on the right-hand side and is a pitch for the book by someone other than the author. It is doubtful that many people read them; most turn directly to the action. The name of the contributor appears at the end.

THE PREFACE is written by the author and tells why and how he wrote the book. It gets as much attention from the reader as a foreword and appears on the right-hand side. If you have an important message and want to be sure the reader receives it, put it in Chapter one, not in the preface or introduction.

ACKNOWLEDGMENTS are a great sales tool. List everyone who helped you in preparation of your manuscript. People love to see their name in print and each one will become a disciple spreading the word on your great contribution to literature. They may even purchase a copy. On this blank sheet in your binder, add names of contributors as you encounter them so that you don't forget anyone.

THE INTRODUCTION was covered above in the discussion of the preface.

THE LIST OF ABBREVIATIONS is only required in some very technical books.

THE REPEATED BASTARD TITLE is next, is optional and is a waste of space.

Obviously, if all the front matter pages listed above were included in your book, you would have a number of pages already. You don't need them all and it is recommended that you do away with most except the title page, copyright page, acknowledgments and table of contents. Check over several other books for the layout, especially old hardbound books which followed convention.

THE TEXT of the book is the meaty part on which the front matter and end pages hang. This is the second or main section.

Start your book off with an "action" chapter. Like the introductory part of a speech, it should arouse the reader and whet his appetite. Too many authors want to start from the "beginning" and put a history chapter first. The reader wants to know where-to and how-to. Don't lose him in the first chapter.

DIVISIONS are sometimes made in long books with distinct but related sections. Their title pages contain the name and number of the section and their reverse sides are usually blank.

CHAPTER TITLES should reveal the subject of the chapter to aid the reader in finding what he wants. He may be skimming the book in a store pending possible purchase or he may be referring back to something he read. In either case, you want the description to be as clear as possible.

THE SUBHEAD is a secondary heading or title, usually set in less prominent type than the main heading, to divide the entries under a subject. They can contribute a logical progression, aid in finding needed material and help to break up long chapters.

FOOTNOTES aren't needed except in technical publications. If your book will be used as a research tool, the readers may want the footnotes so they can follow up on the material. Where they must be used, some people recommend they be placed at the end of the chapter or in the appendix as it is more time consuming and therefore costly to place them at the bottom of the page.

THE BACK MATTER is that reference material placed at the end of the book. It is less expensive to revise lists at the end of a book when reprinting; don't print lists which may change in the text.

THE APPENDIX contains important charts, graphs, lists, etc. and it may be composed of several sections. It is permissible to print it in smaller type.

THE ADDENDUM has brief, late, additional data. It is printed as part of the book or on a loose sheet.

ERRATA are errors discovered after printing. The list is printed on a separate sheet and may be pasted in or loose.

AUTHOR'S NOTES come next and include additional information in chapter order.

THE GLOSSARY is an alphabetically arranged dictionary of terms peculiar to the subject of the book. Some authors like to save space by combining the glossary and the index.

> ". . . writing. It was a private thing that I could do. I could just send it out and see what it did. If someone laughed, I could stand up and say, 'I did that' " – Erma Bombeck in The Writer.

THE BIBLIOGRAPHY lists the books you used in writing your book.

THE INDEX aids the reader in locating specific information in the pages and is particularly important in reference works. Assembling the index is very time consuming and the added pages increase the cost of the finished book. The index must be revised every time the book is updated because the page numbers change. Professional book indexers feel very strongly about their work and are quite vocal about the need for good indexes. They may soon find their work a lot easier with the introduction of computerized text editing equipment as it will automatically find any word every place it is used in the text. Some authors prefer to add lengthy subheadings, with or without individual page numbers, to their Table of Contents instead.

THE AFTERWORD is sometimes seen in manuals. Often it is a personal message from the author to the reader wishing the best of luck and/or requesting suggestions for improvement.

"COLOPHON" is Greek for "finishing touch" and details the production facts by listing the type style, designer, printer, kind of paper, plate maker, binder, etc. It is not as common as it once was but is used more and more today in special "labor of love" type publications.

Make a page for each of the sections listed above that you wish to include and fill in as much information as you now have. Keep adding with a pencil as you progress. It doesn't have to be neat or in order, the important thing is that now you have a place to store your material. As you add pages, as the book fills up, you will have more work to carry as you venture away from home on the job, etc. When you find a few idle moments, open the book, draft and revise it, bit by bit. Tighten your writing, change words, cut out those which fail to add to your message. Revise and improve.

EDITING your manuscript is where you cut, rearrange and add material. You will probably make fewer changes than you predict. Go through the manuscript section by section and clean it up. Ask a couple of friends to read it over and to pencil in their suggestions.

THE MANUSCRIPT must be typed, never handwritten. It should be neatly double spaced on one side of 8½ x 11 white paper and contain a minimum number of changes. Check all spelling, punctuation and grammar. Using a binder to hold the manuscript, it is easy to change, add or subtract material. To delete, line it out. To change, type it out in new copy and paste it over the old. To add, just insert an additional page and give it the same number as the previous page with the suffix "a", as in 16a. The result will be several strips of paper pasted onto each page. Fill an empty Elmer's Glue-All bottle with rubber cement to simplify the job.

PHOTOS AND DRAWINGS are easily indicated in the manuscript with page and position numbers. The second photo on page 40 of chapter 3 would be marked "3-40-B", for example. Mark both the location in the manuscript and the back of the photo or drawing. Mark the photo near its edge and don't press too hard, you may press through to damage the photo. Incidentally, it is sometimes

Indicating the photo on the page.

necessary to indicate which side of the photo goes up as it is not obvious to someone not familiar with the subject. Type the captions into the manuscript under the photo position number. Make a photocopy of the photos or contact prints and paste them into the manuscript (set the machine on "light"). This will make the draft clearer to both you and the printer. Never paste in the photos themselves, they're hard to get off and make a mess.

HELP is available to those who still can't write even after learning the tricks mentioned above. If you can talk, you can write, so get a tape recorder. Do the transcriptions yourself or hire it out. Type it as you said it. Then either correct the language or leave it as it is. Sometimes a basic speaking style adds to the book. Many big name authors can't type or spell so they hire people who can. To contact people in the "word game," go to libraries, PR firms, advertising agencies, college English departments and see the *Writer's Digest Yearbook*. There are a lot of people out there who will be happy to work for you cheap. If you still can't get your thoughts to paper, try a "ghostwriter." You'll need a contract saying the book will be in your name and that he or she will be on straight salary only.

Many people who are not professional writers get into print. If they can't pick up the skills, they ask for help. You can too.

TYPING THE MANUSCRIPT. If you lack either the ability or desire to type the final draft of the manuscript, there are many typists who specialize in this work. Check with your printer, call other printers, business schools and see the Yellow Pages. Their rates are moderate. If you are preparing a manual and can accept space-grabbing larger type, you might have the typist do it with an IBM Correcting Selectric typewriter and a carbon ribbon. This will eliminate typesetting and you can go directly to press. Your printer will explain all this to you before you complete the final draft.

START EACH CHAPTER about one-third of the way from the top of the page and make it appear just as you want it in the book by listing the chapter number and title. At the top of each page, type your name and the chapter/page number. Leave about a one inch margin all around the page so you and the printer will have room for penciling in notes. If you maintain consistency in line length and in lines per page, it will be easier to project the length of the finished book. If you type the final draft yourself, you'll have an opportunity to clean it up and make the text flow better.

TYPESETTING NOTES should be made on a page in the front of the manuscript. List your name, address and telephone number; they may wish to call you to clarify something in the manuscript. Include the hours you expect to be by the telephone if you aren't always there. List the typestyles you want for each type face used in the manuscript. Some subjects use words that are similar and easy to interchange. For example, one set in aviation is "altitude" and "attitude." Tell them to watch for these. And you may have some other special notes to include.

TYPE STYLES may be indicated in the manuscript in a couple of ways. The usual system is to code each one with a number and then to mark the manuscript with them only when there is a change. The typesetter doesn't want the text all cluttered up with notes such as "10/11 Bodoni Bold." Another very neat way is to use different IBM type balls in a Selectric typewriter. Whatever your system, place an explanation in front of the manuscript for the typesetter. For an explanation of type, see Chapter Four.

"If you don't know where you're going — you're there."

33

NOTES TO TYPESETTER.

Type Styles: I have used various IBM type faces to indicate the type styles I want in the book. This eliminates constant marking in the text.

1, CHAPTER HEADINGS

2, CHAPTER SUBHEADINGS

3, Normal body type

4, *Italics for quotes and book titles*

5, Small bold type for captions

7, The Appendix will be in smaller type

CHAPTER FOUR, EMER

CAUSES, AVOIDANCE AND CU

are dealing with machines (aircraft), ne

"The gull sees farthest who flies highes

At an angle: the air is deflected around the b

Parachuting Publications

PROOFREADING has to be done again and again. You will proof your manuscript for content and style, and then you will proof the book as it makes its way through the various stages of production.

Ask friends to proofread your manuscript for grammar, punctuation and content. Do they find it easy to read? Do they understand it? If no one has time to read the whole book, ask them to go over an interesting chapter. For technical proofing, send chapters off to various experts. Just make a photocopy of your draft and ask them to make notes right on the copy. Remember to give them credit in the acknowledgments. You will not only produce the very best book, you will gain their support for it and this is very important to its marketing. Incidentally, to these experts an honorarium of, say, $50 for a book length manuscript is normal procedure and it is worth much more to you.

The manuscript must be proofed and marked prior to final typing, the final draft has to be proofed for the printer, the set type or "boards" have to be proofed and the blueline prints of the book signatures have to be proofed. You'll have some errors anyway but without careful proofreading, you'll have more. Being familiar with your own writing style, you will find it difficult to catch all the errors. Try reading syllable by syllable, slowly. Find a friend to proof for you. There is an interesting story about a professor who wanted to publish the error-free book. He brought it out in mimeographed form and offered his students 10¢ for each error they could find in the course of the term. They found quite a few. Then he corrected the stencils and ran off another set. This time he offered the new class 25¢ per error. They searched harder and found fewer. By the fourth time around at $1 per error, only a very few turned up and the professor was satisfied. Incidentally, this proved to be an effective way to encourage the class to read the required text thoroughly.

Proof well. Get it right the first time. "What you (don't) see is what you get." There is no practical way to take ink off paper.

Some printers will want you to proof the "galleys," the composition before it is pasted down on the boards. This is a holdover from letterpress when it was less expensive to make changes at this point. (Actually in letterpress, this is the last chance to proofread before the plates go on the press.) The only good reason to proof galleys today is if the

"Most people work at only 10% of their mental potential. There is much capacity for improvement."

author turned in a messy manuscript. The printer should proof his own galleys for typographical errors and proceed with the pasteup.

Proofing the "boards" is what you'll do if the book is being printed offset. These are the pasted-up pages and the printer will provide you with a photocopy to mark up. Usually the printer will proof the boards before sending them to you. They will catch the obvious punctuation and spelling errors but not the technical or look-alike words (altitude and attitude). Many of the errors will be from the typesetter, not from your manuscript. Proof carefully; a page is not error free just because it looks clean. You will not be charged for errors made by the printer, so correct them no matter how small. On the other hand, you will be charged for any deviations from your submitted manuscript. But if they are important, this is the cheapest place to make them. Do it now.

Proofing the blueline prints comes next. These are large folded blueprints of the actual stripped-in negatives which were photographed from the pasteup boards. They are assembled into signatures just like the proposed book. They enable the printer to make sure the pages are in order and that everything is in place. This is your last chance to proofread. Check especially the numbering, sentence continuation from one page to the next, the chapter page numbers in the table of contents, proper insertion of the illustrations and captions, the numbers on the copyright page, the price and ISBN on the cover, etc. To change even a punctuation mark at this point, it is necessary to reset the entire line, paste it on the board, reshoot the negative, strip it into the flat and reshoot the blueline. Expensive! If you delete or add words, entire pages may have to be reset and this may affect more than one page. It may be necessary to reset the rest of the chapter or even the rest of the book. So count the characters and make the new line the same length as the one it replaces. Ask for a tour of the plant and you'll better understand the situation.

Compare the set type with your manuscript. Use "PE" (printer's error) next to your correction in the manuscript where the printer made the mistake so you won't be charged for the change. If the change is your fault, it is called an "author's alteration" and they cost. Use a red pen to mark the proofs so your notes cannot be missed. Don't proof blueprints outdoors; the sun will turn them solid blue fast. Write in small corrections but type out and paste in large ones. Proof with a dictionary. Double check all numbers, dates and facts. Recheck the spelling of names, places and unusual words.

"Press proofs" are where the printer runs off a few sheets and then lets you do a final proofing. It is very expensive to leave a press idle. Press proofs should not be necessary, you had your chance with the blueline prints.

No matter how carefully you proofread, some errors will always show up in the final printed book. Don't be concerned; resign yourself to it, you can't catch them all.

Many publishers like to make a small 5,000 unit press run the first time to help them catch the errors. Keep a "correction copy" of the book near your desk and pencil in changes as they come to your attention. Then when you are ready to reprint, you'll be ready to go. Major errors may require the insertion of an "erratum" slip. They are slipped into the front of each printed book.

PROOFREADER'S MARKS are standardized to enable you to communicate clearly with your printer. A complete set can be found in your dictionary under "proofreader's marks." Stick to the standard marks. If you make up your own, you'll only confuse your printer. Use these marks throughout the editing/proofreading process.

"The horizon is larger in the West. And there's enough freedom for a small publisher to take a chance on a book that wouldn't get off the ground in New York" – David Dreis in *West Coast Review of Books.*

PROOFREADER'S MARKS

ℓ	delete; take it out
◡	close up; print as one word
ℬ	delete and close up
Λ or > or ⋏	caret; insert here (something)
#	insert a space
eq#	space evenly where indicated
stet	let marked text stand as set
tr	transpose change/order the
/	used to separate two or more marks and often as a concluding stroke at the end of an insertion
⌐	set farther to the left
⌐set⌐	set farther to the right
⌢	set ae or fl as ligatures æ or fl
=	straighten alignment
‖	straighten or allign
X	imperfect or broken character
☐	indent or insert em quad space
¶	begin a new paragraph
(sp)	spell out (set 5 lbs. as five pounds)
cap	set in capitals (CAPITALS)

S.C. or sm.cap	set in small capitals (SMALL CAPITALS)
lc	set in lowercase (lowercase)
ital	set in italic (*italic*)
rom	set in roman (roman)
bf	set in boldface (**boldface**)
= or -/ or ⌃/ or /=/	hyphen
1/N or en or /N/	en dash (1965-72)
1/M or em or /M/	em — or long — dash
V	superscript or superior ($\overset{2}{V}$ as in r^2)
∧	subscript or inferior ($\underset{2}{\wedge}$ as in H$_2$O)
⌃ or X	centered (⌃ for a centered dot in p · q)
⌃	comma
⌄	apostrophe
⊙	period
; or ;/	semicolon
: or ⊙	colon
" " or ⌄ ⌄	quotation marks
(/)	parentheses
[/]	brackets
ok/?	query to author: has this been set as intended?

ARTWORK consists of line work and halftones. Line work is a clean black on white drawing without any shading. They may be pasted directly on the boards unless their size must be enlarged or reduced. Camera work costs extra. Halftones are made from photographs, or drawings with shading, by taking a photograph of them through a screen. You will notice the result using a magnifying glass to look closely at a printed photograph. It is composed on many tiny dots of various sizes (shading). This takes camera work and you will be charged for each one. Camera charges are a start-up cost and are spread over the entire printing. Therefore the cost of an individual photo when spread over the entire print run is very small. It is foolish to be cheap at this point.

If you need line work and can't draw, you can hire a commercial artist. Most printers have illustrators on their staff or know some and they usually work inexpensively. Your printer will also have a large file of "clip art" and you may find something there you can use. These are commercially provided drawings on a large variety of subjects. Many people lift art from reprints of old Sears catalogues and other publications where the copyright has expired. Depending on your subject, you may be able to clip drawings from certain military and government publications which are in the public domain or are supposed to be yours under the Freedom of Information act.

PHOTOGRAPHS, rarely seen in fiction, are almost a requirement in nonfiction, especially how-to books. The most successful how-to books are those that manage to integrate words and pictures into an attractive teaching tool. Unless you are writing an art-type, book, you will use black and white rather than the more expensive color. Color requires four trips through the press plus "color separations." The best photos are large, (they become sharper when reduced) glossy, black and whites with a lot of contrast. Color photos and slides may be reproduced in black and white but won't be as clear. Photographs which have already been printed once may be pasted in direct or reduced and rescreened but the results are not as good as with an original glossy photo. When in doubt about the suitability of a photo, ask your printer. Sometimes the screening actually improves the photo.

CAMERAS. Unless you are an accomplished photographer with a good set of equipment, you'll want to consider the following: get a good camera with attachments and buy a book on how to use it. There are many types of cameras but the most popular and versatile is the single lens reflex. Many used models and accessories are available at your discount photo shop and they have good resale value. If all your subjects are still, you can get by with a cheaper match-needle model. If you are shooting fast-moving people or objects, you may need a camera with automatic features and/or motor drive. (Aircraft mounts may dictate these and a remote firing device too.) And don't overlook the new zoom lenses which make framing faster and easier. Olympus has the fastest motor drive, (five per second) and that still isn't fast enough to get a series of photos to show the windup and throw of a Frisbee disc. But it is fast enough for most subjects and allows you to keep your eye on the subject rather than pulling away to advance the film. Some good automatic cameras are the Olympus OM-2, Nikon FE, Minolta XD-11, Canon A-1 and the Konica C35-AF.

USING THE CAMERA. As you compile your manuscript, make a photo list so you'll know what you need. Then set out with your gear to take them. Try to frame your shots on the object, person or activity you are trying to show; avoid distracting clutter. For good black and white contrast, avoid tonal shades. Put people in your photos. If you are showing a number of pieces of equipment which are better modeled, such as parachutes, invite as many different people as possible to wear them. You can bet that each one will buy a copy of the book. When taking still shots of people, make them smile. Get their teeth in the picture. Most people don't know how to pose for a photo and complain that they don't photograph well. Catch them smiling and they'll love you for it. Try to capture action in your photos, make them move. Seek the unusual, tell a story, look for human interest, shoot from a different angle. Then have your film processed by a custom photo lab. Don't send it out through your supermarket. Slides don't matter as much but in b/w processing the negative must be focused with the enlarger onto the print paper. The jiffy photo places hire cheap labor who do "close enough" work for the general public. The prints will be comparatively muddy and will not reproduce well.

Photo release forms are advisable, particularly for pictures of minors. Permission might cost $20-500 but normally your subjects are just tickled to be in the book. A news photo does not require a release unless it is used in an advertisement. Permission fees are paid by the author on publication. However, you will often overlook getting permission and occasionally a subject will inquire about his rights. The best way to handle this is to tell him that you are about to go back to press with a revised printing and while it will cost you to replace his photo, you can take him out. I have never heard of a subject who wanted to be deleted from a book.

Other photo sources abound. Freelancers with a stock of photos will sell them for a couple of dollars each. Or you can have them custom shot for $5-$20 per photo. Photo syndicates are in the business of selling stock photos. The chamber of commerce, private firms, trade associations and some governmental departments have public relations departments who pass out photos as part of their function. Libraries and museums sometimes have photo files. Photos from old books with expired copyrights are easily copied with your camera. Just carry them over to the light, lay them out flat and snap a photo of them. They come out very nicely. When covering an event, make contact with the other photographers and get their card. They may have just what you need. Picture sources are listed in *Writer's Market.*

Handle negatives and photos carefully, you have a lot invested in them. Keep them clean and mail them flat between cardboard sheets. When you wish the printer to crop them, don't take out the scissors, make crop marks on the edges. If a photo needs re-touching, such as to remove an extraneous object like your camera bag, let the printer do it. Don't use paper clips. When writing on the back, concentrate on the edge and don't push down too hard. Make sure the ink is dry before restacking the photos and to be safe, ship them back to back and face to face. For more information on cameras and photography, see the discussion in *Writer's Market.*

CHOOSING A TITLE for your book. You should be thinking about a title while you are creating the manuscript. It is discussed here because the choice doesn't have to be made until the manuscript is completed. Make the book easy to find. It will be listed in Bowker's *Books In Print* by title, author and subject. If the title and subject are the same, you have doubled your exposure. Book listings print only the title, not a description of the contents so get more mileage with a title and a sub-title to tell what the book is about. For example, *PARACHUTING, the skydivers' handbook* is listed under the most common heading "parachuting" but the word "skydiving" may be more recognizable to some. And it is a how-to handbook, not fiction or history. Many self-published books are sold by mail order and to be marketed they must be advertised. Here the title must grab the attention of the reader and make him a promise such as: "buy this book and make a million." Test proposed titles out on your friends and acquaintances or run test ads to compare their pulling power. Good book titles are your best teaser copy whether they are selling the book from a magazine advertisement or the cover of the book itself. Brainstorm it and come up with a good "one-liner" which tells a complete and compelling story. The title is perhaps the single most important piece of promotional copy you will draft for the book.

MAILING THE MANUSCRIPT. If you aren't dealing with a nearby printer, you will have to ship the manuscript to him. Stack the photos and drawings and enclose them in cardboard to avoid folding. Send the manuscript in a binder. Enclose both in plastic bags and pack them in a sturdy cardboard carton. The Post Office does offer a special manuscript rate (same as book rate) but most authors prefer United Parcel Service because the service is good and the parcel must be signed for on the receiving end. Another alternative if you are not near a UPS office is certified, priority (air) mail through the Post Office. A couple of extra dollars now is well worth the expense. Be sure the carton contains your complete return address.

Always keep a copy of the manuscript. This is to protect you in case the original is lost in the mail or by the printer and it is your ready reference when the printer calls with questions. Take the manuscript to a copy center which has a plain paper dry type Xerox or IBM copier. They usually give reduced rates for overnight service and are quite cheap. After the book is printed, turn the copies over; the paper makes a fine scratch pad and people love to get notes on it.

If you are shipping a manuscript off to a publisher, make it arrive on Tuesday, Wednesday or Thursday, his better days. Send it Special Delivery so it doesn't come with the rest of his mail. Put a cover letter on top of the box and include postage for the return trip.

Writing a book is easy if you have the organization. With an understanding of this book, a decision to go and some discipline, you will start a whole new rewarding life.

The author has operated, and worked for, large firms and now has opted to go it alone. In terms of both dollar volume and books sold, he is probably the world's largest one-person publishing company. And this is by design.

Because he has committed himself to the luxury of a one-person enterprise, he must operate efficiently. He must concentrate on those areas which will provide a maximum return on investment of time and money: the highest profit and best results for the time and energy expended (invested).

He knows small business and small publishing inside-out because he plays both roles: he sets policy as management and implements it as labor. Consequently, he has developed simple systems to handle every task.

Most publishers with his amount of business have 5-7 employees. Dan works more efficiently and keeps all the pay cheques.

Dan is a small business man. His background is in marketing and mail order. He didn't come from the publishing industry and, consequently, he doesn't make their mistakes.

Starting a small publishing company is easy. It won't interfere with your writing as there is very little you have to do.

CHAPTER THREE

STARTING YOUR OWN PUBLISHING COMPANY

Forming your own publishing company is not difficult and many of the normal requirements may be postponed until you are ready to send your manuscript off to the printer. You do need a system and must get into the habit of using it. This is, after all, a business.

There are three forms of businesses: sole proprietorship, partnership and corporation and each choice has advantages and disadvantages which you will have to weigh. You don't have to make the choice right now. If you don't file anything, you will be operating as a sole proprietorship anyway. Here are a very few things to keep in mind while you are concentrating on the most important project: your manuscript.

In a sole proprietorship you have the choice of keeping your financial records on a cash basis or an accrual basis; the cash system makes more sense to a small business. Accrual requires more bookkeeping and you may always switch to it when you grow larger. But you must get IRS permission to make any switch

In a corporation, you are an employee, not the company itself. This means more accounting, payroll taxes, paperwork, annual meetings with published minutes, more taxes and annual registration fees. In California it is $200 per year.

Corporations are separate legal "beings" and can be sued but their stockholders cannot be touched. A sole proprietor does not have the protection of this "limited liability" and could lose his home and other possessions. There is more to consider in publishing than just the debts of the business. Someday, a reader is going to sue, claiming a book mislead him to his great damage. In fact, this has already happened with a cook book and a diet book. He will, of course, join both the author and publisher as defendants trying to collect from both you and your incorporated company. Since you are the author, incorporation won't protect you from suits.

Libel might be another reason to sue, but again, the plaintiff would seek damages from both. Keeping some of these problems in mind and considering your topic, talk to other people around you in small business and to your accountant and attorney.

PUBLICATIONS. When your manuscript is near completion and you have a "product," you will want to concentrate on the business end of publishing to get it printed and off to market. The Small Business Administration has many free publications and some at a slight charge which should help you. Write SBA, Washington, DC 10416 and request publication order forms #115-A and 115-B as well as Booklet #71, a checklist for going into business.

> *"Many of us are small because we want to be"* – Charles Nurnberg in *Publishers Weekly.*

It is strongly recommended that you subscribe to *Publishers Weekly* and *Writer's Digest* magazines. You'll learn about the writing/publishing trade, gain many ideas and build enthusiasm. Purchase a business book such as Kamoroff's *Small Time Operator* (see the Appendix).

SCORE is an SBA division the letters of which stand for "Service Corps of Retired Executives." These are retired executives who will call on you to assist in your problems. There is no charge for this service except for occasional out-of-pocket traveling expenses. There are several hundred SCORE chapters around the country. Call the SBA office nearest you to see if there is a nearby SCORE chapter. Look in the White Pages under U.S. Small Business Administration. Tell them what you need and they'll find someone tailored to you and your business. Naturally, it is always best to get this advice before you get into trouble; do it sooner, not later.

YOUR COMPANY NAME will have to be decided before you go to press so keep thinking about it. You could name it after yourself, say Ed Vickery Enterprises or Lon Nordeen Publishing Co., but these choices don't make you look as big as a separate name. The use of "enterprises" is the sign of a rank beginner. Don't do it. Looking big may be important when applying for credit from your vendors or asking a paper mill for samples. A company name will create the impression that you have a going business.

Geographical names can be limiting. Which sounds larger, East Weedpatch Press or North American Publishing? Which would you rather run and what happens if you move to West Weedpatch? If the business succeeds and one day you decide to sell out, the name will be sold with it. A good name will have more value. After all, what is the value of Scott Hamilton Publishing without Scott Hamilton? To find a new name, one that isn't being used in the publising industry, go to the library and look through *Writer's Market, International Directory of Little Magazines and Small Presses, Books in Print, Literary Market Place* and your local telephone directory. This is fun and you will note that the newer companies have some pretty weird names. As a new, little outfit, it doesn't hurt to have a handle that attracts attention. Pick a name that isn't being used by anyone else.

YOUR LOGO is a graphic image, an easily recognizable symbol; it may consist of a drawing or just the company name in a distinctive style of type. If you can dream up something clever and easily recognizable, start putting it on all of your letterheads, labels, business cards, etc.

YOUR PLACE OF BUSINESS will be your home for quite a while. You don't need a lot of space to write or even to store and ship books initially. When you have several titles and need more space and employees, you will have to move out, but for now home has many advantages. Working out of your home (house, mobile home, camper, wherever you live) will save additional rent, utilities, the headaches of a second property, etc. and, as we'll discuss later in this chapter, you can write off part of it on your tax return. Before you actually begin sorting, shipping and selling books in your front room, quietly check the zoning ordinances. Local regulations may allow one or two firms in one house. Your business will be small at first and as long as you don't have employees and large trucks aren't pulling into the drive every few minutes, no one is likely to complain. Avoid walk-in traffic and refer to yourself as an "author" rather than a "publisher" and you shouldn't encounter any difficulty. Sometimes when local regulations prohibit operating a business in a residential neighborhood, author/publishers post their business licenses at a friend's store and continue to quietly work out of their home. In the U.S., two percent of the work force enjoys the "short commute." If you are worried that a vendor or client might not be favorably impressed with your setup, make a lunch date in a restaurant.

Actually, he'll probably envy you. Working out of your home is more comfortable, efficient and cheaper.

P.O. BOX OR STREET ADDRESS. There are many good arguments for each one. Some feel quite strongly that a street address is more effective in a mail order ad because the business reflects more substance and stability. But today, even the big firms are using boxes. This is probably the result of the high incidence of urban crime. There was a time when the mail was sacred and no crook would dare to touch it, but not anymore. Depending on your address ("1234 Northwest Whispering Valley Parkway" or "Box 3") it could cost you more in classified ads where they charge by the word.

You will have to go to the Post Office regularly to ship books so you might as well pick up your mail while there. Another advantage is that you can maintain the same address even though you move (the Post Office forwards mail for only one year). But, perhaps the most important reason is to keep your excited, loyal readers from dropping in at all hours to meet their author who must be interested in them and their project. With a box, you'll be able to pick up your mail a few hours earlier each day. Apply for a box now and ask for a big one. In some areas they are in short supply and there is quite a waiting list. It may take you months to get one. Write your name, your company name and the title of your book on the box registration card so you will get your mail no matter how it is addressed. Remember, all your stationery and business references need an address so get a box now. They cost just a few dollars per year.

YOUR STATIONERY is you. It should look nice but you don't want to tie up a lot of money here. One attractive, inexpensive, simple system is available from The Drawing Board (Box 505, Dallas, TX 75221); write for a catalogue. All you'll need are #10 window envelopes, #ML5-N72 memo sized letterhead (without reply) and some invoice forms to fit. Windowed envelopes save time as you only type the name and address once. Also order business cards and a rubber stamp with your company name and address.

YOUR TELEPHONE may be listed under your name or the company name and if you request a commercial listing or a Yellow Page ad, you'll get hit with the higher commercial rate. Keep costs down by dialing direct during the evenings and on weekends for your research. For exact hours, consult the initial pages of your telephone directory.

YOUR TYPEWRITER is your most important piece of machinery; spend the money and get a good one. You are a "wordsmith" now and require the best word processing machine you can afford. For example, an IBM Correcting Selectric II is less tiring to operate than many machines and it will make your work look better. It can be used to create brochures, forms, etc. because of its clear, sharp type. There are a few on the used machine market and there will be more now that offices are switching to computerized, video display text editing equipment. See an office supply store. Even if you have to go new, consider paying for it over several months or years. After all, you'll be using it over a long period. If you are already in a high tax bracket, you should consider leasing all your office equipment. The costs are tax deductible and you tie up less money. Ask your accountant.

THE BETTER BUSINESS BUREAU may offer some credibility to a mail order business operating out of a Post Office box with a name like "Joe Smith Enterprises" and many people recommend joining. Look them up in your telephone directory and call to request

"You're a living, breathing, embodiment of the American Dream — free enterprise division".

literature on what they have to offer. Membership fees vary from one locality to the next and often run $100 per year for small business.

THE LEGAL REQUIREMENTS of operating a business are covered in many parts of this book just as you will encounter them in every facet of your daily publishing life. The following is what you need to run your business, but remember that most of it may be postponed until you are ready to go to press, move out of the house or hire employees. These tips, of course, are food for thought, not a substitute for legal counsel.

Interview a friend or acquaintance who has recently set up a small business in your community. They will be happy to tell you what happened to them, where to get various licenses, recommend an accountant, etc. In some areas you must register your business with local authorities, but not in all. Ask this same friend where to find the office. As a sole proprietorship, you won't need a separate bank account and until you hire employees, you will avoid tax numbers and special accounts.

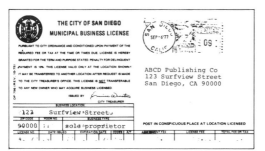

SALES TAXES. Most states have a sales tax. If your state does, you will be required to collect it ONLY on those sales shipped within the state which are NOT for resale by another dealer. The sales tax is collected only once at the retail level from the ultimate purchaser. In some states, shipping supplies are not subject to the sales tax. Other states exempt certain non-profit or public institutions such as libraries and schools. As a commercial firm, you must either collect the sales tax, show by the shipping address on the invoice that the goods are going out of state or claim to be selling them "for resale." Many states will require you to maintain a file of customer resale numbers. Sometimes they are listed on purchase orders but usually you have to send a standard resale number request card, available from your stationer, with the invoice. Type "for resale" on the invoice and record the resale number there if you have it.

Before you go to press, obtain your resale permit so you won't have to pay sales taxes on your books when you pick them up from the printer. Find the office in the telephone directory. In California it is called the Department of Equalization, in Massachusetts it is the Sales and Use Tax Bureau of the Department of Corporations and Taxation. Check the posted permit at a nearby store, the name of the controlling agency will be on it.

When you apply for your resale license or seller's permit, say you are just starting out as an author and hope to sell a few of your books. Tell them that most sales will be wholesale to bookstores or shipped out of state. This way you may be able to avoid giving them a deposit and you'll be allowed to report annually instead of quarterly, thus saving both money and paperwork. For example, in California, if you say your taxable sales (retail and within the state) might amount to more than $300 per month, you must place at least $100 on deposit with the Board of Equalization before you start. If you say

---

"We don't charge sales tax here, we just collect it."

you might be collecting over $12.50 per month in sales taxes, they'll want you to fill out the forms and remit the taxes quarterly instead of annually. When you apply, the tax office will supply you with an explanatory sheet detailing your responsibilities toward the sales tax in your state.

FIRM NAME _____

I HEREBY CERTIFY,
That I hold valid seller's permit No. _____
issued pursuant to the Sales and Use Tax Law: that I am engaged in the business of selling

_____

that the tangible personal property described herein which I shall purchase from:

_____

will be resold by me in the form of tangible personal property; PROVIDED, however, that in the event any of such property is used for any purpose other than retention, demonstration, or display while holding it for sale in the regular course of business, it is understood that I am required by the Sales and Use Tax Law to report and pay the tax, measured by the purchase price of such property.

Description of property to be purchased: _____

Dated: _____ 19 _____   Signature _____

at _____   By and Title _____

Phone _____   Address _____

Example of a California resale number request card.

When drafting ads, don't say: "California residents, please add 6% sales tax." This is a sure way to lose sales. Your potential buyer is not a mathematician and he will be embarrassed because he doesn't know how to figure percentages. Just ask for so many cents for sales tax. For example: "Californians please add 54¢ sales tax."

THE LAW YOU MUST KNOW as an author/publisher concerns copyright, defamation (libel), right of privacy and illegal reproduction. Briefly, copyrights work both ways: they protect your work from others and their work from you. Take pride, do your own original work and make it better. For a detailed explanation of the copyright, see Chapter 5.

DEFAMATION is libel in the printed word and slander when spoken. Black's Law Dictionary defines it as: "The offense of injuring a person's character, fame or reputation by false and malicious statements." It may take the form of either words or pictures. The offense is in the "publication" of the matter so you aren't "covered" if you read it somewhere else first. You are safe if the statement is true; this is the perfect defense, but check the source. The best advice is never to say anything nasty about anyone. You will need all the support you can get to sell your book. If you disagree with another authority, write "some people will argue. . ." or "many authorities believe. . ." and then tear up the position with your view. If you don't like someone, the worst thing you can do to them is to leave them out of your book altogether. Cover yourself and stay out of court; it's expensive.

RIGHT OF PRIVACY is another area of law you may face. Unless part of a news event, a person has a right to keep his photo out of publications. Most people love to see their

"More trouble than you ever dreamed may be as close as your nearest tax office."

photo in a book and, in fact, they are prime customers for the finished product. But if you suspect there may be a problem, have them sign a written release.

ILLEGAL REPRODUCTION covers the promoting of lotteries, stamps, financial schemes, fraudulent activities, securities, etc. In other words, don't print money. If you are writing about these subjects, you probably already know about the problems and the Postal laws, etc., relating to them. If not, seek legal advice.

TAXES are one place an author/publisher gets a big break. Not only are the costs of printing your book deductible, so are all the direct expenses incurred while writing it. If you are writing about your favorite hobby, you can deduct the expenses in pursuing it, too. There are sales and publicity tours and you can even write off a portion of your home, its rent or mortgage, utilities, etc. Assuming you are already employed and Uncle Sam is withholding 30% or more from your weekly cheque, that amounts to thousands of dollars a year. The game is to see how much you can get back. How much did you pay last year? Would you like to get a full refund? It's fun and rewarding. Of course, if your book is a great success, you'll make more money and have to pay taxes on it. For complete details, purchase a copy of the *Small Business Tax Guide* from your nearest IRS office. Under "record keeping", below, we'll detail possible deductions.

RECORDKEEPING must be done from the beginning of your writing because you can't deduct what you don't have written down. Many small business people get themselves into a jam by coming up with a great business idea and then charging off in pursuit of it. At the end of the year they suddenly realize that they've forgotten to fill out forms or record expenses. At that point their only choice is to hire an accountant to straighten out the mess. He charges much more for this sort of work and he will never be able to completely reconstruct the records or take all the deductions the business is entitled to take. The IRS is plugged into your bank and when they notice that $25,000 went through your bank account when you reported only $15,000, they'll be by with questions. And you can't really avoid the bank as you have to cash all those cheques which come in the mail for your book.

Dun & Bradstreet claims that 80% of all business failures are due to poor records. A University of Pittsburgh survey found that 40% of the retailers surveyed did not keep proper records. It's silly — no, tragic — because recordkeeping is easy with a simple system. Of course, as the business grows, you will also need financial information on your past to properly project the future.

Start right now. Pick up a few sheets of ledger paper from your office supply store; get some with at least 20 columns. Label the columns in the expense ledger as follows: meals & lodging, gas/lube/ wash, office supplies, shipping & postage, advertising, entertainment, air, etc. fares, travel expenses, cost of supplies (books), dues & licenses, subscriptions, telephone, electricity, water, mortgage/rent, parking

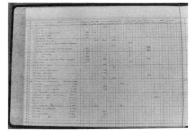
Sample ledger page.

& tolls, car repairs, car tires & supplies, refunds and miscellaneous. The income ledger sheet will probably only reflect sales from your wholesale invoices and retail labels (see Chapter 10). For a detailed explanation of the items that fit into these columns, see the IRS publication *Small Business Tax Guide* mentioned above. The best way to get into the habit and to learn what is deductible is to list EVERY cent you spend the first year. Get receipts whenever possible, at the Post Office, for parking, tolls, meals, motels, etc. Your accountant will decide what is deductible when he does your taxes.

You have already decided to carry pen and paper at all times to record your thoughts for your manuscript so carry one more sheet for recording expenditures. Write down every cent. As you learn what is deductible, you will find that you become generous where it can be written off and stingy where it can't. This is good discipline and good business. Keep an envelope in the car. Each day as you get in and start the car, let it warm up a moment as you record the date, mileage reading and places you intend to go. Use the envelope to hold the receipts you acquire during the day. Use a new envelope every month.

Every few months or even at the end of the year, sit down at the ledger and post the expenses for each month from your pocket notes, car envelope and cheque book. If you are not sure what column an expenditure might go in, place it in miscellaneous. In March, total up the columns and take the ledger and totaled figures to your accountant. He will do the rest and the charge will be reasonable. You'll be amazed at the size of your refund and he will compliment you on your work. It is so easy and yet many people think there is some great mystery to accounting.

You don't even have to make money to claim deductions. You can claim a loss for up to three years in a row before the IRS deems you to be a hobbyist rather than an author/publisher. Keep good records and you'll be able to easily prove you are in business. See the tax discussion in *Writer's Market*.

RAISING THE MONEY YOU NEED to finance the production and promotion of your book will take you into the world of finance unless you have a lot of loose, ready cash lying about. Insufficient capitalization is one of the greatest problems facing most new businesses. Money won't come looking for you. You have to find it by selling yourself and your book. But it is there, it is available. To begin, you won't run up bills by hiring help or renting space and you'll even save some leisuretime money by staying home to write. So you won't have any immediate needs for large sums of cash. Most people have more money than they really need for necessities. They throw away their disposable income on frivolous purchases. Going without booze, cigarettes and nights out is not only healthier, the time can be better spent writing a book.

Some people advise the use of "OPM" (other people's money) rather than your own. Then if your business goes bust, you still have your own money in reserve. But as you tuck your prized manuscript under your arm and venture off in your search for funds, you're going to find it takes some searching.

THE SMALL BUSINESS ADMINISTRATION has prohibited financial assistance to book publishers ever since it came into being in 1953. But then they treat the whole opinion-molding media this way. This is to avoid financing radicals who might print seditious literature and then file for bankruptcy. This would leave the taxpayers with a social problem and the bill for starting it.

BANKS don't search for loan applicants in the publishing industry. They like "going" firms with upbeat balance sheets; like everyone else, they are in business to stay in business. Banks look on manuscripts/books as "speculative." Even armed with a detailed market research report on your product, you may find that you can't even get an appointment with the loan officer. A stack of books isn't considered good collateral to a bank; if you defaulted, they wouldn't know how to turn the books back into money. If you ask for money to go into business, the bank won't be interested. You are better off working

---

"You can't deduct it if it isn't recorded. If you don't make a note now, you'll forget it."

your new publishing company part time. Then if it fails, at least you aren't out of a job, too.

Basically, there are two ways to borrow money from a bank. The first is the "term" loan which is normally used to finance purchases such as a car. It is paid back monthly and is usually limited to 36 months. The second is an ordinary signature loan with interest at the prime rate plus about 5%. It runs six months and you pay it off at the due date. But while the loan is written for six months, it is common to pay just the interest and renew it for another six. Many authors have been successful in acquiring money by leaving the manuscript at home and asking for a "vacation" loan.

You may need collateral, perhaps a second mortgage. If you have enough real and personal property, you will be able to get the money on your signature alone. Don't think small, large amounts are often easier to borrow.

All banks are not the same, shop around not only for loans but for the bank itself. They aren't doing you any favors, you are doing them a favor by dealing with them. Stop in at several and pick up pamphlets on their chequing account and loan policies. Take the brochures home and compare them. Do they charge for each cheque deposited? You will be receiving a lot of small cheques and any cheque charge will add up fast. Do they pay interest on chequing accounts and if so, what is the minimum required balance? Will they let you bank by mail and will they pay the postage? Don't just think of your present needs, think of the future.

PRE-PUBLICATION SALES are often used to raise money. Before going to press, send a brochure out to all who might be interested in the book and offer them a break on the price for a pre-publication order. Emphasize that the manuscript is complete and that the book is on the press. Tell them you won't cash their cheque until the book is shipped. Mention a shipping date but give yourself an extra month or two.

SELLING STOCK in your business is another way but there are a lot of problems. You aren't big enough to make it worth your while and you should give it a great deal of thought before sharing the rewards of your work. If you can find someone to risk an investment in your book, you can find one to give you a straight loan at a good rate of interest where his risk is lower.

GRANTS are available from numerous foundations for worthwhile publishing projects. The Glide Foundation tells you all about them in *The Bread Game*. Check into the National Endowment for the Arts (Government), Alicia Patterson Foundation (private) and see the listings in *Grants and Awards Available to Writers*. Additional listings may be found in *Literary Market Place,* UNESCO's handbook *Study Abroad* as well as in magazines such as *CODA: Poets and Writers Newsletter* and *The Writer.* The Dramatists Guild and the Theatre Communications Group also publish useful periodicals. See listings in the Appendix. Most of the grants and fellowships are for fiction and poetry. If your book qualifies, it can mean a lot of money but there is a lot of paperwork to go along with it.

WRITERS' COLONIES often supply free room and board to support budding authors. Some have rigid rules limiting the length and number of stays. For a list, see *Writer's Market.*

YOUR PRINTER may be interested in helping you in exchange for an interest in the book. Typically, the printing company would absorb the printing costs and would receive 10-15% of the sales in return.

"High cash flow": Taking in lots of money but being unable to find any of it.

PARENTS will lend on a book. They have faith in their offspring and ᴠ
name on a book as much as you do. But if you do borrow from friends o
the same presentation to them that you would to a bank. Talk figures an
tional. Then pay them the 10-13% interest that you would pay the bank
a business basis and keep the friendship. It's all deductible and you'll get more of your
withholding taxes back anyway.

OTHER POSSIBILITIES include credit unions, retirement plans, the Veterans Administration (if appropriate) and the Farm Home Loan Association which is said to be very
liberal in its definition of a "farm community." Shop around.

HOW MUCH you will need is an important question and this will take some research. At
1979 prices, it might cost you $12,000 to launch a nice book. This would be 5,000
copies of a 6 x 9 paperback with 200 pages, lots of photographs and a four color cover.
Initially you might spend $2,000 for research trips, photographic work and office supplies.
The printing might cost $8,000 and then the shipping supplies and early promotion may
run another $2,000. A book with fewer photos and a one color cover could run much less
but without a good looking book and some promotion money, the book won't sell. For
details, see the chapters on pricing and promotion. Get a quote from your printer to firm
up the middle number. Try to be more exact with amounts and dates. On the first venture, the printer will probably want his money in installments: 1/3 when the composition
is set, 1/3 when the paste-ups are made and 1/3 on the completion of the printing. After
a book or two, he'll no doubt give you normal 30 day terms and want his money a month
after he delivers the books to you. If he wants installments, agree to them and then request a "2% discount for cash." (2% of $8,000 is $160.) In fact, you should always take
cash discounts when paying bills even if you have to borrow to do so. Invoices with terms
marked "2% ten" mean you can knock off 2% if you pay on the 10th instead of the 30th
day. This is the equivalent of 36% per year. If you pay money before it is due, you are
financing someone else's business without receiving interest; unless they offer ten day
terms, pay on the 30th day.

Realistically, not wishfully, project your other expenses. Then work up a projected
income chart. How much money do you expect to come in, from where and how fast?
Now you know what you'll need.

If you wait until you need the money to approach the source, you've waited too
long. For if you can find it at all at this point, it is likely to be very expensive. Line up
your sources of credit now but don't borrow the money until you need it. Borrow the
funds for one, two or three years, whatever you project the needs to be, and make sure
you won't be penalized for paying it back early.

Run a streamlined, efficient operation. Do everything yourself and buy only those
services you cannot perform. Avoid employees, they cost you time (management), money
and paperwork. When contracting for services, remember that everyone is in business for
himself first, you come second. The graphic artist, accountant and all the rest will try to
sell you more than you need. They don't care about your business as much as you do because they have less to lose.

Keep on top of costs. If you can save $1,000 per year by streamlining procedures
and your net profit is normally 3%, the effect is the same as if you increased sales by
$30,000.

Don't waste anything. Save the stamps from the incoming mail. Stamp collecting
is big business and you can sell them to the big stamp companies.

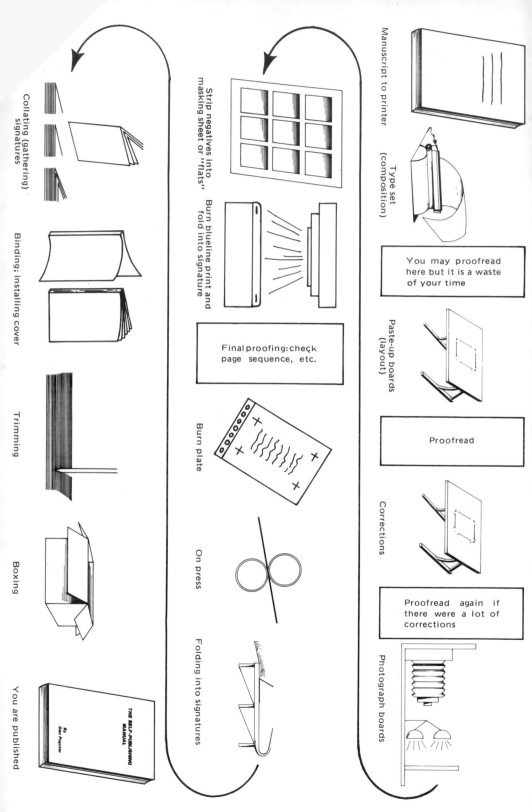

Manuscript to printer

Type set (composition)

You may proofread here but it is a waste of your time

Paste-up boards (layout)

Proofread

Corrections

Proofread again if there were a lot of corrections

Photograph boards

Strip negatives into masking sheet or "flats"

Burn blueline print and fold into signature

Final proofing: check page sequence, etc.

Burn plate

On press

Folding into signatures

Collating (gathering) signatures

Binding; installing cover

Trimming

Boxing

THE SELF-PUBLISHING MANUAL

By
Dan Poynter

You are published

CHAPTER FOUR

PRINTING YOUR BOOK

THE PRINTING PROCESS   DESIGN OF BOOKS
BOOK MATERIALS

Here is what you can expect when your book enters the production stage. This explanation of the printing process is meant to be brief and yet provide you with enough information to deal with your printer. There are many excellent books on the printing trade. See your library. One good one is *Printing It* by Clifford Burke. See the Appendix.

You have the information and have written the manuscript. Now the project is to decide how to package the information to make it saleable. Some packages will bring in more money than others. You might print it in a series of magazine articles, present it at a seminar or print it in a book. Or you might concentrate on one of them, such as the book, and spin off part to the rest. People are paying good money for well packaged information today. Some manuals cost $75 and some seminars run $200 per day. Obviously, the "package" must appear to be worth the asking price. It must be a professionally run seminar, a nicely printed book or an attractive article in a prestigious magazine. Here is what you should know about printing. This will help you to select an appropriate design for your book.

PRINTING PROCESSES. There are two methods which may be used to print your book. Letterpress is the older one. It uses a linotype machine to set "hot type" or cast metal which is set into the press. It is more costly as it requires highly skilled tradesmen, usually unionized and it is less flexible than your other choice. Photo offset is a newer process where the original work ("cold type") is set by typewriter, composer (like a typewriter but much more versatile with variable type size, proportional spacing and a justified right-hand margin) or a computerized photo composition machine with a video screen. The pasted copy of type, line drawings and screened photos are transferred to a thin printing plate photographically. The "plates" are lighter, type is set faster, illustrations (and you'll have a lot of photos) are easier to handle, the quality is better, accuracy is improved and it is more versatile. Most printers have switched to offset today, so unless you go to a specialized firm or a very small press which concentrates on letterpress work, all you will find is offset. You will hear of other modern methods of producing books such as Web offset and belt press but these are used for large and very large print runs.

Conversely, there are also some less expensive, short run methods. Wire stitched (stapled) booklets with up to about 60-5½ x 8½ pages can be reproduced very nicely on photocopy machines from typewritten material. Machines such as the Xerox 9200 and

> *"Quality often becomes diluted if you publish a lot, whereas to a small publisher each publishing decision is a crutial one – you commit everything to each book, without hoping to counterbalance a wrong choice with a more successful one"* – Glenn Johns of Rodale Press.

9400 will print both sides of the paper and collate them. They will even handle heavy cover stock. Other machines will even print in color. Drop by a Xerox office for a demonstration. Short run booklets may also be inexpensively produced by your local "instant print" shop. Ask them for a brochure.

This book will concern itself with squarebound soft cover and hardcover books, those you normally see in a bookstore. If you have a book-length manuscript, one which will fill a book of 100 pages or more, you'll want a clean, sharp, professional-appearing product, one that will sell. You will be proud of it and it will be more acceptable to the stores.

You can figure on about a month to print, bind and deliver your books to you but it may be slower if your printer can't do all the work in-house and has to farm some of it out. What will take a lot of time, perhaps months, will be the composition and layout. The variables here are the number of photos, number of pages, amount of corrections and whether you can get in to keep up with the proofreading. Hardbound books will take a couple of weeks more because they must be sent out, in most cases, to install the cover. They take longer to bind.

BOOK DESIGN serves two purposes. It organizes the material for the reader to aid communication and it organizes the material for the printer for efficiency. Most publishers have book designers who rough out the book layout and make up dummies. They show the position of the type on the pages, especially in the front and back matter. You may wish to give your printer specific instructions on some of your pages but there is no need to make up a dummy of the whole book. You already know what will go where because of your binder layout.

With a colored pencil, so it won't be confused with copy, write your notes on the pages. Use the same color pencil throughout for consistency. Only occasionally will you have special instructions for the layout of a page. Most of the copy and illustrations will simply be stripped in. There is no need to illustrate the obvious. Use other attractive books as a guide. You may vary from their format but strive for consistency throughout your book. Note that chapters start on a right-hand page. If this leaves you with a blank on the left, fill it with a photograph. Just supply the printer with a few extra photos and tell him to fill any blank pages with them.

"Running heads" are lines of type which appear across the top of the book page. Usually the title of the book appears on the left-hand page while the chapter title is on the right. They are a good sales device and educationally useful as they reinforce your message, but they may be omitted. The "folio" is the page number. They may be placed in the top outside corner, bottom middle or even on the side. In a die-cut circular book, the side might look best. Traditionally, pages receive Roman numerals in the front matter and Arabic numbers in the text. But today, many publishers take a tip from the magazine companies and start the count, though not the numbering, from the title page. This makes the final page count higher and makes the purchaser feel he is getting more for his money. The argument goes: "I paid for those pages so I'm going to count them."

Sometimes there is a good marketing reason to vary from the standard. The book is nestled into the disc and shrink wrapped.

STANDARDIZE AND SAVE MONEY. If you vary from the norm, it'll cost you. Occasionally this can be justified, as in a die-cut circular book on Frisbee play, but make sure the special work will contribute to the sales of the book. Remember, too, that libraries and bookstores have standardized shelving. You want your book to fit. Ask for a tour of your printer's plant and take his advice. As long as he can produce your book at a competitive price, it doesn't really matter how he does it. According to *Publishers Weekly,* most short run books are 6 x 9, perfect bound (glued) paperbacks with or without photos and drawings on a 50-pound stock. The cover is printed on a 65-pound uncoated stock. Beyond this basic volume, a number of variations are possible. Each page will accept about 400 words, less with illustrations. The conventional 6 x 9 is suitable for both hardcover and soft, it is one of the most economical, fits a library shelf well and is by far the most popular size. Whatever size you select, make all your books the same so as to standardize your shipping bags and cartons.

NUMBER OF PAGES. You need 24 to qualify for the Post Office's "book rate", 50 to get a Library of Congress Catalog Card Number and 100 pages to qualify for a listing in H. W. Wilson's *Cumulative Book Index.* Over 100 is psychologically good and will help to justify your price so if you have just 99 pages, add some copy or an illustration.

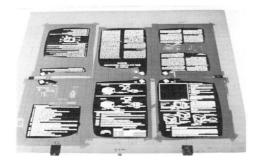

A stripped-in flat.

The photographic negatives of the pasted-up boards are "stripped-in" (positioned) to the masking sheet or "flat" prior to being "burned-in" to the thin metal printing plate.

Your book will be printed on several very large sheets of paper which will be folded down into "signatures." The number of book pages which will be in each will depend on the size of your printer's press, but 16 is common. This means that eight of the pages will be printed on one side ("eight up") and eight will be printed on the other. Therefore, you will figure the pages in your book in multiples of 16.

Ask your printer how many pages his press can fit onto a sheet and you'll be able to figure how many signatures will be required. Now, depending upon the size of the signatures, probably multiples of 16, try to come out close to even. 113 pages will cost much more than 112 (16 x 7) because of the extra press run which will be required for just one page. You might like to cut some material or choose a slightly smaller type style. The dimensions of your books have to be considered. One hundred-twenty 6 x 9 pages make a much nicer book than 60-8½ x 11 pages. The only good reason to go oversize is if the product is a workbook requiring larger areas for drawings, etc.

You will know the exact page count once the boards are pasted up and it will take a week or more before you will take delivery of the books. If you need the page count sooner, simply look through books of the same size (6 x 9, etc.) and find a type size and spacing you like. Count the words on the full page. Then count the words on a typical

"We think that small presses and self-publishing individuals frequently preceed the market because they can more easily become involved in a new trend at the conceptual level and can bypass a lot of the red tape that slows things down in larger houses." — Bob Speer of Southwest Book Services.

full page of your manuscript and add in more pages for photos depending on their to-be-reproduced size and number. Don't forget to count the front matter and back matter separately. While your printer can come up with an exact count through a long, involved computation, this will be close enough. In your brochures, refer to the page count as: "More than 150 pages"; you don't have to be exact but people do like to know what they are paying for.

Poetry gets different treatment. Unless very short, each poem should get its own page.

EXAMPLES OF TYPE FACES

TYPE FACES are many and varied; no printer could stock all the styles and sizes. With the help of your printer, you will select the type size and style, the width of the columns (128mm or 5" in a 6 x9 book) and whether you want the right-hand side justified (even or ragged right margin). Books set with a ragged right don't look professional and find it difficult to gain acceptance in bookstores and libraries. Four factors affect legibility: type style (sans serif, italics, etc. are harder to read), type size, leading (rhymes with "heading" and is the space between the lines) and the column width (the eye was trained on narrow newspaper columns). To give your book some variation, you may use italics, boldface, small caps and larger sizes for chapter heads, captions, subheads and for lending emphasis.

8/9
Univers
lite

10/10
Univers
Med.
Condensed

Here are some more type terms to make you sound as though you know what you are talking about. "Point size" is the height of a capital letter (and its mount) as in "10 pt. type." There are 72 points to the inch. "Pica" is the printer's standard measurement for the length of a line and the depth of a page. There are 12 points to a pica and six picas to the inch. Therefore, "24
picas" means a four inch wide column. "Leading" or slug is the space between the lines. Printers used to use a strip of lead, hence the name. So, if you have nine points of type plus two points of leading, it would be written out as "9/11."

10/11
Theme
italic

10/12
Press
Roman Bld.

Nine on eleven is about as small as you should go for a legible book.
Ten on twelve is very common though children and older people with failing eyesight prefer a 12/14. This book, for the most part, was set in 10/11 which is legible and economical. What you will decide to use will depend to a great degree on the length of the finished book. Look through books you like and ask your printer for samples.

11/11
Univers
Condensed
Lite

Some composing machines put more type on a page than others using identical type face, size and leading. "11/13 Century x 24 picas" is not always the same; it all depends on how the machine was originally programmed. You will want a sample of your printer's work in order to estimate pages.

11/11
Theme
Medium

You may even set your own type with a typewriter but you'll get a more professional book if it is typeset. If you use a typewriter, buy or rent an IBM Correcting Selectric II with a carbon ribbon and type on "repro paper" which is whiter and provides cleaner, sharper copy.

11/12
Univers
Medium

Compare the various type faces.

6 Helvetica
7 Helvetica
8 Helvetica
8½ Helvetica
9 Helvetica
10 Helvetica
11 Helvetica
12 Helvetica
13 Helvetica
14 Helvetica
15 Helvetica
16 Helvetica
17 Helvetica
18 Helvetica
19 Helvetica
20 Helvetica
21 Helvetica
22 Helvetica
23 Helvetica
24 Helvetica

Letter height is measured in "points." There are 72 points to the inch.

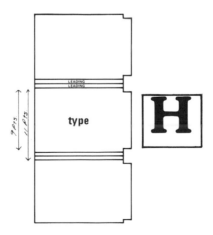

The relationship between type and leading in point size. This is "9/11."
Note that the character is not the full height of the type body. Leading
is used to further separate the lines of type to facilitate reading.

Americana
Americana Italic
Americana Bold
Americana Extra Bold

Aquarian Script

Avant Garde Extra Light
Avant Garde Book
Avant Garde Medium
Avant Garde Demi Bold

Baskerville
Baskerville Italic
Baskerville Bold

Bauhaus Light
Bauhaus Medium
Bauhaus Demi Bold
Bauhaus Bold

Bembo
Bembo Italic
Bembo Bold
Bembo Bold Italic
Brush

Caslon Antique
Caslon Open

Cheltenham Bold
Cheltenham Bold Condensed

Cheltenham Bold Outline

Commercial Script

Cooper Black
Cooper Black Italic

Deepdene
Deepdene Italic

Eurostile

Type over 12 point is usually set with a headliner.

HEADLINES, such as chapter titles, which are larger than 12 pt. are set on a headlining machine. Your printer will show you the type styles he has to offer. You may also set your own using transfer type available at most stationery stores.

ILLUSTRATIONS will augment the text, enhance the appearance and aid the saleability of the book. Don't be cheap with illustrations. Each one is very inexpensive when the cost is spread out over the entire print run of books. If a photo or drawing will make the book more attractive, readable or useful to the buyer, include it.

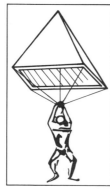

Line drawing.

Extra lines were crowded into this line drawing to give it an appearance of shading.

Photo printed unscreened.

Same photo screened.
Study with a magnifying glass or lupe.

LINE ART may consist of type, charts, sketches, etc. If you draw your own artwork or have it done, use a fine-point felt tip pen with black ink.

"Clip Art" is sold by the book or sheet and consists of line drawings on almost every possible subject. It lacks originality but it is less expensive than hiring an artist. Your printer can tell you where to get clip art and he may have a lot of it himself. Art may be taken from old magazines and books, too. If the copyright has expired, it is in the public domain. Prior to 1 January 1978, copyright protection was for 28 years and was renewable for an additional 28 years. Therefore, anything printed prior to 1922 is safe and anything in print prior to 1950 is probably safe.

HALFTONES must be made of artwork which is not solid black-white, such as photographs. The original copy is re-photographed through a screen and the resulting print is composed of dots of various sizes. The eye blends the dots together into a continuous tone. Making a halftone of a photo, pencil drawing, water color, etc. costs $4 to $7 each. This is a one-time charge if you save the negatives; you won't have to pay again to screen photos for the next press run.

Screens come in several values and are measured in dots per linear inch. The more dots, the crisper the printed halftone. Newspapers commonly use a 65- or 85-line screen (85 dots per running inch) while books are commonly done in 120, 133 or even 150 line. Black and white photographs screen best. Color prints tend to get muddy.

Photos taken from other magazines and books have already been screened and may be pasted right onto the boards. However, if they are to be enlarged or reduced, they must be re-screened and this usually reduces the quality.

With both photos and drawings, reductions are preferable to enlargements. Reductions become sharper while enlargements only magnify flaws, losing clarity.

A DUOTONE is a two color process which is usually done for technique and makes a halftoned photograph look different from a plain black and white. Using a black and white original photograph, the paper goes through the press twice to be inked with black and one other color.

FOUR COLOR PRINTING should be used on covers but it is normally too expensive for inside pages. To reproduce a color photo or slide, it is re-photographed four times, each time with a different colored filter over the lens. This produces four negatives consisting of the three primary colors (red, blue and yellow) plus black. This is called a "four color separation." Then the paper is run through the press four times, each with one of the colors and the color photo is re-created. Naturally, this is all more expensive because of the additional camera work and press time. Always ask for a "color key" before your color pages are run through the press. When checking these four plastic color overlays, remember simply that the sky is blue, the grass is green, clouds are white, wood is brown, etc. What you see is what you get.

Drawings may be pasted right down on the board. If they are to be reduced, this is done photographically and there is a camera charge. You will be able to check them for position in your first proofreading. If there are just a few halftones (photographs), the board will only have empty spaces for them, you won't check them until the page negatives have been stripped into the flats. If, however, your text has several hundred halftones, your printer may wish to make screened prints of the photos and paste them onto the boards. This allows you to catch the errors sooner and is ultimately cheaper. It is frustrating to proof copy without the accompanying photographs; you just cannot visualize the completed page or comprehend the entire message.

PAPER is even more confusing than type faces, and while you should know what to look for, you will need the guidance of your printer to make a final choice. In times of tight supply, not all types of paper in any quantity are always available. Some printers stock a very few grades in a narrow range of colors while others order paper for each job they do. Basically, you have four general choices:
1. Newsprint: this is inexpensive but it looks cheap and the photo reproduction is poor.
2. Uncoated book stock: looks good, photos OK.
3. Coated book stock (matte, coated or gloss): looks great, photos great, more expensive.
4. Fancy textured papers: may be hard to print, especially photos. Expensive.
Unless you are doing an art book, an uncoated book stock is what you need. Your printer will probably suggest a "50-pound or 60-pound offset."
Paper comes by the sheet or the roll (cut into sheets after printing). Usually 16 pages are printed and then the paper is folded down into signatures for the book. There are many variables which must be considered when selecting paper.
1. Weight is expressed in pounds per 500 sheets but the full size of the sheet varies according to the category to which the paper belongs. 60-pound cover stock and 60-pound book papers are not the same. Generally, heavier paper is more expensive though some of the newer lightweight papers, developed for combating Postal rates, are even higher in price. If the paper is too thin, the book will look and feel "cheap"; if it is too heavy, the book may not fold flat and, in any case, you have wasted your money.
2. Texture. Some highly textured paper does not accept ink well, especially photos.
3. Opacity. You don't want the type on the other side of the page to show through. Light paper can be very opaque, especially when coated. Opacity may be tested by placing a printed sheet under the sample to see how much shows through.
4. Bulking factor is expressed in pages per inch (PPI). An 800 page book of 60-pound stock might have a PPI of 1 7/8ths while the same book in 45-pound paper would have a PPI of 1 3/8ths. Bulking depends on the fiber content and the milling process used; A high bulk may also be produced by whipping air into the paper during manufacture. This produces a thicker paper without increasing weight. However, this fluffed-up paper allows ink to diffuse more, so halftones are not as crisp. PPI is measured by the even inch.
5. Grain is important if you plan to fold the paper, since it may fold better in one direction than another. Important in greeting card manufacture using heavy stock.
6. Grade refers to the type of paper, be it writing grade, book, cover stock, envelope, gummed, blotting, chipboard, etc.
7. Coating is done with a clay-like material and produces a smooth, shiny finish. Since the ink dries on the surface, rather than down in the fibers of the paper, it looks crisper and cleaner. Coated stock, while more expensive, makes half-

tones look much better. It is a must for art books. Smooth finishes may also be produced by drawing the paper over a blade edge or calendering (a heat and pressure roller process). The result may be a duller finish which is easier on the eyes.

Paper comes in a large variety of types and paper salesmen will be happy to deluge you with beautifully printed samples of all their wares. Don't buy paper any more expensive than you need. Ask your printer if he has any stock left over from another run. Perhaps you can shorten your press run and swing a sweet deal.

If you attend one of the many publishing seminars, you will probably be advised to purchase your own paper and "save about 15%." This makes about as much sense as taking your own oil to the gas station when you want it changed. The printer won't be happy about losing his markup and will probably charge you a "handling fee" or he may raise your price later claiming the job was "hard to print." If you buy your own paper, you'll have to pay for it sooner, will be faced with storage and transportation problems and might lose it all if the printer botches a press run. It is far safer to simply get several quotes on the finished product and let the printer worry about the materials. After all, what you want is the least hassle and best price. Incidentally, printers and paper salespeople continually use the same pressure tactic claiming there will be a paper shortage soon. Expect it.

INK comes in a lot of colors and types, too, but both you and your printer will probably want black. If you are doing something special, ask to see his ink color sample books. Remember that inks are transparent. If you print a drawing in blue and then overprint part in red, that part will become purple. Similarly, if you print blue ink on yellow paper, the print will be green. Unless you are doing a special art-type book, you will stick to the traditional black ink on white paper.

PAPERBACK AND/OR HARDCOVER.
Traditionally, publishers printed in hard-cover at a high price and would wait until sales dropped to come out with a cheaper softcover version. They might also publish a "library edition" with a supposedly reinforced hard cover, may-be an extra fancy "deluxe edition" on special paper, with gold stamped leather covers and even numbered and auto-

Examples of the same title in both paperback and hardcover.

graphed. Then there might be "large type" editions for the elderly and, finally, even an inexpensive "mass market paperback" edition. But what has emerged more recently is the very popular "oversize paperback," also known as the quality, trade, large format, large size, special or higher priced paperbacks. They fill the gap between the mass market pocket-sized book and the hardcover version. So this narrows your field to the hardcover and the quality paperback or simply "softcover."

Years ago, hardcover books carried a certain prestige while paperbacks were considered cheap and less desirable. But, primarily because of increased production costs, this is no longer true. Today, many publishers issue their books in the softcover only.

By far, most of your sales will be in the soft cover but you should produce some in hard not only for the libraries but for those special presentation copies you'll want for yourself. But with two editions, you want to make sure that they sell at the same rate

"Larger paperbacks . . . represent the greatest potential for growth in the book business today" – Publishers Weekly.

so that you won't have a lot of one left over when you run out of the other and are printing a revision. On a 5000 book press run, you might consider doing 4000 in paper, 200 in hardcover and holding the texts of the remaining 800 to be covered later. But you must tell your printer to do this prior to the folding operation. Similarly, you must tell the printer you intend to use the same photo on all the covers so he will make the color separation just slightly oversize. This allows for wrap-around on the hardcover while a small amount is trimmed off on the paperback.

Hardcover books are expensive to produce and must carry a higher cover (list) price, but libraries like them and you don't want to miss out on this important market. However, libraries know how many times books can be loaned out (about 18 for paperback) before they fall apart. If the price difference between the two is too great, it becomes less expensive to purchase copies of the paperback and replace them more often. Often, libraries send paperbacks out to be "Permabound" with laminated hard covers. It costs about $2.50 to extend the book's life in this manner. Hardcover bindings are often used for reference works and it is estimated that about 20% are purchased as gifts. They do make a nicer presentation than a paperback.

More and more softcover books are showing up as school texts today. Paper editions are lighter in weight and take up less space, making them easier to carry and cheaper to mail. Their lower manufacturing costs result in wider distribution, thus bringing the author greater fame and fortune.

DUST JACKETS OR PRINTED CLOTH. You have a choice in the covering of your hardbound edition. The traditional method is to wrap the book in a colorful jacket. The problem is that the jackets are not durable and don't last long. In fact, many bookstores ask for extras to keep the stock looking fresh. Another way is to print the cloth before it is installed on the book; this makes it far more attractive, especially on library shelves.

Dust jacket and printed cloth covers.
A printed cloth cover lasts longer.

DUST JACKETS often contain a synopsis of the book on the inside front flap and a photo with a biography of the author on the inside back. If you use the printed cloth cover instead of a jacket, then like your paperback, you won't have any flaps. The alternative is to place the biographical information, lists of previous works, etc., in the front matter or back matter of the book.

THE COVER OF YOUR BOOK has two purposes: to protect the contents and to be a selling tool. According to *The Wall Street Journal*, the average book store browser who picks up a book spends 8 seconds reading the front cover and 15 seconds reading the back. And this assumes the book stood out enough to catch his attention enticing him to pick it up in the first place. In mass market (small size, high volume) paperbacks, this "hype" consists of about 12 words on the front cover and 75 on the back. The blurbs use words like "stunning," "dazzling," "moving" and "tumultuous."

The cover should include the title, subtitle (helps to identify the subject), the name of the author and a related photograph or drawing with impact. The print shouldn't be so fancy that it is hard to read at a glance. It is said that red attracts and sells best and many

> *"You can't tell — but you can sell — a book by its cover"* — The Wall Street Journal

cover designers like to use it. Color definitely sells and the money should be spent to send the cover through the press four times. At the very minimum, two strongly-contrasting colors should be used. It depends upon your subject. In an action sport, an eye-catching color photo is preferable to straight lines of type.

Some of the things your cover should do are to make the author look like the ultimate expert on the subject. It should promise the buyer something such as health, wealth, entertainment or a better life. It must be bold, distinctive, intriguing so as to catch the eye and sell; it must stand out from the thousands of books around it. Depending upon the subject, you might include documentation and source material such as testing, surveys, case histories, etc. Stress the promise that the buyer is getting more than his money's worth. Important new information, such as a prestigious book review, may be printed on a sticker. Make the sticker a contrasting color and apply it at an angle so it doesn't look printed on.

THE SPINE usually has the title, the name of the author and an eye-catching symbol. If it is a dog book, include the outline of a dog. The symbol may attract the buyer more easily than the printed word. If there is room, you may include the subtitle, but make sure the title is big enough to be legible. Traditionally, the name of the publisher was included here but in this case, you are the publisher and no one has heard of your company at this point. Some publishers also include the International Standard Book Number (ISBN) here. But beware of too much clutter. Your book will probably end up in the bookstore with only the spine showing from the shelf. Make it an eye-grabber.

THE BACK COVER usually has another attractive illustration or group of them, a blurb on the book, the price and the ISBN. Use whatever will sell the book. Many books have a photo and biographical sketch of the author. If you are an obvious expert and can't find anything better to put here, do it — but watch the ego trips. Many publishers print testimonials here. To get them, they send galley proofs out for review months before the book is completed. You will be anxious to get into print and onto the shelf so it is unlikely that you will have them prior to your second printing. You can always print the reviews of your relevant previous titles. Bookstores want a price on the cover. It is often recommended that you use small stickers to allow flexibility. But this requires extra work and expense and even in these inflationary times, it makes little sense to raise the price once your printing bill is paid. Remember that changing prices, up or down, means new brochures, notifying *Books In Print,* etc. Sometimes the back cover is used to promote other books by the author but this valuable selling space probably shouldn't be wasted in this manner.

Make every word on the front cover, spine and back cover count. There is no way to predict how the store will display your book.

DIFFERENT MARKETS are used to looking for different things on book covers. Target your primary audience and then try to cater to as many others as possible.

Mass market (smaller) paperbacks use a lot of color and "hype" because they have to compete with magazines for attention. It is assumed they are aimed at the less sophisticated people who don't frequent bookstores.

Mail-order books don't have to be flashy but their type must be large and clear so as to show up well in photographs in brochures and ads. The back covers don't show in the ads so they are often used to sell other books.

> *"The designer is expected to approach covers as though they were posters or ads"*
> — John Huenefeld.

Trade books aimed at bookstores need a poster-like cover to aid in their sale. The back should also have a sales message as it is the next place a potential customer will look after the cover.

Textbook covers must be much more conservative or they'll "turn off" the educators who make the purchasing decisions.

Don't be confined by convention. The unorthodox cover may catch the eye better. Unless it is offensive, it will be the first step in selling the book. But look over other books you admire. Most follow the same pattern in layout. There must be a reason and you can bet it isn't lack of Madison Avenue imagination.

If the cover is not doing its job, consider changing it when you go back to press for a second printing. Once it is in print the first time, you will come up with a number of ideas for changes. Ask your printer to send you a half dozen of the paper covers flat. He will take them off the line before they are scored, folded and installed on the texts. These covers are beautiful and look very nice framed. You'll be proud to hang one on your wall and you might like to send others to those who provided you with a lot of help, such as the photographer of the cover shot.

COVERING MATERIALS for your paperback edition will probably consist of a heavy, glossy, white coated paper. There is a great variety of cover stock to choose from. Your printer will tell you which is least expensive and easiest to print. After printing, the cover usually gets another trip through the press to apply press wax or varnish to seal in the ink and protect the cover from fingerprints. You can also get special materials some of which look like leatherette such as Lexotone, Kivar, Graphitek, etc. Your printer will have samples.

Examples of binding styles: binder, wire, comb, perfect, cloth, saddle stitch and side stitch.

BINDING is your book packaging, the final touch. Consider your market (to whom will you sell it?) and the expected usage (will it be read once or used as a manual?). Because of the great expense of traditional hard binding, there may well be a cross between the hardcover and the paperback one day. In Japan, it is common to place a dust jacket on soft cover books already. The choices are many and here are the most common types:

1. Perfect binding is the standard glued-on cover you see on most paperbacks. The pages are folded into signatures, often of 16 pages each, stacked and then the cover is wrapped around and glued on. The greatest advantage, besides lower cost, is that it presents a squared-off spine on which the title and name of the author may be printed.
2. Cloth binding (case binding or hard binding) usually consists of Smyth sewing or side stitching the individual signatures together. Then they are installed (and glued) between two hard paper boards. They will accept a lot more flexing because they depend on thread, not glue, to retain the pages.
3. Wire stitches are staples and may be used in binding paperback books. This is the least expensive way and many highly automated printing plants are set up for it. Wire stitches may be "saddle stitched" where the staple is on the fold or "side stitched" where the staple is driven through from the front to back cover. Saddle stitching will handle 80 pages or less while side stitching may be used to bind even several hundred pages. Side stitching won't open up to lay flat so it

shouldn't be used in manuals. Sometimes "Holland tape" is used to cover the binding and the staples making the book more attractive. The "stitches" come from a roll of wire and are adjustable in length.

4. Spiral wire binding will allow the book to open up and lay flat but it looks cheap. It is poor on the shelf because the title doesn't show and libraries don't care for them. Consider your market.

5. Plastic comb binding allows the book to open and lay flat and is often used for mail order books directed at professionals. It is relatively expensive but looks cheap, the pages tear out and they don't stack well making shipping a chore.

6. Vello Bind is similar to side wire stitches but uses melted plastic rivets.

7. Xerox-Cheshire has an interesting hard and soft cover binding machine which is good for short-run production.

8. Binders are sometimes used in very expensive manuals directed toward professionals. They have the usual advantages of a binder but they are expensive and the pages tear out easily.

TO ESTIMATE BOOK PRODUCTION COSTS, send a request for quotation to a number of printers. Request that all quotes for composition, layout, printing, halftones, reductions, etc. be made on a per item and per page basis. If your quotes are not figured this way, reduce them to these page/item figures yourself. Then when the book is finished and the exact number of pages, photos, etc. are known, both you and the printer, individually and objectively, will come up with the same figure for the bill.

Old quotes may be used to make estimates of the costs of new books but 1% per month, since the date of the quote, should be cranked in for inflation.

With the per page figures and the known number of pages, you will be able to calculate the unit cost (what you are paying for each book). This will help you to select the best number to run both the first time and for reprints.

Even if you keep up your end of the bargain on the delivery schedule, your printer will probably be late. Just count on it, they all are.

SELECTING YOUR PRINTER. Solicit several printing quotes, a half dozen or more. You will find some to be three times higher than others. It's amazing and it obviously pays to shop around. Some printers are too big for you, some are too specialized and some are too busy. You need a good one who is hungry and specializes in "short run" printing. If your state has an inventory tax, you might consider avoiding it by printing in another state and shipping books in batches so as to avoid the tax date (1 March in California). Both the Post Office and trucking companies give special rates for "bound books." Your printer may even be willing to drop ship large quantities for you so you can ship direct to major customers. Some authors have found considerable savings on certain processes outside the U.S. They have printing done in Taiwan, color separations made in Italy, color printing done in Singapore, etc.

There are over 40,000 independent commercial printing companies in the U.S., so there are plenty to choose from. In order to learn the ropes, it may be best to deal with a local printer the first time around if you can find one with a competitive price.

Book printers are set up for books only and offer very good prices. Many are located in Michigan and some require camera-ready copy. This means you have to have your composition and layout done locally. Many of them advertise in *Writer's Digest*.

Printing brokers can often provide better service and prices. They know the industry and which manufacturers can do which part of the book most efficiently as well as who is busy and who is looking for work. They have buying power and often supply the paper making their profit on the paper mark up. Check under "printing brokers" in the Yellow Pages.

(Your letterhead)

REQUEST FOR QUOTATION

To:

Please quote your best price and delivery in producing the following:

SPECIFICATIONS

Name of book: (The Future of Book Publishing)
Total number of pages including front matter: (152)
Trim Size: (6 x 9)
Quantities: (3,000, 5,000, 10,000)
Type: (10/11 Times Roman)
Paper
        Inside: (60# white offset, book)
        Soft cover: (10 pt. C1S cover)
        Hard cover: (printed cloth)
Binding
        Soft cover: (Perfect 4,000)
        Hard cover: (Printed cloth, Smyth sewn and headbands 500)
Presswork
        Text: (Black throughout)
        Soft cover: (Four color plus varnish)
        Hard cover: (Four color on cloth)
Packaging: (In plastic bags and tightly sealed cartons)
Terms: (Net thirty days from delivery of books)

QUOTE

Composition, per page:
Layout, per page:
(20) halftones requiring reduction and screening, each:
(40) line drawings requiring photo reduction, each:
Delivery charges to our address above:
Delivery will be:_____working days from receipt of manuscript.

Total price:
      First run of 3,000:   5,000:   10,000:
      Later run of 3,000:   5,000:   10,000:

Remarks:

Signed:

Any item in this RFQ takes precedence over any industry convention. The boards and all artwork shall be returned to customer on completion of job.

**Example of a request for quotation.
Sample specifications are in parentheses.**

The bottom line quote is the real difference so get quotes from brokers, book printers, local printers, everyone.

EXCELLENT QUALITY costs more. Tell your printer what you expect and inspect samples of his work. He won't drop his standards to give you a lower price but he may use cheaper processes. You want clean, sharp work because your name is going on it. Communicate with him initially and you won't be disappointed later. If you aren't in a great rush, the printer may be able to schedule your book into his "down time" and give you a better quote. In any case, don't rush the printer and you'll get a better job. "Haste makes waste" and in printing waste can be expensive.

You might even decide to acquire a press and do the printing yourself. Be forewarned, however, that unless you have a simple job and are willing to sacrifice quality, the press run should be left to the professional. You have to decide whether your want to be a writer, printer or to concentrate on sales. Some gain great satisfaction doing the whole job themselves. Unless you can use the printing press to capacity, your own printing won't be competitive in price.

GET IT IN WRITING, get everything in writing. You are new to publishing and what you assume may not be the same as what your printer assumes. Good faith and trust and friendship are fine until the bill arrives. Ask for samples and show him what you like, what you expect. Get a contract with the printer spelling out exactly what each part of the job will cost. Then if you have two more photos than your estimate, you and he will arrive at the same added figure. Count the books you pick up and get copies of the receiving slips. Monitor the production and make sure the book is coming out the way you want. If you see poor press work, tell the printer now. Don't wait to argue after binding. Your name will go on this product, so make sure it is right. After the boards are pasted up and you have an exact page count, ask for a new quote on the press run. You should be able to calculate it using the original quote but it is best to avoid any possible misunderstanding.

You may be able to sell an unattractive book by direct mail where the purchaser can't inspect it first. But you may get it back and you certainly won't sell him anything else, ever. In the mail order publishing business, you need repeat orders.

Make sure your contract includes a clause which states: "Any item in this contract takes precedence over any industry convention." You aren't familiar with the printing industry and aren't interested in how it is normally done. You want an attractive book and you want to know what it will cost.

KEEP YOUR ARTWORK. Maintain a file with a couple of clean copies of the book and all your reproduction materials. If you need them again, and you do hope for many happy reprintings, you don't want to have to regenerate lost material.

Put all the artwork, photos, drawings, etc. into a large envelope. You want to be able to find them easily if you contract for a translation or other foreign edition. Keep the boards and negatives of all promotional material such as brochures and order forms.

The art boards for the book are the publisher's property. Many printers will tell you the large and thin metal printing plates, stripped negatives (flats) and boards belong to them as they are the product of the printer's craftsmanship. A printer who argues this simply wants to make sure you return to him for reprints. The plates are difficult to store and printers often throw them out. Many also discard the boards, keeping only the flats. You may take possession of the plates and flats if you specify their ownership in the printing contract.

You should store the boards for future revisions. Find a cool, dry, clean place; they are subject to yellowing. If you think you might like to switch printers for the revision, you can always specify in the contract that you own everything. On the other hand, allowing the printer to store the flats while you keep the boards is good insurance. If one place burns to the ground, you won't lose everything. Additionally, you will probably want to make revisions when you go back to press. In this case, it is far more valuable to have the boards than the flats.

CHAPTER FIVE

ANNOUNCING YOUR NEW BOOK

TELLING THE WORLD YOU ARE AN AUTHOR AND A PUBLISHER. GETTING LISTED.

THE INTERNATIONAL STANDARD BOOK NUMBER (ISBN) is a world-wide identification system which has been in use since the late sixties. There is a different ISBN for each edition of each book so its use avoids errors in identifying the books ordered, shipped, received, etc. Publishers are finding that with the increased use of computers in the book industry, this system has become an essential element in the distribution of their books. However, while most publishers are using the numbers in their books, catalogues, promotional pieces and ads, fewer than half are noting them on their shipping and billing documents where they would do the most good.

A typical ISBN might be 0-915516-21-7. Here, the initial "0" indicates a book in the English language. The 915516 identifies the publisher. The suffix 21 identifies this particular title and edition of the book, hard cover or paperback. The last number, 7, is a check digit which is a computerized mathmatical function to make sure the rest of the numbers are correct, that they haven't been miscopied or transposed. Once started in the system, you assign each of your new titles an ISBN suffix yourself. Then you print it on the copyright page of the book and on the right foot of the back cover or jacket in 12 pt. type.

Write to the International Standard Book Numbering Agency, 1180 Avenue of the Americas, New York City, NY 10036 and request a "Title Output Information Request Form," a "User's Manual," and a "Bowker Products and Services" brochure. Since they don't particularly like to list publishers with a single title, it is best to represent yourself as being larger. After all, this won't be your only book. Keep this in mind when filling out the Title output form. For $5, they will send you a card bearing your ISBN Publisher identifier and a log book sheet with enough room for listing 100 different editions.

By now, you are probably finding that there are a lot of agencies and offices catering to the book trade at 1180 Avenue of the Americas. Bowker is a big outfit and they are into many things.

Example of an ISBN log book sheet.

0-915516-25-X
0-915516-26-8
0-915516-27-6
0-915516-28-4
0-915516-29-2
0-915516-30-6
0-915516-31-4
0-915516-32-2
0-915516-33-0
0-915516-34-9
0-915516-34-7
0-915516-36-5
0-915516-37-3
0-915516-38-1
0-915516-39-X
0-915516-40-3
0-915516-41-1
0-915516-42-X
0-915516-43-8
0-915516-44-6
0-915516-45-4
0-915516-46-2
0-915516-47-0
0-915516-48-9
0-915516-49-7

Treat each office separately, as though they were in different buildings, so your mail won't get misdirected or lost.

ADVANCED BOOK INFORMATION is another Bowker service. By filling out their ABI form, your book will be listed in *Publishers' Weekly, Library Journal, Forthcoming Books, Books in Print, Subject Guide to Books in Print* and several other specialized directories. *Books in Print* is published in November of each year and is the most important.

The ABI form.

Everyone in the industry turns to BIP first when looking for a particular book. It lists all available books by subject, title and author. Ask for it at the library and become familiar with this many volumed work.

You should fill in an ABI form about six months before your publication date but don't be too anxious. Wait until you have signed a contract with your printer to produce the book. Some new publishers act prematurely; they list the book and then never get into print. Your "publication date" will probably be six months away anyway, as discussed in Chapter 7.

Write to the ABI Department, R.R. Bowker Co., 1180 Avenue of the Americas, NYC, NY 10036 and request an ABI descriptive brochure and a half dozen ABI forms. There is no charge.

The BIP check list.

Bowker will send you a computer generated ABI checklist every other month to keep your listings up-to-date. Always use the guide book when filling out the ABI form. Some of the questions may mislead a person not familiar with publishing terminology. Photocopy the ABI form before you mail it off and send the copies to book clubs and other subsidiary rights buyers. Ask them if they would like to see an examination copy for bidding purposes. See the discussion in Chapter 7 on subsidiary rights and check the listings of buyers in *Literary Market Place* available in your public library.

With a listing in BIP, a membership in COSMEP and a subscription to *Writer's Digest* you will begin to receive a lot of writing and publishing mail. See the listings in the Appendix.

COPYRIGHT is the subject which most interests potential authors. They want to know how to protect their precious material from others and to know how much they may steal.

A copyright covers exact printed words, not ideas or thoughts so just don't copy word-for-word. The copyright law was completely overhauled on 1 January 1978 and it will be many years before every aspect of it has been interpreted by the courts. The courts seem to deal with each case individually when determining infringement. One test has been whether the original work is any less saleable once it has competition from an alleged infringer. Make it a personal rule never to copy any three words in a row and you should be safe.

TO COPYRIGHT YOUR BOOK, follow these three steps:

1. Print the copyright notice on the copyright page (title page verso). The notice takes the following form: "© 1979 Maryann Murphy." You may use the word "copyright" but the "©" says the same thing and it is necessary for international protection. Also add "all rights reserved" and expand on it if you like. Check other books. This notice must appear in *all* copies of the book to protect you, so double check it and all the numbers on the copyright page every time you proof copy, boards, bluelines, etc.

2. Publish the book. Check for the copyright notice before any of the books are distributed.

3. Register your claim with the Copyright Office within three months of the book coming off the press. To do this, send a completed Form TX, two copies of the "best edition" of the book and a fee of $10. The "best edition" would be the hard cover if both the hardbound and paperback came from the printer at the same time. However, since the hardbound edition takes longer to produce, the softcover is the "best edition at the time of publication." If you send paperback copies, be sure to note that they were produced first.

Your work may be copyrighted before it is published but, unless you are passing a lot of copies around for technical proofing and comment, you might just as well wait for books to come off the press.

The new copyright term is for life plus fifty years. It is now a valuable part of your estate, so be certain your copyrighted material is mentioned in your will.

Copyrights protect you like a patent but they are cheaper and much easier to secure. Like a patent, however, you must always be on the lookout for infringers. The copyright protects your text, photographs, drawings, maps, everything except the title.

> *"From the time Gutenberg lifted the first sheet off the press, there has been a steady demand for books of instruction of all kinds"* — Arnold F. Logan of Petersen Publishing Co.

The copyright form.

Send for Circular R99 and a couple of copies of Form TX for complete details. Write: Copyright Office, Library of Congress, Washington, DC 20559. You may mail your application form, books and cheque free when filing. See Postal Manual 137.22f for details. The Copyright Office will add a registration number and date to the form and will send you a photocopy containing a seal and the Register's signature.

MANY DOCUMENTS ARE NOT COPYRIGHTED. If you want to find whether some material is protected under either the current or pre-1978 law, the Copyright Office will conduct a search for you. Send them as much information as possible, such as the author, title, publisher and publication date. The cost is $10 per hour and they should be able to find two per hour. Government and military publications are in the public domain. Even if they weren't, they would probably be covered by the Freedom of Information Act. If you really need a piece of material, military or civilian, ask for permission. It is safer and cheaper than hiring a lawyer to defend you.

YOUR COPYRIGHTED MATERIAL is valuable property, or it may be so one day. File on all those magazine articles you don't get paid for. You may need the article for inclusion in a book someday and the expenditure on fees will justify to the IRS that you really are in the word business.

If you are asked for permission to reprint some of your work, you might consider a limit of a section or two and stipulate that an editor's note indicate that it was used with your permission and came from your book. This will further indicate you as an expert and is good publicity for the original work. A copyright on your book is not only for protection, it is prestigious; it shows you are a professional. For more information on copyrights, see the discussion in *Writer's Market* and read Johnston's *Copyright Handbook*.

LIBRARY OF CONGRESS CATALOG CARD. Since 1901 the Library of Congress has, through its Card Division, made its printed catalog cards available to libraries throughout the world. Since 1951, the Library has preassigned card numbers to forthcoming books. These numbers appear on the verso of the title page of each book and are also included in the lists and reviews appearing in the leading journals of the book trade. Use of the number enables subscribers to the Library's catalog card service to order cards by number and thus eliminate the searching fee.

About 20,000 libraries from all over the world subscribe to this service and some order almost every catalogued book. Additionally, most of the books are listed in *The National Union Catalogue*, issued several times a year in four editions. Most public and private libraries subscribe to it.

Write to the CIP Office, Library of Congress, Washington, DC 20540 and ask for "Procedures for Securing Preassigned Library of Congress Catalog Card Numbers" and their "Request for Library of Congress Catalog Card Number" application form.

REQUEST FOR LIBRARY OF CONGRESS CATALOG CARD NUMBER

NOTE: This form may be used ONLY for requesting a PREASSIGNED card number, IN ADVANCE OF PUBLICATION. Once a work has been published, a card number can no longer be PREassigned and can be obtained only by DONATING one copy of the published work to the Library.

To receive a PREASSIGNED card number please supply fullest information possible:

Author(s): _____

Title: _____

Edition: _____

Place of publication: _____

Publisher: _____

Proposed date of publication: Month _____ Year ____

Series Title: _____

Number of pages (approximate): _____

Will this publication appear at regular intervals under the same title? Yes _____ No _____

Will work be copyrighted? Yes _____ No _____

Although there is no charge for a PREASSIGNED card number, the Library of Congress requires one copy of the completed book for cataloging purposes. A postage-free, self-addressed label will be sent with the preassigned card number for your convenience in mailing the required copy of the work.

Name and address to which preassigned card number should be sent:

_____

_____

_____

607-7 (rev 6/76)

Library of Congress number request form.

PROCEDURE. The Library of Congress card number must be requested prior to the publication of the book. They do not preassign numbers to books that are already in print.

The publisher sends a list of forthcoming books to: the CIP Office, Library of Congress, Washington, DC 20540. The following information is needed (Use their form or just send the following):

a. Full name of author or editor
b. Title of the book
c. Edition statement
d. Date of publication
e. Name and address of publisher and/or printer
f. Series title and number
g. If a continuing serial (periodical, annual, conference proceedings, etc.)
h. If it is to be copyrighted
i. Approximate number of pages
j. Type of binding (hard, soft, etc.)

If there is a delay in replying of more than six weeks, call (202) 426-6372.

ELIGIBILITY. Catalog card numbers are preassigned only to books which they assume will be added to the collections or for which they anticipate substantial demand for LC printed cards. The types of material which the Library collects only in a very limited way and for which catalog card numbers are generally not available include: calendars, laboratory manuals, booklets of less than 50 pages, brochures, advertisements, bank publications designed for customers, blueprints, certain kinds of light fiction, privately printed books of poems, religious materials for students in Bible schools, catechisms, instructions in devotions, individual sermons and prayers, question and answer books, most elementary and secondary school textbooks, tests except for standard examinations, teachers' manuals, correspondence school lessons, translations from English into foreign languages, picture books, comic strip and coloring books, diaries, log and appointment books, prospectuses and preliminary editions, workbooks, and vanity press publications.

Upon examination, materials in the excepted categories may still be selected for the collections of the Library of Congress and cataloged. Accordingly, rejection of a work for preassignment of a number does not necessarily imply rejection for the collections.

The Library usually prepares only one card for serials, which in library parlance is called an open-entry card. The card number which is assigned to this card may be used for future issues of the serial. In general, because of internal problems in cataloging, the Library prefers not to preassign card numbers to periodicals.

```
Library of Congress Cataloging in Publication Data

Poynter, Dan.
    The self-publishing manual.

    Bibliography:  p.
    Includes index.
    1.  Publishers and publishing--Handbooks, manuals, etc.
2.  Authorship--Handbooks, manuals, etc.  I.  Title.
Z285.5.P69              658.8'09'070573              79-712
ISBN 0-915516-22-5
ISBN 0-915516-21-7 pbk.
```

Catalog Card Number assignment slip.

If the Library determines, on the basis of information submited by a publisher, that the book is to be cataloged, a catalog card number is preassigned and sent to the publisher on a typed 3 x 5 slip giving the author, title, imprint and publication date. The catalog card number appears in the upper right-hand corner of the slip.

The publisher adds this number to the manuscript of the front matter indicating that it be printed on the verso of the title page using the following legend: Library of Congress Catalog Card Number: 79-12946 (for example). The first two digits do not indicate the year of publication, but the year in which the card number is preassigned. If you register after 1 January, your book will appear to be a year newer. Ever wonder why the dates on films are in Roman numerals?

The CIP Office must be advised of all subsequent changes in titles, authors, etc., and cancellations. This notification is important as it prevents duplication of numbers. A new number is not necessary when changes are made. Confirmations of changes will not be acknowledged unless requested by the publisher.

There is no charge for the preassignment of a card number. An *advance* complimentary copy of each publication must be sent to the CIP Office, Library of Congress, Washington, DC 20540. This copy is used for final cataloging so that cards may be printed before the book is released. The CIP Office provides postage-free mailing labels for use in sending these advance publications. This is only for checking so send the less expensive soft cover edition.

The Copyright Office is operationally separate from the CIP Office. But the CIP and Catalog Card offices are the same. See the next paragraph. Catalog card numbers may be applied for per the above or when applying for Cataloging in Publication Data.

CATALOGING IN PUBLICATION was initiated by the Library of Congress in 1971 to aid the cataloging of new books. Under the program, publishers submit photocopies or galleys of all or part of their books in production to the CIP Office. Within ten working days, the Office sends the CIP data and the catalog card number so the publisher may print the information on the copyright page of the new book.

This information is required by librarians who prefer to prepare their own Library of Congress catalog cards. It enables them to rapidly and economically process new titles for library users. Once a number has been assigned to a book, it will never be used again, even if the book goes out of print.

Write the CIP Office, Library of Congress, Washington, DC 20540 and request: "Cataloging in Publication — Information for Participating Publishers" and some "Publisher's Response" forms. They are eager to help and can be reached at (202) 426-6372. They even provide postage-paid mailing labels for the materials you are expected to send them. Here is a line-by-line explanation of the CIP data:

1. **Library of Congress Cataloging in Publication Data.**
2. Poynter, Daniel F., 1938-
3. Parachuting, The Skydivers' Handbook.
4. 1, Parachuting. 2, Skydiving. I Title
5. GV 770.P69   797.56   77-83469
6. ISBN 0-915516-16-0 Paperback
7. ISBN 0-915516-17-9 Hardcover

Typical CIP data block.

1. The heading is made distinctive by setting in bold typeface.
2. The author's name, date of birth and, if applicable, death.
3. The title of the book.
4. The LC subject headings.
5. The "GV 770" is the LC classification number. The "P69" is keyed into the last name of the author. In this case "Poynter." The second number group is the Dewey Decimal Classification Number (see *The Dewey Decimal Classification and Relative Index)* and the last is the LC Card Number.

6 & 7 The International Standard Book Numbers.

AUTHOR NUMBER TABLE

Aa	— 15	Ba-Bb	— 3	Sa-Sc	— 2
Ab-Ac	— 2	Be-Bh	— 4	Sch-Sd	— 3
Ad-Ak	— 3	Bi-Bn	— 5	Se-Sg	— 4
Al-Am	— 4	Bo-Bq	— 6	Sh-Sl	— 5
An-Ao	— 5	Br-Bt	— 7	Sm-Ss	— 6
Ap-Aq	— 6	Bu-	— 8	St-	— 7-8
Ar-As	— 7			Su-	— 9
Ast	— 8	Same for other			
Same for other		initial consonants		Q-Qt	— 3
initial vowels.		except S		Qu-	— 4

Letters not included are assigned next higher or lower numbers as required.

TO OBTAIN YOUR CIP DATA, send photocopies of the front matter of your pasted up boards and a filled-out LCC Data sheet to the CIP Office. This enables them to select the proper classification numbers. They also like to have any other information you might have, such as a descriptive brochure on the book, a photocopy of your ABI form and a biographical sketch of the author.

They don't always catalogue the book just as you might want it. Give them as much information on it as possible and read their "Information For Participating Publishers" carefully. You may even supply suggested data. Pay particular attention to the "subject tracings" (line 4 above). How a book gets catalogued can be just as important to small presses as how it gets reviewed or advertised.

THE LIBRARY OF CONGRESS	1. Date Form Completed
LC CATALOGING DATA SHEET No. 1-2 * (Use with galley; if no galley available, answer item 17 in full.)	2. Form Completed by

3. Name of Publisher — Phone

4. Name of In-House Editor — Phone

5. Authors' Names Appearing on the Title Page (last, first, middle) — Birthdate

6. Title

7. If this is a *translation* from a foreign language, give *original* title:

8. Give title(s) of any *other* English language edition(s) if *different* from this title:

9. If this is a copublished book, give name of copublisher:

10. Projected date of Publication:
    month _____ year _____

11. Check here if book has:
    ☐ bibliography   ☐ Index

12. If title comprises more than one physical volume, the number of volumes planned is:

This is the galley for volume number:

13. If title belongs to a series of monographs having a comprehensive title, and it will appear in the book, the series title is:

14. If the series is numbered, the number for this title is:

15. Work is essentially a
    ☐ novel   ☐ biography   ☐ essays
    ☐ textbook   ☐ other _____ (specify)

16. Primary audience for whom book is intended:
    ☐ general   ☐ nurses   ☐ engineers   ☐ college students
    ☐ children   ☐ other _____ (age level) (specify)

17. Primary subject of the books OR Precis of the book in detail if galley is not available. (Be as specific as possible, continuing on a separate sheet if necessary.)

18. The following information items are related for cataloging purposes. Use a single line for each ISBN involved, giving the rest of the information as fully as you can.

ISBN(s) and FORMAT OR VOLUME NUMBER	LC CARD NUMBER IF PREASSIGNED	PRICE (Specify if sold only as set)

19. Person and address to which CIP entry should be mailed

607-6 (rev 10/73)   Use previous issues until exhausted.   * Use Cataloging Data Sheet No. 3 for photo offset reprints.

The LC Cataloging data sheet.

INFORMATION SLIP

Description of new book for FREE record in Cumulative Book Index, published by The H. W. Wilson Company, 950 University Ave., Bronx, N.Y. 10452

The Cumulative Book Index is published monthly.   A copy of the book or descriptive material will be appreciated.

Author ....
(Full Name) (Please print)

Title ....
(Verbatim)

....

Subject ....

Series and Number ....

Edition .... No. of vols .... Size .... No. of pages .... Illustrations ....

Binding .... Retail price .... Date of publication ....
(In your currency)   (Exact)

Name and Address of Publisher ....
(From whom the book may be obtained)

For IMPORTATIONS the following additional information is REQUIRED: (a) Are you the sole U.S. agent for the book? .... (b) What is the U.S. publication date? .... (c) How many copies will be on hand in this country on the U.S. publication date? (or are on hand now)? ....

11-65—50M(2687)M.A. Printed in U.S.A.

Cumulative Book Index Information Slip
If a copy of the book is sent, this slip is not required.

THE CUMULATIVE BOOK INDEX is an international bibliography of new publications in the English language. All the bibliographical information necessary to identify a book is provided: full name of author, complete title, date of publication, edition, paging, price, publisher, International Standard Book Number, and Library of Congress card number.

In addition to bibliographical information, CUMULATIVE BOOK INDEX also provides subject headings to describe the contents of the book. These headings can usually be determined by an examination of the table of contents and a reading of the preface; sometimes, a careful examination of the text is necessary. Books must have at least 100 pages and a minimum press run of 500 copies to be eligible for inclusion in the Index.

A listing in CUMULATIVE BOOK INDEX gives your publication valuable publicity. Subscribers include most of the major libraries and booksellers here and abroad. No charge is made for a listing in CUMULATIVE BOOK INDEX, but in order to record accurately the bibliographical description and subject content of each book, it is most helpful to base the listing on an examination of the book itself.

Although other units within the company such as the *Vertical File Index* will make further use of the book, only one copy is necessary. Send books to: Cumulative Book Index, H.W. Wilson Co., 950 University Avenue, Bronx, NY 10452.

BOOK PUBLISHERS OF THE UNITED STATES AND CANADA is a directory in which you may have a free listing. For an application form, write: Gale Research Company, Book Tower, Detroit, MI 48226.

PUBLISHER'S TRADE LIST ANNUAL is another Bowker publication. It is used by the publishing industry to announce books. Advertising rates for small ads are not high but many small presses find they get very little return on their investment. For information and an ad rate card, write: R. R. Bowker Co., P.O. Box 1807, Ann Arbor, MI 48106.

CONTEMPORARY AUTHORS is a large reference book containing over 54,000 biographical sketches. Authors of technical and vanity press books are not eligible. Send for a form to: Contemporary Authors, Gale Research Company, Book Tower, Detroit, MI 48226. After you fill it out, make a few photocopies so you'll be ready when someone else asks for extensive biographical information. The listing is free.

COSMEP is the international association of independent publishers. The name Committee of Small Magazine Editors and Publishers is, however, misleading. They publish a very informative monthly newletter, and membership will establish many valuable contacts. Send $35 to COSMEP, P.O. Box 703, San Francisco, CA 94101.

LOCAL COSMEP CHAPTERS are being established all over the world. They provide an opportunity to meet other area publishers in order to share mutual successes and problems. For the address of your nearest COSMEP chapter, write the San Francisco headquarters (address above).

INTERNATIONAL DIRECTORY OF LITTLE MAGAZINES AND SMALL PRESSES is another place you'll want to list your new firm. Send for a form and send one copy of your book to: Dustbooks, P.O. Box 100-P, Paradise, CA 95969. Request information on their other directories, too.

PUBLISHERS' INTERNATIONAL DIRECTORY is published by the K. G. Saur Publishing Co., 175 Fifth Avenue, NYC, NY 10010. Write for information and a questionnaire.

LITERARY MARKET PLACE is one of the most important reference books in the publishing industry. It lists every major publisher, publicity outlet, and supplier. An inclusion here will help your customers and suppliers to find you. Many firms use it to locate publishers as it is so much less expensive than *Books In Print*. To be listed in this annual reference, send for an application form to *Literary Market Place,* Attn: Janice Blaufox, Editor, 1180 Avenue of the Americas, New York City, NY 10036.

CHAPTER SIX

WHAT IS YOUR BOOK WORTH?

PRICES, DISCOUNTS, TERMS, COLLECTIONS AND RETURNS

BOOK PRICING is a complicated affair which strikes a compromise between a price high enough for the publisher to stay in business and low enough to overcome customer price resistance.There are, perhaps, three reasons people write books: 1, fame, 2, fortune and 3, enjoyment. Since few people fall into the last category, we'll concentrate on the first two. Your first book is usually for recognition, and once that is out of your system, the second is for money. Consequently, the author is likely to underprice his first book but work with a very sharp pencil on the price of the next.

THE LIST PRICE of your book will not be easy to set. Many first-time author/publishers ask themselves whether they want maximum financial return or maximum distribution, feeling they can't have both. Usually they wind up with a price on the cover which is too low. As a result, many small publishers have warehouses full of books which they can't afford to market effectively. It takes advertising to sell books and they neglected to budget this item when setting the price.

Some publishers make the mistaken rationalization that a lower price will give them a competitive advantage. But only in the textbook market are prices really compared. Books are becoming more and more expensive; visit a bookstore and compare prices. In a how-to book, you are selling information, not entertainment or stacks of paper; the selling price is not nearly so frightening to the buyer as it is to the author.

You must also consider that the price printed on the cover is not what you will receive for it. Dealers require a percentage for their selling efforts. Your promotion costs, to let people know the book exists, are likely to be much higher than you originally anticipated. Both discounts and advertising take a big chunk out of the selling price.

According to *Publishers Weekly,* the average prices for books in 1977 were as follows.

Hardcover: $19.22 (Some areas more specifically were: Business $18.00, Science $24.88, Sports & Recreation $12.28, Travel $18.44, etc.).

Quality paperback: $5.93 (Business $7.09, Science $8.81, Sports & Recreation $4.87, Travel $5.21, etc.).

Mass market paperback: $1.72 (Business $2.06, Science $1.92, Sports & Recreation $1.86, Travel $2.07, etc.).

These are 1977 prices, the latest available and they are going up. Add one percent per month since January 1978 to estimate current average list prices.

"Book buyers are less influenced by price differentials than almost any category of customers" — John Huenefeld.

Some publishers like to test prices before deciding on them. There are times when a higher price will make a product seem more valuable and will make it sell better. They run identical ads except for the price and then check the returns. Mail order book buyers are said to be the least price-conscious of all.

Your book is unique. Like you, it is one of a kind. While a customer won't pay more than what he figures to be a fair price, if your book is a good one and he wants it bad enough, he will pay what you ask. Underpricing a book to increase sales is often a very big mistake. In fact, it may even undermine the credibility of the book. And remember, price has a reverse impact when a book is purchased as a gift.

Books you intend to sell through bookstores and mail order should be priced at 8 times unit production cost, textbooks at five times. Total unit production cost includes all composition, layout, printing, binding, etc. Pricing the book any lower than this is courting financial disaster because of the high discounts to dealers, shipping expenses and the necessary promotional costs. Roughly half of the cover price will cover your internal costs, such as manufacturing, overhead and profit. The remaining half covers dealer discounts and promotion on wholesale orders and advertising for mail order sales. If the projected list price seems too high, consider reducing the print run, cutting out some of the copy or photographs or selecting a smaller type and narrower leading to get more on each page. Check with your printer for ways to reduce costs. Now, if the price still seems too high, you picked the wrong subject to write about.

The 8X formula does not fit every case; there may be some exceptions. Consider your audience and the cost of reaching them. If you write a pictorial history of your town and the Chamber of Commerce is buying them all to give to tourists, your promotion and distribution costs will be much lower. If 8X seems like a lot, you should know that audio-visual materials are often marked up 11X.

It may seem old and silly, but $9.95 is still a lot cheaper to the subconscious mind than $10 and there is no good argument for a mid-price like $9.50.

Recheck your costs at reprint time; you may wish to raise the cover price. Also remember to change your ads, brochures, etc. and send off a press release to *Publishers Weekly*. (Every little mention helps.) To ease the blow on your better dealers who have you listed in their catalogue, consider offering them a one-time buy on the new edition at the old price in order to protect their catalogue price. This will also generate quick cash to help you pay your printing bill.

One major reason small publishers stay small is their failure to think objectively about pricing their books. Low prices make you work harder for less and limit your growth.

HOW MANY BOOKS? Once again, we must consider your purpose for writing the book and how many you can expect to sell. Do you want just a few to family and friends? Is it a high-priced mail order book with a small audience? Do you want to take a crack at the big chain bookstores and hope you have a bestseller? How many will be review copies, gifts and other freebees?

INITIAL PRESS RUNS should normally be limited to the number of books one can reasonably estimate will be sold in the first year. If the book is 100% accurate and 99% complete, go to press. That one last photo and that one extra item can wait for the reprint. If you wait, you are tying up your money longer and you are missing the market. Unless you have a substantial number of prepublication sales, it is a good idea to limit the first

---

"The higher your markup, the better you can afford mistakes"

printing to 5,000. No matter how diligently you proofread, some errors won't surface until they appear in ink. Also, once you see the book in its final state, you will wish you had done some things differently. By printing only 5,000, you can use the next few months to catch your errors and make some design changes. Then you will be much happier about the revised second edition.

Set the first press run conservatively. It is better to sell out and have to go back to press than to find yourself with a garage full of unsold books. You will be spending a lot of money on promotion so it is best to hedge your bets by tying up less in the book even though you have to pay a slight premium in printing costs to do so.

The economics of printing are as follows: the greater the quantity of books, the higher your bill but the less each book will cost you. And the "start-up costs" make the first press run much more expensive than reprints. The major expenses, in fact, are the start-up costs of composition, layout, camerawork, stripping, etc. Once the type is set, you only pay for the paper and press time. The more copies printed at one time, the lower the price per copy. This is only true up to a point since the differences become smaller and smaller as the press runs. Again you must consider the number of books you may be able to sell in one year, because the price breaks fail to maintain significance after 9,000 copies. Normally, between nine and ten thousand, you save so little that it isn't worth the storage space or the price of borrowing money at the bank. Therefore you don't want to print over 9,000 unless that number will move out within the year.

For example, you might get quotes such as:

Number of copies	500	1000	3000	5000	7000	9000	10000
Total cost	$1495.00	$1784.00	$4485.00	$6778.00	$8750.00	$10530.00	$11300.00
Unit cost	$ 2.99	$ 1.78	$ 1.49	$ 1.36	$ 1.25	$ 1.17	$ 1.13

So it is to your advantage to order as many books as possible in order to get the best unit price. And you want the best price as long as you are fairly sure you can sell the higher number.

Remember that a printer makes money on printing. Don't let him talk you into more books than you need. There is economy in scale but there are no savings in paying for books you can't turn into cash. Consider the total printing bill as well.

ESTIMATING SALES for that first year will be difficult with your first book because you don't have other books with which to compare it. You may get an idea from your own previous work experience and may be able to find out what similar books have done. But remember that bigger publishers have more clout in the trade and already have the connections for placing their titles; you won't do as well initially. Check also with anyone you may know with other publishing companies for their educated estimate. With proper promotion, any reasonably good non-fiction book should sell 5,000 copies in its first year. If you can't objectively project sales of 5,000 copies for the first year, you will have to raise the price substantially to justify printing the book.

REPRINTS have to be timed just right. If you order a reprint too early, you may tie up more money before the first run is paid for. And, many of those books could be sitting on the shelves in the stores - unsold. It is a good idea to make some telephone calls to find if the book is actually moving. On the other hand, if you wait too long to reprint, you run the risk of being out of stock and losing the all-important sales momentum the book is enjoying.

Coordinate with your printer so you can get a fast reprint if necessary. Consider reprint time, seasonal demand, etc. Then, considering the size of your storage space, amount of money you can invest, need for future revisions, inventory tax dates, etc., print a one- to two-year supply. One great advantage of these annual printings is the ability to make revisions, keeping the text up-to-date.

DISCOUNTS must be set down in a definite policy right from the beginning. It must be clear to both you and your customers to avoid any misunderstanding.

Ultimate consumers placing individual orders usually pay the full retail price and send cash with their order (CWO). When an order is received without a cheque, it is best to return it with a copy of your brochure and a note requesting payment in advance. Circle your prices and terms on the brochure; some people order asking to be billed because they don't know what the full price will be. Asking for payment in advance will lose only a very few orders but it will stop credit losses and cut billing costs. Customarily, you pay the postage unless you have stipulated otherwise in your brochure. COD shipments necessitate too much paperwork for a small sale and the collection charges often upset the customer.

DEALER DISCOUNTS. The terms publishers extend to the trade (booksellers, etc.) vary so much from firm to firm that the American Booksellers Association publishes a loose-leaf handbook trying to list them all. Discounts are supposed to be based on the theory that there is a saving in bulk shipments. However, bookselling tradition has based the discount rate on the category of the wholesale customer, arguing that certain clients need a bigger piece of the pie to stay in business.

Discounts to the industry start at 40% and this comes as a shock to many new publishers. But one has to consider the high overhead retailers have in the form of rent, taxes, salaries, utilities, insurance, etc. They need it to stay in business. It is, incidentally, lower than the discount on the merchandise found in gift, sporting goods and other stores; they often get 50% or more. The publishing industry has been able to justify the lower discount by making the books returnable if they aren't sold. Fortunately, books are uniform in size, easy to store, simple to ship and are unbreakable. The discount must be high enough to encourage the retailer to get out and sell your product; it has to be worth his while.

WHOLESALERS get 50% on the theory that they purchase large quantities for resale to retailers and libraries. Often they are regional suppliers providing both one-stop-shopping and a short supply line for quick and easy restocking. In order to maintain large library accounts, they usually extend to them discounts of 20-33%. Bookstores get up to 40% depending on the size of their order but they are usually allowed to mix titles. Wholesalers pay the shipping (FOB origin) when purchasing from the publisher.

RETAIL BOOKSTORES get 40% off the list price, as mentioned, and they pay the shipping costs. They need this typical retailer's discount to survive.

TEXTBOOK publishers give the college bookstores 20-25% off on the books to be sold to students. Here the quantity is often large and any books not sold after the school term begins are returned. There is very little risk as the store is just acting as an order taker. This "short discount" results in a lower price to the consuming student.

These short discounts are sometimes applied to regular books and when this is done, all sales literature should be clearly marked. The book trade won't be too enthusiastic about the poor discount but they can't complain if they are buying in ones and twos and have been informed of the short discount in advance.

LIBRARIES usually get 20% off but many orders will arrive with a cheque made out for the list price. They don't often care about discounts because the acquisition librarians are not spending their own money. Wholesalers get 76% of the library orders by offering good discounts and one-stop shopping.

TEACHERS and other "professional book users" often expect a 10-25% discount too, but don't give it unless they ask and then only if you can justify it with the possibility of future sales.

Discounts are not extended to ultimate consumers except occasionally as a sales inducement in an advertisement. The Federal Trade Commission (FTC) requires that the discounts you offer one dealer be offered to all dealers who are purchasing the same quantity. You aren't required to extend credit, but if they are paying cash and want the same quantity, you must sell at the same discount.

A "UNIVERSAL DISCOUNT SCHEDULE" is being used by many publishers in deference to discriminatory tradition. It is based not on the classification of the customer but on the order quantity.

The theory is that the wholesaler will earn a better discount by buying in larger quantities. Bookstores and libraries ordering smaller quantities get a "courtesy discount." This encourages them to consider ordering from wholesalers with a great title mix where they can get a better deal and to reduce their paperwork with one-stop shopping. Remember that these small quantity special orders from the stores aren't getting your books on the shelf. They have already been sold and will go straight to the customer.

1 book — no discount	50 - 74 books — 44% off
2 - 4 books — 20% off	75 - 99 books — 46% off
5 - 9 books — 30% off	100 - 199 books — 48% off
10 - 24 books — 40% off	200 or more books — 50% off
25 - 49 books — 42% off	

A typical universal discount schedule

These prices are offered on assorted titles except where there is a great difference in price, that is, you wouldn't mix a $1.50 title normally wholesaled 500 at a time with a $30 book usually purchased three at a time.

Don't confuse "discount" with "markup." A discount of 50% from $2 to $1 is the same as a 100% markup from $1 to $2.

When figuring your discounts, total the order and then subtract the discount. You will come out with a higher figure than if you figure the discount per book and then extend it out. For example, buying 200 $5.95 books at 50% off there is one dollar difference. $5.95 x 200 - 50% = $595.00, but $5.95 - 50% = $2.97 x 200 = $594.00.

No single plan fits all types of publishers. For example, if you cater primarily to a specific class of people bound together in a trade, club or sport, you expect to have several large, good dealers who purchase hundreds of books at a time.

> *"Before you can sell a person anything you have to make him or her want it more than the money it costs."*

The **PARACHUTING MANUAL with Log** is an inexpensive, compact yet complete basic sport parachuting manual. " The first jump course in your pocket." ISBN: 0-915516-11-X. List price $1.50.

QUANTITY	DISCOUNT	PRICE EACH	PRICE TOTAL	U.S. SHIPPING	TOTAL DELIVERED
3 up	40%	.90	$ 2.70	$ .64	$ 3.34
200	50%	.75	$150.00	$2.04	$152.04
500	-40% -25%	.67	$337.50	$3.64	$341.14

When moving books in quantities, it is a good idea to let your cutomer know exactly what the cost will be.

Whatever discount schedule you chose, make it simple. You will have to use it to compute each order. Occasionally you will receive an order from a dealer with a cheque and taking a 20 to 40% discount. Most publishers find it easier and cheaper to simply fill the order than to attempt to enforce their discount schedule.

Consignments make you into a banker as well as a publisher. This is where the dealer takes delivery on the books but doesn't pay the publisher until they are sold. The biggest problem is that since this inventory is free, the dealer pushes his paid-for inventory harder. He has no incentive to move your book when he can move another. This is particularly true of wholesalers who are trying to persuade retailers to take just some of the many titles they have to offer. "Delayed billings" are a little of the same thing and only constitute a loan from the publisher to the dealer. Money costs money. You can check today's price for it at your bank.

Pre-publication specials are sometimes used to generate capital to pay the print bill. The offer is often 55% off for 500 or 1,000 copies on a non-returnable basis and it is made to wholesalers, organizations and anyone else who might be interested in a quantity. This will be almost impossible on your first book but once you have established yourself as a writer of good material, the chances are much better.

Your discounts and terms should be printed in your dealer bulletins, on your invoices, etc. where they will be continually seen by your dealers. A copy should also be sent for inclusion in ABA's *Book Buyers Handbook* (122 East 42nd Street, NYC, NY 10017).

Once you have published your prices and terms, stick to them. Besides the FTC rules, it just isn't profitable to deviate from those figures which took you so long to calculate. Some dealers are always asking for a better deal and some publishers feel that any sale above their cost is a good one. But since you are the one building up the demand for the book, it will probably sell anyway — through another dealer or direct from you. Your valuable time should be used to generate additional net income not more marginal gross.

SHIPPING CHARGES are usually included in the price on individual retail sales. The book may be advertised at "5.95pp" (postpaid). While you have made an allowance for postage in the list (cover) price, the buyer feels he is getting something for nothing. Occasionally, the publisher will pay the shipping where a wholesaler has sent cash with order (CWO). Normally, however, the dealer pays the shipping (FOB origin). Book rate postage is spiraling upwards and both publishers and booksellers are becoming very conscious of the shipping expenses. Similarly, the cost of packing materials and labor are high and some publishers try to offset some of these with a "handling charge." The term "handling charge" is sure to evoke a nasty response from the customer no matter how small it may be. If "postage" is not exactly the same as the amount on the package, you will also hear about it. If you do plan to tack on a little extra to pay for the invoice, its First Class mailing, envelopes and shipping supplies, call the postage and handling charge "shipping." Some publishers tack a processing charge of 50¢ onto all orders. This is a lot

"In this world a man must be either an anvil or a hammer" — Longfellow

on a single book but is only a penny each on a carton of fifty. Processing the orders costs the same. Those dealers who object to the additional 50¢ charge usually just scratch it off the invoice when paying the bill, but very few notice. Shipments over 100 lbs. are usually shipped via truck, collect (for the shipping charges). The "bound books" classification is very inexpensive. For smaller shipments compare the latest UPS rate with the Post Office's "book rate;" they are constantly changing.

SCOP stands for "Single Copy Order Plan" and, like STOP or "Single Title Order Plan," consists of a special multipart order form which arrives with a cheque. Because the store is paying in advance, they assume a discount of 20-40%. The cheque is either made out already or is blank and restricted to a certain top amount. Sometimes the directions ask that the book be shipped direct to the customer and other times to the store. Part of the purchase order may be used as a shipping label. It is cheaper and easier to fill these orders than to haggle over the discount in those cases where the store has assumed too much.

TERMS and credit are different in the book trade. Most wholesalers and bookstores routinely take 60 days to pay, many take 90 and some get around to mailing out cheques every six or eight months. This forces the publisher into a frustrating banking situation. There are very few small publishers who can either afford to finance the inventories of their dealers or take substantial losses.

The customary terms for the book industry are that invoices should be paid within 30 days of an end-of-the-month statement (30 EOM). This is up to 30 days longer than "net 30 day" terms. Some publishers, eyeing other industries, offer "2% ten day" terms, but the dealer usually pays late and still takes the 2%. Another way to get most of your money faster is to offer 5% for "cash (or cheque) with order" (CWO). Unfortunately, this offer is usually taken by the financially sound "good pay" customer who would pay on time anyway, not by the slow pay customer you'll have to chase for months. Many of the newer small publishers don't subscribe to the 30 EOM terms or discounts for fast pay, they quote strictly "net 30 days."

"Advance dating" of invoices is sometimes done for seasonal business and catalogue houses. This provides them with the opportunity to get the books into stock before the rush; important where timing is critical.

Once you have decided on your terms and have published them, stick to them religiously. Any sign of relaxation will be evidence that you don't mean what you say and some dealers will take advantage of you. You are a publisher, not a banker, and if you were in the loan business you would charge interest.

Many publishers offer discounts only when their invoices are paid within 60 days; late payments must be for the full amount. They call overdue customers explaining the lack of timely payment and their terms, then offer to extend the discount period ten more days (only). This personal attention and extra pressure often works.

CREDIT. New accounts should be shipped right away. You will receive all sorts of small orders from distant bookstores and it is not worth the time and effort to run a credit check on each one. It may cost $50 or more to run a credit check even if you do it all yourself by telephone and it will take a lot of time. On small orders, credit checks aren't worth the effort for the occasional bad pay or bankruptcy.

Set a limit of say $50 for any dealer order coming in on a letterhead or purchase order. Enclose your brochure, statement of terms and return policy with the invoice. You might also like to slip in a form letter welcoming their account and explaining that you are happy to extend credit and that prompt payment of this invoice will raise their limit to $100. Beyond that you'll need trade and bank references. Those who don't stand your test or who are awaiting a credit check for a large purchase may be urged to pay in advance via a "pro forma invoice" (you make out a complete invoice to include shipping charges but you don't ship the books until the invoice is paid).

Schools, libraries, state and federal governments are "good pay" but often "slow pay." They have taxing authority so it's hard to go bankrupt no matter how badly managed they are. Just make sure their request comes on their purchase order. Too often someone in the Park Department will write you on city letterhead asking for a book with no mention of money. This may well be an unauthorized order. Join a local publishing association and meet some of the people in other book firms. If you question an account, often a call to one of your contemporaries will provide the information you seek.

Foreign orders may be treated in the same way as domestic ones. There will be a difference in shipping charges, sometimes higher and sometimes lower. Unless they pay in dollars drawn on a U.S. bank, there may be a cheque cashing charge. Foreigners have about the same payment history as U.S. customers.

COLLECTIONS. When the money doesn't come in on time you have to exercise your collection process. Wholesalers and bookstores are accustomed to receiving end-of-the-month statements of their account; they want a recapitulation of the many small orders they have placed. Statements aren't a requirement but they may speed payment. You can type up statement forms but initially it will be cheaper to photocopy your invoices or to use a four part invoice form saving one copy for these end-of-month statement mailings. Check the Yellow Pages and make some calls. Often the copy centers near colleges charge as little as 3¢ each for photocopies.

```
┌─────────────────────────────┐
│                             │
│                             │
│         (clear plastic)     │
│                             │
│                             │
├─────────────────────────────┤
│                             │
│       (collection message)  │
│                             │
└─────────────────────────────┘
```

The quickest, easiest and most efficient way to make a statement of account is to use a photocopy machine collection overlay. Simply tape the plastic sheet to the top of the machine. Place the invoice on the overlay and make a photocopy. Then just stuff the copy into a windowed #10 envelope. The plastic sheet makes use of the bottom 1/3rd of the page which is normally wasted. This system avoids separate statements, transposition errors, small envelopes, typing and collection stickers. The collection messages may include:
1. Is there any reason why this past due bill has not been paid?
2. If you are unable to pay the whole bill, won't you evidence your good faith by sending us a partial payment?
3. We subscribe to Dun & Bradstreet's Commercial Collection service.
4. If payment is not received within ten days, we will be forced to turn this matter over to our attorney for collection.

When typing invoices, always include the name of the person signing the order on the second line. This focuses your claim on a specific individual where it will have more impact than if simply sent to the company. Now pen a nice personal note on the bottom of the statement to this particular person.

If they go another month without responding, pen a stronger note on the bottom of the statement. Then wait two weeks and make a telephone call. If they don't pay in 90 days, cut them off. You don't need customers like them.

After this, there are a couple of options. You may arrange with your attorney to send a standard collection letter which he will have typed out automatically on a mag card typewriter. The charge may be $10 - $15 and he may give you a better price on a quantity of them. You may also consider a collection agency. Your local firm will have "affiliates" all over North America or you might contact a large firm with many offices such as Dun & Bradstreet. They usually take one-third as their collection fee and they prefer the easy cases. They have little power and usually get their money through a personal visit which embarrasses the bookseller. They will threaten legal action and will turn the case over to a local attorney if they fail to collect. Generally, the older the debt, the harder it is to collect.

Whatever collection system you select, make it automatic so that you can be objective and won't allow deadbeats to negotiate delays. Let them know you mean business.

The telephone is a powerful collection instrument and a good supplement to dunning notices. Many callers use "guide scripts" to make sure they get their complete message across quickly.

Remember, it is better to have the books returned unsold than to have the books sold and not get paid.

THE ACCOUNTS RECEIVABLE OPERATION is one of the most pleasant. It is always fun to count your money. As the cheques arrive to pay for due bills, match them with the invoices (if only everyone would note the invoice numbers on their cheques!). Mark the invoice with a date stamp to indicate when the payment was credited. Put this pink file copy in a record storage box. See the invoice handling discussion in Chapter 10.

FOR DEPOSIT ONLY
C98-079971

Cheques may be made out to the publishing company, the author or the name of the book. All may be simply covered with a rubber stamp with the account number and the words "For deposit only."

DEPOSITS may be made up every week or so. Endorse the cheques with a rubber stamp and list them on an adding machine tape. If your bank wants you to list each cheque individually on the deposit slip, threaten to go to another bank. Big corporations don't have to do this and you won't either if you stand your ground. Keep it simple!

RETURNS are one of the biggest controversies in the book business. Both wholesalers and bookstores expect to be able to return all books they can't sell and they return 30 to 35 percent. This almost amounts to a consignment and the publisher is caught in a bind because if the booksellers didn't have the return privilege, they would be far less likely to carry his books. The publisher wants his books displayed and so has to take the chance of having a number of them come back. Therefore, there is little difference between consignment and a no-strings return policy.

PARACHUTING PUBLICATIONS

Books By Dan Poynter
POST OFFICE BOX 4232
SANTA BARBARA, CA 93103 USA
Telephone: (805) 968-7277

BOOK RETURN POLICY

1, Books in saleable condition may be returned for credit not less than 90 days, nor more than 12 months, after date of publisher's invoice.

2, Bookseller must request and receive permission from publisher before shipping returns.

3, Return requests must give quantity, title, author, original invoice number and invoice date. Books returned with this information will be credited with 100% of the invoice price minus postage. Otherwise, it will be assumed that the original discount was 60%.

4, Returns must be shipped via Parcel Post (book rate) prepaid to: P.O. Box 4232, Santa Barbara, CA 93103, or UPS prepaid to: Rt #1 (Barney's route), Goleta, CA 93017.

5, Books must arrive in good resaleable condition. They should be packaged so as to keep them clean and so they won't shift in the carton. We recommend plastic bags and tight packing.

6, A credit memo will be issued toward future purchases. To simplify bookkeeping, cash refunds will be made 180 days following date of return.

Sample return policy statement.

Libraries rarely return a book but textbook dealers return a high percentage. They deliberately overstock in order to be sure to have enough books for the new term.

Most publishers will allow returns between ninety days and twelve months of the invoice date. They specify ninety days because they want to make sure the books were

"Make effective use of your most important asset, your time."

given a fair trial on the shelves, but twelve months because they don't want them sitting around too long; the title may go into a new printing.

Usually the bookseller is required to request permission and specific shipping instructions first but few do. They just ship the books back.

Returns should identify the original invoice number under which they were purchased. The publisher wants to credit the bookseller with the correct amount, the amount they paid. He also wants to make sure the books came from him. If they were purchased from a wholesaler, they should be returned to the wholesaler.

Books must arrive back at the publisher in good, unblemished resaleable condition so that they may be returned to stock. This is the biggest failing of the bookstores. They never pack the books properly. They just throw them in a carton, often without cushioning material and send them back. During the long trip, the books chafe against each other and the carton and, consequently, they arrive in a scuffed, battered condition. These have to be set aside while a letter is written asking the dealer where he wants his books shipped.

Large publishing firms usually do not send refunds on returns. They issue credits because they are dealing with the customer on a continuing basis. Small publishers, with few other titles to offer, should send a refund cheque promptly.

Some publishers are charging a penalty of 10% or so for returns. This helps to offset their processing costs.

Damaged and lost books should be replaced by the publisher. Your only alternative is to insure each one and the cost and paperwork are not worth the effort. It is far cheaper to "self-insure" and replace the occasional lost or damaged book.

CHAPTER SEVEN

PROMOTING YOUR BOOK
MAKING THE PUBLIC AWARE OF YOUR BOOK WITHOUT SPENDING FOR ADVERTISING

If you intend to be a successful author, you will measure your success with money. To make a profit, you will depend on good promotion and marketing. This chapter covers promotion: those methods which require some time and effort but no big advertising dollars. Of course, there will be a certain amount of overlap. Probably your most important reference book will be *Literary Market Place*. While you may use the one in your local library, it is worth buying for use at your desk.

Competition for space is a tough proposition. Over 100 titles are published for every day the bookstores are open; the crowd is thicker in the fall than the spring. It is difficult to compete for attention in such a crowded field and against much larger, more knowledgable firms. But you must jump into the fray, exploiting the media through press releases, review copies, radio and T.V. appearances, autograph parties, lectures, etc.

Large publishers are lucky if 40% of their titles make money and they have departments of experts to launch their promotion. They also have built up thousands of key contacts during their many years in the business. You have only one book, your first, and therefore, you have only one chance to make it. But look at the brighter side. The big firms often work through routine and without imagination. Your overhead is much lower and you are cutting out the middlemen by publishing yourself. While your manuscript might not be wide enough in scope to interest the big publishers, there could be enough in the sales for "little" you. You will also do a more effective job of promotion because you have a greater interest in the book than a publisher who is looking after several titles at one time.

By doing the promotion yourself, you are avoiding the most common problem in author/publisher relationships: differing views on the amount of money which should be invested in promotion and advertising. The author cannot be objective about his product and is convinced that the book would sell better if only the publisher would promote it. The publisher, on the other hand, needs more sales to convince him it is worth investing more dollars in advertising.

Before we plan the attack, we have to analyze the current state and trend of the industry. We have to understand their approach to selling books. The big New York publishers are being absorbed by the bigger multinational conglomerates such as ITT and Gulf & Western. Normally, their main interest is to serve their stockholders by generating maximum return on their investment. To do this, they employ sophisticated marketing techniques to move books. They concentrate their efforts on sure bets and high volume, often tying in films and merchandise offers to build public interest. Their

---

"Analyze carefully the kind of person who is a prospective purchaser of your book. This is, perhaps, the single most important thing to consider."

---

marketing dovetails perfectly with the approach by the large chains such as Walden and B. Dalton. Most of their material comes from well-known celebrities or is custom written for a pre-defined audience.

Many of the small publishers, on the other hand, accept "good literature" manuscripts and then try to interest the public in their book. Because of this approach, the book often lacks a well-defined audience. The problem is compounded by a lack of resources for proper promotion.

It is nearly impossible to compete with the large publisher on his ground because you don't have his money. You don't want to follow the small publisher because he isn't making much money. There is a lot of room for the very small independent publisher with imagination and initiative. The competition is easy; it's a challenge. All you have to do is think.

ANALYZE YOUR MARKET by determining who might purchase your book and then figure the best way to reach them (direct mail advertising, space ads, classified ads, T.V., etc.). If your book is on auto repair, you will want to send news releases, review copies, ads and maybe even articles to auto magazines. If you are approaching book stores, college book stores, public libraries or school libraries, you want to determine their seasonal buying patterns. If you are pursuing direct mail sales, you'll want to set up a system of mailings and emphasize the program in certain seasons. (There aren't too many little old ladies who are going to purchase a book on sport parachuting so you don't want to waste your time pursuing them.) The keys to your promotion are targeting and timing.

As you read through this chapter and the next, think about your book and its market. Make a list of, or underline, those ideas mentioned that best fit your book. Then go back and work out a promotional schedule by the week for a period of several months. List ad deadlines, dates for mailings, etc. Set a schedule so you won't lose sight of it later when you are busy typing orders and stuffing boxes.

You can expect your sales to take on an airfoil shape if your prior promotion is good. Sales will climb rapidly, level out, taper off and become steady. Thereafter you will notice bumps in response to seasonal changes or when your advertising or promotional work is successful.

The big initial jump is due to your pre-publication publicity and resulting orders; they all hit at once. By contrast, the big New York publishers market books in the same way Hollywood sells a motion picture. They throw it out on the market to see if anyone likes it. If it gets a response, they dump in a lot of promotional money. Then they push it for a couple of months. When the interest cools, they bring out another film and start all over.

As a small publisher, it makes more sense to market your book like breakfast food or soap. Develop your product, pour on the promotion, carve a nitch in the market and then continue to sell at the same level for years. This can be done with a non-fiction book which is revised at each printing.

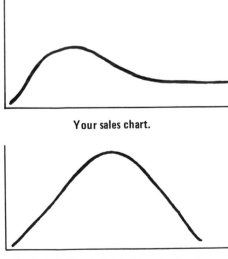

Your sales chart.

Typical big firm individual book sales chart.

"If your book fails to sell, you don't know your market."

"BEST SELLERS" are only a name, a myth. This is not like a gold record in the music industry or another service to the trade run by Bowker. National best seller lists (and there are several) are assembled exclusively from certain bookstore sales reports. Even if you move a million books via mail order distribution, you won't make a best seller list. On the other hand, it may be the best selling book in its field and there is no reason why you can't mention this in your advertising.

PROMOTION IS UP TO YOU. Whether you are a self-publisher or are only the author, it is up to you to make your book a success. Publishers have several titles to be concerned about and they rely on the author for a lot of the promotion. If the publisher fails to properly promote a book, then the author must do it. So there is a lot to learn from this chapter even if you aren't self-publishing.

Bookstores make your book available but they do not promote it. They provide availability but you must supply the promotion. If your book is a hot seller, they will want to carry it. If no one asks for it, they won't touch it. You must create the demand.

KEY CONTACTS are those people who can help you move the greatest volume of books with the least expenditure of time and money. They must be developed if you are going to properly promote your book. The only difference between you and a professional book publicist is that he already has the media contacts. There are many wholesalers, T.V. people and subsidiary rights buyers who are just waiting to "discover" you and your book. While most are very busy, they want you; that's what their job is all about. You will meet a great number of nice, helpful people but only a few "key" contacts will do you a great amount of good. What you have to do is to locate and then carefully cultivate them. Some of the people will be listed in *Literary Market Place* and other directories available at your library. For others, you may have to call the company and ask for the name of the "small press buyer," etc. Tell the company operator who you are and ask who you should properly correspond with. Write or call this contact and field your sales pitch; establish a rapport. Maintain credibility and remember that they are everyone else's key contact, too. Don't expect them to return calls. Send review copies of your book and follow them up in a few days with a telephone call asking "have you received it?" If this is a chain or a wholesaler, be bold and ask for an order.

With chains and wholesalers, the important mission is to get into their system with a large stocking order. This doesn't mean you should oversell them. They'll return what they can't move so it is always safer to go low. It also maintains your credibility with the buyer who is more likely to take your suggestion for an initial stocking order next time.

Start files on these key contacts and fill them with letters and notes of your telephone conversations. Note their personal likes and dislikes so you can bring them up in future conversations. Treat them well and they will be there to help you with your next book, too.

ADDRESS CODES will assess the return on your promotional investment. Just add an extra letter or number to your street address or box. Code everything! Every brochure, ad, order blank, press release, directory listing, everything. Then, you will receive only a few orders you can't trace. Some people will be influenced by your promotion and will seek your book through their library or bookstore. But coding will indicate the source of most of your orders.

"The main difference between marketing a book and marketing soap is that a book is a one-shot deal . . . a book usually only has 90 days to make it or it's dead" – Carole Dolph, promotional director, Doubleday & Co.

Ad response log.

List your address as "48 Walker Street, Suite 712," or in a classified where every word costs, "48-712 Walker." Many customers figure out the obvious codes and, knowing they aren't important to the address, leave them off. So, if you are advertising in *Popular Science* in August 1979, Don't use "48 Walker Street, Dept. PS-8-9." This is even more important with press releases and those items not going directly to the general public because the media are conscious of these codes and won't repeat them. An address code is of no value to you if it doesn't get used.

List all the places to which you are mailing ads and other promotional material and give a short code to each. Letters are good for a start but there aren't enough of them and some can be confused when rendered in script on an envelope. Avoid "I" & "1", "u" & "v", "G" & "6", "0" & "O", etc. They are often difficult to decipher when handwritten.

If you have more than one title and are advertising or promoting two or more in the same market, you will want to make a notation as to which was ordered on the envelope as you process the orders. Then total up the responses at the end of the month and record them by code letter or number on a spread sheet. Also enter on the sheet when certain advertising and promotion hit so you can better visualize the results.

These tallies aren't hard work and can even be done spread out on the floor in front of the T.V. set. It is terribly revealing where some of your orders come from. How else would you know, for example, that a mention in a *Changing Times* article brought in 140 orders? With this information, you will be able to assess what works and where you can most effectively spend your time and money to generate more sales. After a couple of months you'll wonder why address coding wasn't obvious to you from the beginning.

YOUR PUBLICATION DATE is a place in the future, well after your books are off the press, when your promotion hits and your books are available in the stores. It is a matter of good timing. The idea is to have the product accessible when public attention peaks in response to your promotion. You want to time book reviews, T.V. appearances, space advertising, autograph parties, etc. with bookstore deliveries. The big important pre-publication reviewers need 12-15 weeks lead time so you'll have to pick a publication date at least three months away.

Production is always subject to delay so it is recommended that for your first book, and until you learn the problems of the printing trade, you wait until the book is on the press before you set your publication date. Set it 3-4 months away and then start publicizing and selling books. The publication date is a fiction for the benefit of the big, important reviewers and only gives you a target for promotion and distribution. There is nothing to stop you from selling and shipping books.

If you have achieved sufficient pre-publication promotion momentum, you should make a significant amount of sales before the printing bill arrives. It is a matter of planning, scheduling, timing and work. The big publishers expend 90% of their promotional effort by the publication date. You, of course, will keep up the pressure.

The best publication dates are probably in the first quarter of the year. Most of the big publishers aim for the second half. This also gives you maximum mileage for your copyright date. People want a new book and if you publish in December, you become a "year old" in just a few weeks. Mail order sales are traditionally best in the spring. There are many considerations.

> *"While publicity, misused, can be nothing but an ego trip for the author, well used it can be a powerful sales tool"* – Al Lind.

PROMOTIONAL MATERIALS take many forms and many are already at hand. Think of the ways you can use photocopies of your manuscript, folded and gathered pages, over-runs on covers, photocopies of the boards, etc. Combine the jacket with a cover letter and an order blank for a mailing.

PROFESSIONAL BOOK PROMOTION SERVICES are available for those who haven't the time or desire to do their own. They can be a great help, especially on your first book when you are just learning the ropes. Typically, they charge $750 for the first city they service such as a big one like Los Angeles and $250 plus expenses for each additional city. One is Irwin Zucker, 9255-P Sunset Blvd., West Hollywood, CA 90069. Others can be found in *Literary Market Place.* Write for details.

TESTIMONIALS. Many people feel that there is no better promotion than a recommendation from a satisified customer. The best way to get them is to ask for them. If you want to use the testimonials on the back cover of the book, you'll need them early. You can send photocopies of the boards to prominent people and ask them for a few well chosen words. Or if, as suggested in Chapter 2, you have sent certain chapters of your book to various experts during the drafting stage for a critique or technical proofing, you can solicit a testimonial from them. Get permission, preferably a legal release in writing. Most people will jump at the chance to be included.

Full names and occupation are best but if you haven't time to get permission, sign the testimonial such as " J. S. H., Attorney, Denver."

NEWS RELEASES generate publicity and invite book reviews. While being cheap and easy to produce, they are particularly effective. They may be used to announce publication of your new book to newspapers, magazines, libraries, radio and T.V. In fact, they should be sent to anyone who will listen.

On your first book, while you are still learning about the printing trade and your own schedules are apt to slip, it is probably best to send your first press release out when the manuscript is actually delivered to the printer. When you are writing your next book, you may send the release out earlier.

Some authors don't like to reveal their project too early and hold off on their releases. They are afraid someone else might pick up on their good idea. But others purposely get their release out very early in the hope of scaring off the competition. These early releases should contain a more generalized publication date such as "March 1980." Later it may be moved or the specific day may be added.

jb Jāma books

Post Office Box 30751 / Santa Barbara, California 93105 / (805) 687-9325

news release

FOR IMMEDIATE RELEASE
Contact: J. Magee Dugan

Santa Barbara, California is not only one of the country's most beautiful cities, but it's past is rich with exploring Spaniards, buccaneers, Russian otter hunters, Indians, and early movie-makers. An attractive new book, SANTA BARBARA:Highlights & History ($3.95 softcover, $9.95 hard), contains a fascinating look at the town's colorful past, as well as information for present-day explorers. In nearly 60 pages, handsomely illustrated with photos (some in full color), drawings, and maps, SANTA BARBARA: Highlights & History serves the reader as both a guide and an attractive remembrance of this unique

THE FORMAT of the release is standardized. The easiest method is to simply type "NEWS RELEASE" on your own letterhead stationery. It will look fancier if you use "press-on type." By using your own stationery, the important information such as company name and address will be at the top. Then just type in the release date or "For Immediate Release" and a contact name and telephone number. Type a clever and catchy headline in capital letters. Then space down and get into the body of your release.

Begin with the most important information first and end with the least important. This way, if they cut part of it, the major message will still be in. The release should begin by describing the contents of the book; make it provocative. Give the price and mention that the book is available from the publisher as well as the stores. List your address so they'll know where to send the money. Continue with some background on the topic and show why your book is unique, useful and timely. Spend a paragraph on yourself and tell why you are an expert on the subject.

Double space and write in newspaper style. It may be any length but a one-page release is usually best.

Type up the release and have it duplicated at the "instant print" shop by photocopy or offset depending on the number you need. Ship them off with a photo of the book if you have one, one of yourself if you don't. Also enclose a reviewer response card (below).

Send the releases to all appropriate magazines (below), book clubs (see Chapter 6), to subsidiary rights contacts (Chapter 6), wholesalers, libraries, sales representatives, hometown papers, etc. Don't forget alumni, fraternal trade or church publications with which you may have a connection. Spread them around.

Use news releases liberally. Every time you go back to press, issue a press release to herald it. Magazines such as the prestigious *Publishers Weekly* will give you a few lines if you just let them know. Releases should also be issued to announce speaking engagements, T.V. appearances, autograph parties and any other newsworthy event. Remember, the media are in the news gathering and publishing business, they want your releases. Take your time and compose a good release. Not all news gatherers do their own work and it may appear verbatim in print. It may even be reprinted word-for-word as a book review.

Photocopies of your ABI form (see the discussion in Chapter 5) may be enclosed with your news releases to provide additional information.

To: Ottley Management Corporation
Attn: Al King
805 Fifteenth Street NW # 718
Washington, DC 20005
We have received your News Release about (title): _____
by (author): _____ We will take the following action: _____
Your book will be featured on (date): _____
Your book will be featured in the near future: _____ (check).
Please send a complimentary copy of your book: _____ (check).
Name: _____
Title: _____
Publication or station: _____
Address: _____
Comments: _____

**Example of a Release Response Reply Card.
The other side is addressed to you and stamped.**

Enclose a Release Response Reply Card. This will alert you to the publicity so you can be ready to collect samples and will provide leads for book reviews. Remember that media people work in a pressure-cooker world. Be polite, they won't expect it. You will get a lot of mileage out of one kind word.

PRE-PUBLICATION BONUS DISCOUNTS are sometimes used to encourage the stores to stock the book by the publication date. Typically, an extra 10% is allowed to stores placing orders three or more weeks before the formal date. But this requires extra record keeping or you'll be paying back too much on the unsold returned copies.

COPYRIGHTS, LISTINGS AND EARLY REVIEWS. In anticipation of your new book coming off the press, address large envelopes to those places listed below and stuff them

"Never talk about what you are going to do until after you have written it." – Mario Puzo

as appropriate with: cover letter, review sheets, photocopied ABI form, 5 x 7 photograph, etc. Then when you receive your first delivery of books, stuff them into the envelopes and send them off according to the following checklist. When mailing to the review magazines, address the package to the specific appropriate editor. Check the current names in *Literary Market Place*. Stuff in brochures, early reviews, etc. to convince them the book has been accepted by others. Don't skimp here.

1.   One copy for LC cataloging. See the discussion in Chapter 5. CIP Office, Library of Congress, Washington, DC 20540. Use their postpaid label.

2.   Two copies for copyright registration, along with your cheque and the copyright form. See the discussion in Chapter 5. Register of Copyrights, Library of Congress, Washington, DC 20540.

3.   One copy to LC Acquisition and Processing along with your brochure and discount schedule. Library of Congress, Attn: Jane Collins, Acquisitions and Processing Division, Crystal Mall Annex, Washington, DC 20540.

4.   One copy to *Publishers Weekly*, Attn: Weekly Record, 1180 Avenue of the Americas, NYC, NY 10036.

5.   One copy to *Library Journal,* Attn: Janet Fletcher, 1180 Avenue of the Americas, NYC, NY 10036.

6.   One copy to *School Library Journal,* Attn: Pamela Pollack, 1180 Avenue of the Americas, NYC, NY 10036.

7.   One copy for listing, per the discussion in Chapter 5, to H.W. Wilson Co., Attn: *Cumulative Book Index,* 950 University Avenue, NYC, NY 10452.

8.   One copy to *The New York Times,* Attn: Daily Book Review Section, Times Square, NYC, NY 10036.

9.   One copy to *The New York Times,* Attn: Sunday Book Review Section, Times Square, NYC, NY 10036. This is one of the most prestigious and valuable review columns. Retail book buyers read this medium and rely on it more than any other.

10.   One copy to *Saturday Review Syndicate,* 380 Madison Avenue, NYC, NY 10017.

11.   One copy to *Choice,* Attn: Louis Sasso, 100 Riverview, Middletown, CT 06457

12.   One copy to American Library Association, Attn: *The Booklist,* 50 East Huron Street, Chicago, IL 60611.

13.   One copy to *Kirkus Reviews,* 200 Park Avenue South, NYC, NY 10003.

14.   One copy to *The Horn Book Magazine,* Attn: Ethel L. Heins, 585 Boylston Street, Boston, MA 02116.

15.   One copy to *Small Press Review*, P.O. Box 100-P, Paradise, CA 95969.

16.   One copy to Gale Research Co., Attn: *Contemporary Authors,* The Book Tower, Detroit, MI 48226.

17.   One copy each to some of the larger wholesalers and chain bookstore buyers. See the discussion in Chapter eight and the listings in the Appendix.

18.   One copy to *Forecast Magazine,* Attn: Patricia Gursky, Baker & Taylor, 1515 Broadway, NYC, NY 10036.

19.   One copy to: The Library of Congress, Card Division, Dept. PWLC, Washington DC 20541 (for the *National Union Catalogue*).

Now is also the time to make use of Bowker's Advanced Book Information (ABI) form. See the discussion in Chapter 5. Send it in now if you haven't already done so. Make photocopies of it and send one to Baker & Taylor Co., Academic Library Services Selection Department, P.O. Box 4500, Somerville, NJ 08876, for their New Book Approval and Current Books for Academic Libraries plans.

BOOK REVIEWS sell books. They aren't difficult to get while they cost you very little in time and money. But there are two types of reviews. They cater to two separate markets and the approach to each is different. They can be labeled: "Pre-publication reviews (wholesale)" and "Publication date reviews (retail)."

But first we must be sure we understand the meaning of, and reason for, the "publication date." As mentioned earlier, the publication date is a fiction for the benefit of the big important reviewers and only provides you with a target for promotion and distribution.

PRE-PUBLICATION REVIEWS are directed toward the industry. Certain publications will review your book prior to publication so that the bookstores and libraries will have the opportunity to stock it before patrons start asking for it. Since 100 new titles are published for each day the stores are open, many book dealers and libraries depend on these concise summaries in making their purchasing choices. Pre-publication reviews are directed at the trade and should not be confused with the regular book reviews aimed at the ultimate consumer/reader.

Ninety or more days prior to your publication date, send photocopies of the pasted boards (or galleys if you are printing letterpress) with a cover letter, reply card and a press release to:

Publishers Weekly, Attn: Forecasts, 1180 Avenue of the Americas, NYC, NY 10036.
Library Journal, Attn: Book Reviews, 1180 Avenue of the Americas, NYC, NY 10036.
Kirkus Reviews, Attn: Library Advance Information Service, 200 Park Avenue South, NYC, NY 10003.
The Booklist, Attn: Book Reviews, 50 East Huron Street, Chicago, IL 60611.
The New York Times, Attn: Daily Book Page, Times Square, NYC, NY 10036.
Forecast, Baker and Taylor Co., 1515 Broadway, NYC, NY 10036.

The cover letter should be addressed to a particular person; current names can be found in *Literary Market Place*, available in your library.

Write a paragraph on each of the following: introduce the book and its contents, tell why the book is important to today's reader, and say that you hope they like the book.

Sample reviews probably won't work with the above publications as they usually do their own work. But it doesn't hurt to try and it will work with some other magazines.

You may send a finished copy of the book to most regular reviewers but those listed above prefer galleys. If you send the finished book, they will think it is too late for a "pre-publication review" and they will probably ignore it. Some reviewers collect galleys feeling they offer more prestige than just books which are available to anyone.

In offset printing there is often less time between typesetting and printing and the new video screen text editing equipment allows authors to set their own type as they write, thus shortening the procedure even more. Eventually, galleys may go the way of the buggy whip. If you do send the finished book only, mention in your cover letter that modern printing methods make sending the galleys impractical, then emphasize your publication date.

Reviews in the above listed publications are the most important. Good reviews in them will get you more reviews in other publications later.

REVIEWS FOR THE ULTIMATE CONSUMER. This is the most effective and least expensive method of promoting your book to the retail market. While few other products can regularly approach the media for free publicity, books have always received rather special treatment. It is almost as though there were an unwritten agreement within the communications communtiy to publicize each others' work.

You want to time most of your reviews to appear on or around your publication date. It won't help sales if they appear before you are able to fill orders or the books aren't available in the stores. Some publications won't even bother to review a book if they can't get into print by the publication date. So mail early or set the publication date late.

It helps to understand the lot of the editor and/or reviewer. Whether they are full time or freelance, they have one thing in common: they are very busy. Some editors live in a pressure cooker world. You can't change this so you might as well understand and take advantage of it.

Your book is a product of yourself. You poured your time, heart and soul into it. But just because you were interested enough to take the time to write it doesn't mean everyone else will be interested enough to take the time to read it. A book critic will read your book but a book reviewer will probably only check the front matter. Most of the reviewer's work will come from your news release and other enclosures. Make them good.

Another problem you will encounter is space. There just aren't enough book review columns to go around. Even the prestigious and prolific Sunday Supplement of the New York Times can only cover about 20% of the books.

However, if your book has special area appeal, you can greatly increase your chances by submitting your book for review to the special publications reaching that particular group. For example, if your book is on hang gliding, you would send review copies to *Hang Gliding* magazine and *Glider Rider*. Then you would consider every aviation, outdoor, sport, recreation, do-it-yourself, teen, men's, etc. magazines you could find. There are some 60,000 magazines being printed in the U.S. today (and a lot more foreign). There must be some which are reaching the group(s) you want.

Be prepared for delays with the smaller association publications. They want to review your book but they have certain staff and budget limitations. Usually they rely on outside free help for book reviews. Typically, the editor will only scan a book before sending it off to an appropriate expert requesting him to review it. Often, the reviewer is very busy too. If you know the editor or reviewer, often the case in an industry publication, give him or her some help. Offer to write the review yourself, sending it to the reviewer for additions or changes. They usually simply sign it and send it in.

SELECTING MAGAZINES and other media for news releases and potential reviews is easy. Go to the library and search through the racks for appropriate magazines. In a large library in a major city, this could take all day. Look for book review columns and copy down the name, title and address of the reviewer. If you don't send the book to the attention of the right person, your book may get ripped-off by someone else on the staff. When this happens, you not only waste a book, you lose out on a review. Pick your publications carefully, there are thousands to choose from. Select only those who are likely to review your book because it is relative to their publication and the interests of their readership. In other words, don't send an aviation book to *Solid Waste Management* magazine until you see garbage trucks with wings. Be objective and realistic.

Reviewers and publications may also be found in: *Writer's Market, Literary Market Place* (with many good lists such as producers of TV talk shows, syndicated columnists, newspaper book reviewers, etc.), the *Ayer Directory of Publications* (lists newspapers and magazines), *Ulrich's International Periodicals Directory* (specialized periodicals), *Bacon's Publicity Checker, International Yearbook* (the key personnel of newspapers), *Broadcast Yearbook* (key radio and TV personnel), *Encyclopedia of Associations* and the *National Trade and Professional Associations Directory* (both list special interest trade and professional organizations).

Depending on your subject, you may find 200 to 400 potential reviewers for your book. Don't be surprised if you come up with 600. Then get to work on them. It will cost you some time and a bit of postage but book reviews are the best promotional investment you can make.

Divide them into two groups: the sure bets and the rest. Send books to the small group of sure bets but send only the literature and a reply postcard to the majority of them.

When the cards come back, send out the books and the literature. You are fishing at this point; you won't hook a fish with every cast but you have narrowed your odds with the postcards. Reviewers don't buy books but their reviews are worth far more than the cost to you. Those freelance reviewers who are not on the staff of the publications often receive only the book as their compensation.

```
To: Para-Resources Publishing Co.
    Attn: Mike Horan
    3183 West Florence-Campbellstown Road
    Eaton, OH 45320

☐ YES, I would like to receive a review/examination copy of:
Title: _____
Author: _____
☐ No, we do not feel this book is suitable for our review.
Name: _____
Title: _____
Publication or station: _____
Address: _____
            _____
Comments: _____
            _____
            _____
```

Review copy reply postcard.

THE REVIEW PACKAGE sent to the reviewer should include the following: a book, brochure, review slip, a sample review, cover letter, reply card and some photographs. Make the reviewer's job easy and provide everything needed.

The cover letter should start by mentioning that this is the complimentary review copy they requested. Help the reviewer. Suggest an interesting or unique local angle. Introduce the book and its contents. Tell why the book is important to today's reader and ask for a review.

Sample reviews (mentioned above) are worth writing. Many reviewers will use them verbatim. In fact, it won't hurt to write up two samples, a short one and a long one. For the more important magazines, check the particular publication and follow their style.

Use the same type of reply card you sent out for the pre-publication reviews.

Artwork will get you a lot more space and make the review more attractive resulting in a higher degree of readership. Enclose 5 x 7 black and white photographs of the book, author and, if the book is well illustrated, a sample illustration.

EXPENSIVE BOOKS

Presents for review . . .

TITLE: The Biggest Ripoff
AUTHOR: Ken deRussy
PUBLICATION
DATE: 1 February 1980
PRICE: $ 9.95 Softbound
       $14.95 Hardbound
       (published simultaneously)

*We would appreciate two
copies of your review.*

Expensive Books Publishing Co.
613 North Milpas Street
Santa Barbara, CA 93103

An example of a book review slip.

**THE SELF-PUBLISHING MANUAL
How To Write, Print And
Sell Your Own Book
Publication date: 5 June 1979
$14.95 hardcover, $9.95 paperback.**

Stamping the book will insure that it isn't returned to you later for a refund.

"When promoting it, speak proudly about your book. You worked hard on it and you should be proud. False modesty will get you nowhere." – Mark Danna

Many books are sent with book review slips listing vital information but a lot of others simply have the title, publication date and price(s) rubber stamped on the inside of the front cover. Some reviewers want the information stamped on for identification in case they lose the book review slip and many publishers do to prevent the reviewer from selling the book to a bookstore. Some stores find they can get more for these rubber stamped review copies and others return the clean ones back to the publisher for credit.

```
To: That New Publishing Company
    Attn: Rusty Walker
    1525 Eielson Street
    Fairbanks, AK 99701
We have received the complimentary review book or galleys you sent of
Title: _____
Author: _____
[ ]   We expect to review this book on (date): _____
[ ]   We did not find this book suitable for our review.
Name: _____
Title: _____
Publication or station: _____
Address: _____
_____
Comments: _____
```

Sample of reply postcard. The other side should contain your return address and a stamp.

Always include a stamped, self-addressed reply postcard so they may indicate the response they plan. You want to be ready to collect the clippings for your files and future promotion.

Don't be too upset by the return rate on the reply postcards. Some will take a long time and others will not be returned at all. Many reviewers just don't know when the review will appear.

Per the discussion above, go to the library and assemble a list of appropriate magazines, newspapers, news services and news syndicates. They can be found in the magazine section, *Literary Market Place, Writer's Market*, and other directories. Hometown newspapers and magazines are easy. They are almost obligated to pick up local color; in a small town weekly you might even make the first page. Hit all your home towns, where you live now, where you grew up, where you went to school, all of them. Address your cover letter to the specific editor and you may not only get a nice review but a special feature story as well.

If you know a freelance or staff reviewer personally, send him or her a review copy. Use every possible "in" you might have.

Some public relations people like to get very personal in review copy mailings. They jot a little personal note to the reviewer hoping to snow them into thinking they've met before or that the reviewer may have made some long forgotten promise at a cock tail party.

Reviewers are cautious people. They are more apt to review your book if it has been treated favorably in pre-publication reviews by big name reviewers. One way to convince them your book is worthy of their attention is to include copies of these early reviews. Just paste them all up on a sheet of paper and make a photocopy.

Follow through on reviewers. If they don't respond right away, contact them and ask: "may I send you some additional information?"

Once you receive a card notifying you a review will appear in a given publication, you may like to advertise in it, too. Some publishers feel this double impact is worth their while though others do not. Many like to see how the review pulls before investing in an ad. They let the review test the medium.

Some of your reviews may be bad and one reason is that some reviewers are bad. Some of these critics are frustrated writers who try to bring all other published authors down to their level. They take cheap shots or use the book as a springboard for lofting their own views. Don't worry about it. Any review is better than no review because people tend to remember the title more than the critique. When you quote from the review, just use the good parts.

Some reviewers still assume that in real publishing, the hardcover edition comes out several months prior to the softcover. If they receive a paperback, they assume the title is old. Similarly, the media have been reluctant to review a book unless it is

Throwing the Book at You

Journal of Aerospace Education

So catch it and get in on the action. *The Frisbee Player's Handbook*—shaped like a Frisbee—is a new and exciting book by Mark Danna (a top world ranked Frisbee player) and Dan Poynter (one of the world's foremost authorities on aviation sports). Specially die cut to a circular format, the book comes nested and shrink wrap packaged in a custom designed Frisbee disc. All this to inspire the world to think circular.

Written for easy reading by both the casual beach player and the accomplished master, this fascinating 187-page book offers a unique training method and a systematic, step-by-step approach to basic, special, and advanced Frisbee throws and catches. Other chapters cover games, competition, Frisbee lore and origin, world records, and even training methods for teaching dogs how to catch a disc. The

appendix lists Frisbee books, magazines, and clubs throughout the world in order to direct the reader to the local action. Enhancing the text are over 400 action photos—including sequential shots and overhead views—nearly all of which were staged by the authors with motorized equipment to illustrate the essential parts of every throw and catch. The *Frisbee Player's Handbook* is indeed the only complete up-to-date, how-to, where-to Frisbee manual, and the disc is sure to become a collector's item.

The price for both the circular book and the custom Frisbee disc together is just $8.95 ($9.95 foreign, Californians add 54¢ sales tax). It is available in many sporting goods, toy, and book stories or directly from the publisher: parachuting Publications, P.O. Box 4232-Y. Santa Barbara, CA 93103.

The New York Times Book Review

Discus plasticus. The oddest-looking book of the year has just arrived from the oddest-named publisher of the year: "The Frisbee Handbook" (Parachuting Publications, Santa Barbara, Calif., $8.95), a 187-page, circular-shaped paperback nestling within a plastic Frisbee, all of it neatly shrink-wrapped. The opus is the collaboration of Mark Danna, a young New Yorker who makes a living as a top-rated Frisbee player, and Dan Poynter, a young Californian who's into such things as parachute-jumping, hang-gliding and publishing books on aviation sports. The picture-filled, amusingly written handbook gives pointers on both solo and team Frisbee play, facts about clubs, competitions and the lore of a sport that has won several hundred thousand devotees, male and female, over the past 20 years.

And how did the Frisbee get its name? It seems that many, many years ago there was a New Haven firm named the Frisbie Baking Co., and Yale men got into the habit of using its empty pie tins to play games with under the elms. ■

PUBLISHERS WEEKLY

A pair of illustrated frisbee books, one for each hand perhaps, are being published this month. The more unusual of the two is "**Frisbee® Players' Handbook**" by Mark Danna and Dan Poynter ($8.95). The difference is in the design. The April paperback from Parachuting Publications (P.O. Box 4232-Y, Santa Barbara, Calif. 93103) is round and fully packed—inside an actual frisbee. The publisher notes that there are more than 100,000 members of the International Frisbee Association and that more than 10-million frisbees are sold annually. Future converts will encounter training methods, frisbee lore, world records and such detailed in this would-be flyer. Danna is about to set out on a 13-week tour for a Coppertone/frisbee promotion.

GAMES

The Frisbee Players Handbook by Mark Danna and Dan Poynter (Parachuting Publications, P.O. Box 4232, Santa Barbara, California 93103, 1978, 187 pages plus Frisbee, paperback, $8.95; Californians add 54 cents sales tax).

With the *Frisbee Players Handbook* you not only get a carefully organized and illustrated manual instructing you in basic throws, advanced throws, basic catches, simple trick catches, advanced trick catches, and special catching maneuvers; you not only learn about throwing multiple discs, about Frisbee games, the official format for Frisbee competition, records for outdoor distance, indoor distance, and maximum time aloft, records accomplished by men, women, seniors, juniors, children, and dogs; you not only find out abbut the lore and origin of the Frisbee, about Frisbee clubs and proficiency standards—you not only get all of this in a book that is shaped so that it can nestle unnoticeably in your Frisbee, but you also get a specially developed training model Frisbee patterned after the World Class 119 G.

Library Journal

Danna, Mark & Dan Poynter. **Frisbee Players' Handbook.**
Parachuting Publications. 1978. 190p. illus. LC 77-79101. ISBN 0-915516-15-2 pap. $8.95.
SPORTS
This is a manual for Frisbee players from beginners to potential world class masters. The authors describe simple throws and catches and more advanced techniques. Many photographs accompany the instruction. There are rules for games and competitive events, and there is a list of current record holders in various events. There is also an explanation of the certification requirements for the four levels of proficiency recognized by the International Frisbee Association. An appendix provides a regional directory of clubs and a list of magazines and books for the player. The book is awkward for libraries, however, because it is rounded to fit into the inner rim of the Frisbee that is sold with it.—*Jack Oakley, Dearborn Dept. of Libs., Mich.*

PREMIUM/INCENTIVE BUSINESS

Frisbee Packs Book In Conventional Disc

Circular 187-page book outlines step-by-step method for learning how to throw a frisbee. Written by a frisbee expert and an authority on

aviation sports, it is neatly packed in a Frisbee. Both Frisbee and book retail for $8.95. FROM: Parachuting Publications.

Circle No. 236 on product card.

Examples of pasted up pre-publication and early reviews.

published in hardcover. Today, with the dominance of the "quality" or "trade" paper-back, this barrier is beginning to be breached and many books are being selected for review on their own merits.

Acknowledge all reviews with a personal letter. Praise and thank the reviewer. They'll remember you when you send your next book. A small amount of time spent on letters here is an investment in the future.

Put a lot of effort into reviews. They are the best promotional investment you can make.

NOTIFY YOUR FRIENDS of your new book by mailing them a press release and an order blank. Send these to friends, relatives and influential people in the field covered by the book. They are prime prospects and will help to promote your book by just talking about it.

RADIO AND TELEVISION offer tremendous exposure for a new author. Talk shows provide an audience in the millions at no cost to you. The shows are constantly looking for fresh material and authors are a prime source. You are an expert on a particular subject, you are interesting.

The big shows are best, of course, as they reach more people. The "Today," "To-night" and "Tomorrow" shows are the most influential in bookselling. The best plug for a book is when Johnny Carson or Merv Griffin takes a personal interest. But these bigger shows are hard to crack. They have lots of material as they are deluged with press releases, visits and other personal contacts by the public relations departments of the big publishers. The competition is great and there just isn't enough air time to go around.

But there are ways to get on the big talk shows as well as to crack the other media; it depends on your subject. For example, if your book is on Frisbee disc play, you would approach the Wham-O Manufacturing Company which makes them. Of course you already know them because they gave you a lot of the material for your book. They have a public relations firm on retainer and it is to their advantage to give your book a lot of promotion. You can use their muscle free. You are actually doing them a favor since your book gets their foot in the media door so they can promote their product. Inciden-tally, such a company would be a prime customer for your book. They would make ideal corporate gifts and could be used in promotions.

Whether or not you can crack into the big shows, do not overlook the smaller and local ones. They are much easier. Many stations have special shows for interviewing authors and most have at least one talk show. The local station will want you on its community affairs program. Depending on your subject, they may even produce a short clip for their news broadcast. Once you have appeared on one local station, don't give up on the others. Use another interesting angle.

To get on a show, find out who the producer is. Locally, you may simply call the station and ask the switchboard operator. For other stations, consult the directories in your library.

Write to the producer enclosing a copy of the book, your news release, a reply card and photocopies of any reviews you have received. Mention two or three of the most interesting aspects of yourself and your book. If one doesn't grab their attention, with luck another will. It helps if you can tie in to some topical problem of the day: local, national or international. Let the producer know, generally, when you'll be available. If the station is local, you may be ready most any time. If you are on tour, you will have a

---

"The publicity departments of publishers would kill for five minutes on Johnny Carson's show" — Ron Nessen, press secretary to former President Ford.

tight schedule. Give as much advance warning as possible. Since radio/T.V. people are used to dealing with a third party, you might have someone else sign the letter.

If you don't hear from the station in a week or so, telephone the producer. Be persistant and polite and you should finally get through. Be prepared. Have a rough script and practice it. Express a positive, lively attitude and exude enthusiasm. This is almost an audition; if you come across well, you'll get on the show.

Set up a city-to-city tour scheduling in the various stations which have responded. You'll need two or three in each town to make the trip worth your while. If a station can't fit you into its schedule, suggest a telephone interview or a recorded one. Ask the producer to send you a list of questions. Then read off the first one into a cassette recorder and answer it. He or she will then ask the question on the air in their own voice and play your answer. It is just as though you were in the studio.

When you go on the air, be prepared. Know your book. Practice public speaking. Think over the best answers to the questions most likely to be asked. Rehearse the stock answers. The talk show host will frustrate you by bouncing from subject to subject so don't be caught with nothing to say. Radio, by the way, is much less demanding than T.V.

Media people are busy and are under a lot of deadline pressure. While your book is the most important thing that has happened to you lately, it is just another news item to them. They aren't impressed, they deal with newsmaking personalities all the time. Be polite, they won't expect it. Everyone around them is tough and short. A kind word from you will go a long way. A thank you note afterwards will leave a nice memory and you'll receive great treatment for your second book.

Sometimes you just have to be ready for an opening. If your book is on parachuting and you hear the radio disc jockey announce that he plans to make his first jump on Saturday, call him up right then and offer to come right over. You'll be on for a week.

When you go on tour, be sure to tie in with local bookshops. Carry a carload of books and visit the bookstore first. Then when you go on the air, you can refer the listeners to the local store. You might even like to follow up the program with an autograph party in the store.

AUTHOR'S TOURS are the way you promote your book out of town and they are very hard work. There was a time when all the author did was to deliver his manuscript to the publisher and then go home to await his royalty cheques. However, with the advent of T.V. and more hype in the book business, the major effort on the part of the writer is now in criss-crossing the country selling the book. According to *The Wall Street Journal,* "For the publisher it is publicity at low cost. For the author it is an endurance test." It's a tough, grueling experience but there is no cheaper way of reaching the book buying public. This means going on as many radio and T.V. shows as possible and visiting bookstores in between. It is terribly discouraging to find that most of the stores don't have it in stock. However, understanding all this, and realizing that the effort is worth it, you can put yourself in the right frame of mind and troop on.

T.V. GIVEAWAY PROGRAMS will provide you with great exposure and all you have to do is donate a book. These programs are presented to raise funds for charitable organizations. Be on the lookout for them.

NEWS CONFERENCES are often staged by big firms who host a lavish party for the press. But there is nothing wrong with a small gathering. If you have something provocative to say on a timely subject, if it would normally be mentioned as a news item, you may be able to draw out the media. You don't have to rent a hotel suite or serve food. Press people just want the information as quickly as possible. Cater to them.

FEATURED ARTICLES ON YOURSELF are another way to gain publicity. Local papers, company magazines, alumni publications, etc. are always looking for interesting news about their people. Let them do a story on you and they'll mention your greatest accomplishment — your book. You are now an expert, an interesting person just because you are a published author.

Mail off the same package you sent to the talk show producers. After several days, call to ask if you may come in for an interview. You are news to every publication with which you are connected, from a national association to a local newspaper. Take advantage of them.

BOOK PROMOTION THROUGH MAGAZINE ARTICLES is another way to gain publicity for your book while furthering your writing career. It is easy to spin off articles from the chapters of your book. You can sell the articles, build your reputation and help to sell the book, too.

First of all, you will be quite pleased to find that you have less difficulty selling to magazines now that you are a published author. You are an expert and magazines want authoritative articles. Of course, you will want to end the article with "Editor's note: Jack Jones is the author of ..." and type it in just as you want it, don't leave it up to the editor. Also try to mention it in the text of the article. Those who read the article will be interested in the subject or they wouldn't be reading it. Many will want to know more and will seek your book. So. while you are making sales on books , you might even get paid for the article.

You might like to consider, however, that if you offer the article free, you have a better chance of its seeing print. Write to the editor, enclosing a few applicable pages from your book, and offer to write an article with the magazine's editorial slant. Offer to send an outline or include it with this first mailing.

SPEAKING ENGAGEMENTS are another way to publicize your book. As an expert on your subject, you are in demand by service organizations, adult education programs, church groups, PTA's, the Chamber of Commerce and others. Many of these groups feature a guest speaker at every meeting. Sometimes they rotate the responsibility among the membership to find a speaker. Your call may actually get someone off the hook.

The possibilities will become obvious once you begin to think of your topic from the marketing standpoint. If yours is a carpentry how-to book, a hardware store or lumber yard might like to build a seminar around you. It might turn into an annual affair. Think of the nurseries which hold pruning classes every spring. You'll make good contacts as well as developing new ideas; it's stimulating.

When you make your appearance, always mention your book. Have one on display and make several copies available for sale and autographs. Prepare a short, powerful speech on one small, very interesting, related item and leave plenty of time for questions and answers.

Speaking engagements will do three things for you: they promote your book, you may receive a fee for speaking and they add to your professional portfolio. Now, in addition to being an author and a publisher, you are a lecturer, too. You must be an expert!

AUTOGRAPH PARTIES are a good ego trip when successful and can help to make your other advertising more effective. Every little bit helps. The best scheduling is to tie in with a radio or T.V. appearance and some local advertising.

Contact a local bookstore and ask if you may set up a table, erect a sign and provide some refreshment. The bookstore may be reluctant to sponsor such an event unless you are willing to underwrite some of the cost. The expense won't be small. In addition to the refreshments and sign, you will have to consider a good deal of advertising via mail and space ads. But the store should pay at least half. Even if they fail to sell a lot of your books, this "event" you are staging will bring new customers into their shop. Once introduced to the bookstore, they are more likely to return in the future.

Once you know a local paper is going to review your book or do a feature article on you, visit the bookstores. Suggest they might like to place an ad in the same edition to draw readers into their store. Offer to stage an autograph party, another fine tie-in.

Don't overlook fund-raising event autograph parties. Here, you would do the selling and would donate part to the club or organization.

To make an autograph party successful, you must pour on the publicity. Send out large numbers of news releases and invitations. Make it sound big and important. Make everyone in town think that everyone else is going, that if they don't go they will be very lonely.

To Rose Pinew
With Best Wishes
Sam Author
JUNE 1979   **Examples of book autographs**

To al Nussbaum
With deep appreciation
for your advice and support—
Sam Author
September, 1979

AUTOGRAPHING BOOKS is something you'll be asked to do both in person and by mail. It is surprising how many prolific authors have never given much thought as to how they might autograph a book. Confronted with an admiring fan, they are suddenly at a loss for words. Most authors simply sign: "To Kathy with best wishes," add their signature and sometimes the date. At times you want to be more personal such as thanking a contributor for his or her help and support on the book. If there is something special about the buyer, include it in your autograph. It is often a question of time. On a mail order book, you can dream up something special while at a well attended autograph party it is difficult to think about a few well chosen words while trying to give witty answers. And, by the way, especially when rushed, make sure you spell their name correctly. In all the hustle, it is easy to draw a blank and mispell the simpliest name or word, ruining a book.

BOOK AWARDS. There is probably no greater satisfaction to a writer than having his book selected for an award. Some are big and well known and some are small. Most are for fiction. There are those that are general while others are quite specialized, but all are awards and winning one looks good in your advertising.

Book awards are listed in *Literary Market Place* and *Writer's Market* available at your library and in a pamphlet entitled *Grants and Awards Available To American Writers* published by P.E.N. American Center. See the Appendix.

Additionally, some more awards are offered by:
1. Aviation/Space Writers Association (aviation and space), Cliffwood Road, Chester, NJ 07930, Attn: William F. Kaiser
2. Pushcart Prize (small press), P.O. Box 845, Yonkers, NY 10701, Attn: Bill Henderson.
3. New York Academy of Sciences (children's science books), 2 East 63rd Street, NYC, NY 10021, Attn: Ann Collins.
4. Book Design Award. Wind Flower Press, P.O. Box 82213, Lincoln, NE 68501.
5. The American Book Awards, One Park Avenue, NYC, NY 10016

RELATED BOOK LISTS can be used to plug your other books. Each of your books should carry a list of all your books and these lists should be updated at each reprinting. The list may appear on the rear jacket or inside the text of the book. This is a way to get your message to potential buyers in the same field at little cost.

BE PREPARED to move when your book takes off. Have your promotional plan organized so you will be able to gain maximum mileage from your publicity. Capitalize on each piece of publicity. Have your releases, ads and letters drafted.

Take advantage of every possible market. Pursue the most lucrative but don't overlook the marginal ones. It costs very little to service them once you've done the initial organization.

CHAPTER EIGHT

WHO WILL BUY YOUR BOOK?

FINDING CUSTOMERS (MARKETS)

Your marketing effort is vital to the success of your book. It may be the greatest ever written but if it fails to reach its intended customer, it won't sell. Money is the measure and your book won't be successful without sales. People will not line up automatically to purchase your book. You have expended a great deal of effort in writing your book but it is the energy you expend now that will make your earlier effort pay off.

Unfortunately, many creative people recoil at the thought of selling their own product. But they must promote their book even when they are not the publisher, too. One function of publishing is to distribute the book to the consuming public.

The role of marketing is to return maximum sales on minimum promotional investment, "to get more bang for your buck." You want to invest your money where you will get the best return. This means advertising where you receive the best response per dollar invested.

An often heard rule of thumb for response percentages — i.e., the number of orders received for a mailing or ad — is 2% and there are many entertaining stories of much better returns. What really counts is the return in sales on the advertising investment. A cheap ad becomes expensive if it fails to bring in any sales. To determine your results, you must total your alternatives before you sign up. The woods are full of ad salespeople and their primary mission, like yours, is staying in business. They'll promise you anything to get into your advertising budget.

Consider the amount of work which will go into the promotion. Total up your office expenses ("licking and sticking") and the direct costs such as stamps and envelopes or ad bills and balance these against the selling price (if to wholesalers, you will get less per book) and the expected response. Total these up and make the decision, but try to be objective. Code your address in all marketing efforts as discussed in Chapter seven, so you can trace the source of your orders.

Each year, some 500 U.S. publishers bring some 30,000 hardcover titles to market, not counting textbooks and reprints. Of these, about 4,000 are fiction. The competition for attention and sales is fierce. *Publishers Weekly* printed some interesting 1977 statistics in June of '78. In adult trade hardcover sales, 46.6% were sold through retailers, 39.6% through wholesalers, 7.9% directly to libraries and institutions, 3% through special sales and 2.5% directly to customers. Over 5% were exported, about half to Canada. But professional books, those including technical, professional, scientific, medical and busi-

> *"The writing of a best seller represents only a fraction of the total effort required to create one"* — Ted Nicholas

ness titles, went directly to consumers 30% of the time with a median price of $12.22. There is also other evidence that the number of books sold direct to the consumer via mail order has been on the increase in recent years.

In Canada, some 65% of the books sold are imports, 25% are Canadian published and the rest are foreign books adapted and manufactured for the Canadian market.

In a November 1976 *Publishers Weekly* article, a poll revealed that only 5% of the population buys six or more books per year (hardcover and paperback) and most were between 18 and 45 years old. While 40% would consider a book as a gift, they weren't sure it was appropriate and thought it would be difficult to choose one the recipient might like. They did feel, however, that books are very personal.

Research and experience will help you select the best places to spend your advertising money. Some of these markets are obvious and you should start planning around them. Then you will want to branch out into the non-traditional markets where the competition is often less. For example, Warner Publishing cracked a new market in 1978 when Karen Lustgarten's *Disco Dancing* was sold in record stores. Your options are so numerous and varied that it is difficult to concentrate on the important areas.

AUDIENCE SPECIALIZATION is concentrating your efforts on the best areas. Before you wrote your book, you analyzed your potential audience and then you slanted your text toward them. In producing your book, you considered how it might be marketed and made your product attractive in this medium. Perhaps you put extra effort into the cover. The selection of your marketing channels is very important. For example, the chains seem to concentrate on fast moving books. If your book doesn't have a wide audience, you don't want to be in the chains. The unsold books will only come back. Even if you get them into an area where there aren't any returns, you want them to sell, not to sit on the shelves forever. So consider who patronizes each of the various outlets and be objective in considering whether they are your audience.

There has been little market research in the general segment of the book industry. Most of the sales effort is based on past experience. In analyzing the market, you will consider your principal marketing concerns, your customers (individuals, schools, libraries, international markets, subsidiary rights, industry, government, etc.) and your distribution channels (mass market outlets, wholesalers, bookstores and book clubs). Your marketing tools are space ads, direct mail advertising, sales representation, etc.

With a specialized non-fiction book you can avoid the expensive traditional big publisher methods of marketing and concentrate on the more profitable areas. Work smarter, not harder. Define your core audience and then pour on the hype. Select your special audience and find a way to reach them. You'll find they are served by magazines, stores, catalogues, broadcast interviewers, specialized book clubs, columnists and others. Remember, you don't have to attack the whole group, you can go after just the cream off the top. Mail to the libraries with the biggest budgets, visit the buyers of the larger chain stores, and select the wealthiest of the direct mail purchasers. Ads and mailing lists can be purchased selectively by region; you don't have to buy the whole country.

Hedge your bets by balancing your markets. Put most of your energy into selling your target group. Sell to the rest, too, but don't spend a lot of time courting them. Invest your time wisely.

REPETITIVE AUDIENCE CONTACT is the key once you have identified your marketing area. A repeated promotion in direct mail advertising, space ads, etc. will normally

> *"It is important to have a book that is appealing enough to its audience that little or no advertising is necessary."*

bring the same response as it did the first time. Naturally the returns will drop off if done too often but many agree that six weeks is sufficient spacing. And, there is some value to repetitive exposure; after a while, people begin to recognize you. It is wise to change your message occasionally as some in your audience will pass over it having seen it before. But don't change for the sake of change. Repeat what works, go with a winner.

You must test each type of advertising on a small sample of the group you are trying to reach. One initial ad rarely produces a bonanza. But each customer who bites is a prime target for similar books on the same subject. People who buy how-to books collect them all. Slowly build your clientele and your product line.

MULTIPLE MARKETS will cost more in time and money but will stabilize your financial position by smoothing out the peaks and valleys. It's wise not to have all your eggs in one basket. With a how-to nonfiction book, you will probably concentrate on space ads and direct mail. Some of your effort will depend on you. If you like personal contact, you might do more talk shows and visit more bookstores. If you like your privacy, you might concentrate on direct mail. This should be fun so do what you enjoy most.

SEASONS will affect your sales and you should plan your marketing efforts around them. The big publishers bring out most of their new titles in the fall targeting them at Christmas. There is a good gift market but the competition is rough. June graduates are a good market. Business books are best moved in the late spring and late fall, not during the summer. Mail order and outdoor books do best in late winter when people are confined indoors and thinking about the activities of the coming summer. Travel books will do well a few months before the applicable travel season.

THE PUBLIC, or ultimate consumer, may be approached directly. Books have been sold door-to-door, hawked on street corners, at street fairs and flea markets. The advantage is the elimination of the middlemen, you keep the entire list price for yourself. But it requires greater effort and the books are sold one at a time. While there is no financial outlay, it is time consuming. The personal touch will sell some books. Dealing face-to-face with the consumer is one of the least-explored methods of selling books. The opportunities, for those with imagination, are unlimited.

The other method of reaching the public is by mail. It is not so personal and the work is different; it appeals to many authors. Direct mail advertising and mail order distribution are discussed in detail in the next two chapters.

Your Christmas card list of friends, acquaintances and relatives provides a ready market for your book. They will buy no matter what the subject just because they know you. Be sure to send them a brochure and it will help if you will include a short, personal note.

DIVISIONS OF THE INDUSTRY. The industry has divided itself by concentrating on certain areas of the product, marketing areas and marketing methods. The balance of this chapter will concentrate on the various marketing channels.

MASS MARKET PAPERBACK DISTRIBUTORS, about 450 in number, merchandise the smaller pocket-sized paperbacks along with magazines. No more than ten firms account for 90% of the total volume. They service some 80,000 outlets including newsstands, drugstores, department and college stores. In 1977, they sold some 531 million books at a median price of $1.50 each. At 4000 to 5000 new titles each year, there are just too many for the rack space available. Print runs usually begin at 50,000 and they are treated like magazines. If they don't sell, the covers are ripped off and returned for credit (to save postage). It is estimated that 36% are returned but 50% on a particular title is not unusual.

It would be nice to have your book in every supermarket in the country but the gamble of low price and high print run is too great; it probably wouldn't sell well enough. To be successful in this market, your book must have vast general appeal. It is virtually impossible to break into it yourself; you almost have to deal with the distributors.

WHOLESALERS AND JOBBERS service bookstores and libraries. They ask a greater discount from you (50%) and often short discount their customer (20% or 33%) but, with regional warehouses, they offer fast service and one-stop shopping. Much of their business is with libraries. It is here they provide a valuable service by combining orders and saving the librarian from thousands of single title orders. Even the big chains make use of them when they run out and are desperate for a book. Often with a call and UPS service they can get the books in a couple of days.

There are a lot of people in the book business who have visualized the big buck and have gone into wholesaling. While the gross may be big, the net is small and it takes a very large and highly efficient operation to be profitable. A number have folded.

SELLING to wholesalers is most effective with a personal visit but you can often make a sale by mail. With a single book, your first, it won't pay to fly across the continent but some wholesalers may be close by and you might be able to get to others while on a business trip or vacation. The best months are January and July in anticipation of the peak selling seasons.

You will find these contacts very educational; these visits shouldn't be left to sales reps. Make an appointment so your trip isn't made only to find the small press buyer on vacation. Be prepared. Take copies of your book, in both softcover and hard if available, your dealer price list, copies of the your reviews, your return policy, photographs of the book, everything. Prepare a summary of recent purchases and returns if they have ordered from you already. A lot of small orders may indicate a demand requiring a larger single order. Remember that the buyer is not there to help you and won't be judging your book on its literary merits. He's thinking about whether it will move and if so, how many.

If they have purchased from you before, check their stock. They may even let you into the warehouse. Some wholesalers have very poor inventory feedback systems and aren't even aware that they are out of your book until you mention it. You will build a lot of good will by suggesting they return stock that isn't moving.

Wholesalers don't often return books since when one is returned by a bookstore, it simply gets recycled off to another one. Your book may fail in one store because of its unusual clientele or because the book was "lost" under the counter and not displayed.

A good reorder rule of thumb is to take half the quantity that has sold during the last three months. If you make the suggestion, it will ease the decision making. Don't shoot too high or the buyer will have to lower the number. If the buyer can get a discount break by adding a few more books to the order, mention it. Don't forget to offer any catalogue or display materials you may have such as photographs, posters or dumps (shipping cartons that become display stands).

Familiarize the wholesaler with your terms and return policy and have an order blank ready with his name and address already filled in to save time. Get a purchase order number and always leave him a copy.

Make up a "call report" just as you would demand one from a salesman working for you. It is a good working habit and, filed away until you next have to contact that buyer, will provide revealing information which has slipped your mind.

Then follow through by mailing your brochure, etc. to the buyer with a note. Follow up later with a telephone call to ask if you can answer any questions. Look up the buyer at book shows, establish a person-to-person contact.

Most of your volume will be through a half dozen wholesale accounts if you have a general interest book. They move quantity; that's maximum books for minimum processing paperwork. Accordingly, they are very important to you. In fact, if your dealer price list requires a large number of books for a discount, it will force more stores to order from wholesalers which may simplify your business. Remember that wholesalers only fill orders, they don't create demand. Even if you don't contact them, they will order from you sooner or later. Then you will know that your promotional efforts have encouraged one of their clients to order. But single copies are not enough, you must get into their system. Once they place a number of small orders, bring this to their attention and suggest a larger stocking order.

The two big wholesalers are Baker & Taylor and Ingram. There are also many small good ones such as Bookpeople in Berkeley. You can find them listed along with the others in *Literary Market Place*. The *American Book Trade Directory* also has a list and even provides contact names. You want the "small press buyer."

CHAIN BOOKSTORES offer your book great exposure potential. There are about 60 of them, with Walden and B. Dalton-Pickwick (Dayton-Hudson) being by far the largest. Walden has over 400 stores and is growing rapidly while Dalton is moving up fast with over 350. According to *Publishers Weekly*, Dalton is the largest hardcover retailer in the U.S. and they have the lowest unsold book return rate in the industry. Their operations are computerized so they know what is selling and can plan reorders. They purchase by category matching books to the individual store's clientele.

Many of the chain stores have their cash registers tied into the central computer to monitor sales. Often the computer will throw a large number of books out to a store as a test only to be sent back if unsold after a period of time. This instant access to sales information enables the headquarters to stay on top of fast-breaking books. They can reorder sooner to maintain inventory levels. The biggest problem you will have with chains is they send large orders but they consist of one or two books to each individual store. This means paperwork and lots of it. On the other hand, receiving an order for several hundred books and knowing that your book will get exposure nationwide is very nice.

Most chains learn of new titles from personal sales visits to their headquarters and many publishers feel this is by far the best way to close a sale. But they also respond to direct mail promotion, reviews and space advertising in *Publishers Weekly*. They are certainly worth a review copy but send it to the right person. If your book doesn't get to the small press buyer, or whoever is in charge of publishers like you, you just threw it away and blew your chance.

Establish and maintain key contacts at the chain headquarters but don't overlook sales visits to their individual stores. Most are authorized to make small purchases and they are especially receptive to regional books.

Chains expect a 40% discount FOB origin and many pay in 60-90 days. A listing of them can be found at your library in the *American Book Trade Directory*.

BOOKSTORES, individual but not necessarily independent, are a diverse group of retailers. They include the downtown bookstore, the college store, the member of a chain, the religious bookstore and others. Over 12,000 in number, they come in all sizes: some sell books exclusively while others carry them as a sideline, some are general and some specialized, and some are attached to museums or libraries. With the introduction of new marketing techniques, the stores are proliferating but their quality is dropping as they confine their selections to the fast moving titles. According to *Publishers Weekly* the number of stores increased 196.4% between 1954 and 1972, while the population of the U.S. increased only 27.8%. Sales, on the other hand, increased by 285.4%.

The patron profile of the bookstore consists of the regularly purchasing book addict and the occasional buyer. Then there are those who never come in. Modern booksellers are faced with trying to attract and sell to all these people. To do so, they have to locate in high rent heavy-traffic areas and they carry too many titles. Stores report an inventory turnover of 2 to 5 times a year with the average about 3.3 times. If a book hasn't moved in six months on the shelf, it is usually returned. According to *The Wall Street Journal*, 30-35% of the new books are returned. This places the new author/publisher between the Scylla of wide exposure and the Charybdis of massive returns.

Publishers reach the bookstore market through personal sales visits, direct mail and space ads, particularly in *Publishers Weekly*. But a lot of orders are generated by customer requests from those influenced by an ad, a TV appearance or other promotion. Bookstores, too, only make your book available for sale; you still have to do the promoting.

Large publishers with many titles send their representatives to call on bookstores. With one or two titles, it is hardly worth your time. But, these sales calls can be a good learning experience. Start small with a local bookstore; learn the ropes before branching out.

Ideally, bookstores should be visited four times a year: in advance of the two selling seasons and then in the winter and summer to check the stock. Mailings should be confined to the spring and fall. The big publishing reps carry only the dust jackets of new books to show the buyer. You have an advantage by carrying in the actual book. You can also offer to drop off the books and save them the postage.

The best time to visit a store is between 3:30 and 4:30 in the afternoon when there are the fewest customers. Ask to speak with the store manager or paperback buyer. They can be very busy and you may have to set up an appointment.

Bookstores rely on sales reps for recommendations so the buyer should be receptive. He or she may ask about your promotion plans. Tell them you are a local author and, therefore, local people might be interested in your book. Mention any local publicity such as talk shows which are planned. If the book is professionally produced, a sale should not be difficult. Be ready with the stock phrase: "I can offer you the books at a full 40% discount, without delivery charges and they are fully returnable, of course."

If you still can't persuade the buyer, you might like to try "consignment." Here the store pays for the books only after they are sold, or more typically, when they need more of them. With consignment, the discount should be dropped to 25-35%. The whole pitch should take you less than five minutes.

Keep the initial order small. It won't help to overload the store only to get them back in a few months. It is better to keep the inventory turning over.

You might like to try offering posters, displays and racks but most stores won't have room for them. Experiment with your local store.

College, school and text stores also respond best to face-to-face sales calls. About one-third of their orders are through wholesalers who offer speedy service and one-stop shopping. There are some 2,800 college stores serving 2,200 U.S. colleges and universities with over 11-million students. Quite a market. These stores are on their own schedule depending upon whether they are on the semester, quarter or early semester system. Graduation time is another good opportunity to move books.

The 100 plus big publishers have too much clout to take head-on in the bookstore market. They routinely dump thousands of dollars into promotion and have their sales-

---

"Booksellers as a group have not been aggressive enough. There are too many individuals just selling books and constantly crying to publishers, 'Give us a better discount' " — David Cioffi, Dartmouth Bookstore.

men in the stores negotiating favorable display locations. You'll be more successful concentrating on and servicing a small selection of stores than trying to blitz all 12,000.

If you like personal contact, load up the car and visit the stores. If you would rather stay home, you can hit more of them via direct mail advertising. A list can be found in your library in the *American Book Trade Directory*. Obviously, visiting wholesalers and chain buyers is a far more efficient use of your time. Many small publishers tolerate but don't pursue small individual bookstores.

Once you have established an account, you can use the telephone for a certain amount of restocking but you can't beat a personal visit and you do want to keep your book on the shelf.

LIBRARIES come in several types: public, private, special, school, government, etc. There are almost 10,000 public libraries, 3,000 can be found in colleges, 12,000 are special and there are around 20,000 in high schools. They spend around $450-million a year for books, buying some 14% of those published. Many of their purchases are for books with press runs under 5,000 which would not get published without their support.

Even though orders are for smaller quantities, libraries offer greater potential than bookstores to the small publisher. The size of the market is hard to verify, however. Some 76% of them will respond to your mailings by ordering from a wholesaler and 75% of those orders go to Baker & Taylor. Rather than place thousands of orders with individual publishers for single titles, libraries save time by sending all orders to a wholesaler. They are extended a 20-33% discount so they are receiving both price and service. Their problem is money. The cost of ordering and processing a new title can cost as much as the book itself. In many libraries, personnel expenses make up half the budget. Many libraries are spreading their already tight budgets even thinner now by adding audio-visual and other non-print items.

Many wholesalers serve their library accounts automatically by sending blocks of books "on approval" allowing the library to reject the unwanted titles. They rarely do. Obviously, it is to your great advantage to have your book included in these computer matched offerings, especially the Baker & Taylor system.

Less than 1,000 libraries have an annual book budget of $25,000 or more and most have much less. They have to be selective in their purchases. Many libraries buy more for topic than quality. They have to justify their budgets to the community (if public) and try to get something for everyone. Whether the book is good, covering the topic adequately, is less important. It is said that better judgement is shown in the purchasing of childrens' books and fiction. One librarian recently explained: "When material is scarce on a topic and interest is high, we will often buy any reasonably priced new book through an ad in *Library Journal* or even a flyer. However, we usually don't buy if it receives a bad review."

If you intend to pursue the library market, you will want to take part in the Cataloging In Publication program run by the Library of Congress. See the discussion in Chapter 5.

Library mailing lists may be rented from the R.R. Bowker Mailing List Department and The Educational Directory (see the Appendix). The list can be broken down according to book budget, etc., so you can reach just the well-heeled ones if you like. To reach libraries, the best magazines for space advertising are *Library Journal* and *Booklist* and the best places to exhibit are at the annual convention of the American Library Association and the state library association conventions.

Libraries tend to do most of their ordering around the beginning/ends of their fiscal year (usually December 31 or June 30) when they try to use up their old budget or break into a new one. This is when they show less buying discrimination. Your book might be selected at this time even if it is an afterthought, not a first choice. At the three-quarter point in their fiscal year they are usually out of funds. School libraries usually use the slow summer months to work on ordering.

Some libraries have acquisition librarians while in others title selection is done by committee. Because more than one person is often involved in acquisitions in the larger libraries, it is wise to send more than one copy of each piece of literature. It helps to build consumer demand and most libraries respond when a title is requested. School libraries are responsive to the wishes of their faculties.

Don't send your promotional material to the "head" or "acquisition" librarian. It is best to direct it toward the subject area supervisor who makes the actual buying decisions. These supervisors are in charge of areas such as: "childrens' books," "adult fiction," "reference," etc. For names, consult Bowker's *American Library Directory*.

When you receive an order direct from a library, add it to your list and include the contact name. Send periodic mailings. They react like any other clients to your direct mail advertising.

While only 24% of the public and 55% of the school libraries deal directly with publishers, they will buy from you if your offer looks good. One of the most effective means of promotion is to send them quotes from reviews. They also respond to requests from their patrons.

Many communities have both city and country libraries; hit them all. Large city library systems will need copies for every branch and these multiple orders are very nice. Books wear out, they can be loaned out only so many times. Unless a worn out title has seen a lot of recent use, it usually doesn't get reordered. On the other hand, if it has been very popular, the library may order several copies. Generally, they prefer hardcover books but they do order paperbacks. As could be expected, childrens' books and fiction aren't of any great interest to college libraries.

Book reviews are very important in library selection decisions. Librarians just don't have the time to read and evaluate the some 100 new titles available each day. Librarians rely mostly on *Publishers Weekly, Library Journal, ALA Booklist, Kirkus Reviews, Choice* and *The New York Times Book Review.* These media review about half of all the titles submitted to them each year. Your brochure is also very effective even if it isn't as objective as a review. Some publishers say price isn't a major consideration and that this is because the librarian isn't spending his or her own money. The librarians say they buy to cover a subject; they will buy a high priced book if it meets the need and is the only one available.

Your local library should buy your book just because of the proximity of the author. Some even have a special private room for books by indigenous writers. If so, it may be appropriate for you to donate a copy to this reference section. If you do make such a donation, be sure the local paper is notified so you can get some mileage out of your largesse.

SPRIL or Small Press Racks in Libraries (P.O. Box 76, Berkshire, MA 01224) is a government funded organization which places donated books in libraries. Usually the libraries place them on special display.

THE SCHOOL MARKET spends over a billion dollars each year for text books and while most of these are developed especially for certain courses, many are regular books developed for other markets but adapted as supplementary educational aids. While educators want the very latest information, they are leary of being experimental. They need to be

"The fact is, do-it-yourself books have never been more popular than they are now, and their popularity is growing steadily" — Arnold F. Logan of Petersen Publishing Co.

assured that the book is up-to-date but has been accepted by experts elsewhere. They are the most price-conscious of all the book markets even though they aren't spending their own money. Under pressure from the schools to keep the price of texts down, publishers can only extend a 20% ("short") discount and this is what is expected.

ELEMENTARY AND SECONDARY SCHOOLS. In the U.S. there are some 64,000 public elementary, 24,000 public high and 1,800 combined schools in 18,000 school districts. Additionally, there are some 14,000 private elementary and 4,000 private high schools. Together, they employ 2.3-million teachers.

Half of the schools purchase texts under a state adoption system where titles are approved by a board for a five-year period. This is a hunting license and allows the salespeople to try and sell it to the schools. Even where there is no state adoption system, planning seems to revolve around a five-year cycle. In some areas, publishers have to ship to central depositories where the schools can draw on them as needed. This usually means a consignment inventory and the books aren't paid for until requisitioned by the schools.

COLLEGES AND UNIVERSITIES. Here the marketing efforts are expended on the instructors who must select books for their courses in more than 3,000 schools. This decision is easy for some professors as they pen their own. Normally the purchasing is done by the local bookstore and the instructor notifies them as to his choice by April for the fall term. Of course, there are problems. The choice is made late and the estimate of the number to be needed is frequently off. Then some students avoid buying the text by sharing or making repeated visits to the library. This results in a return rate of more than 20%.

There are three types of bookstores. Some are owned by the institution, some are private and some are college stores with a private leasee.

Teachers expect to get free examination copies and while some treat this privilege with respect, others just collect books or sell them to the bookstore. Often the younger instructors are trying to build up their libraries. The older professors who have more say in book selection do much less collecting. Some publishers like to request more information about the size of the course, the requester's academic position, etc.

It is worth your while to send these desk copies if they reach the right hands; after all, you can't expect an instructor to select a book without inspecting it first. Now, most publishers require specific information about the course to cull those with a genuine interest from the ripoff artists. Then they stamp the cover and title page with "complimentary copy" to preclude resale.

Some publishers follow up by mailing a letter with a reply card asking if the professor has received the book. They offer one copy free for an order of 15 or 20 or, in the alternative, 40% off on the one sent. Some go a step further and include a "conditional invoice;" one that is scrapped if it results in adoption and a sale or if the book is returned. Of course, some instructors won't return the book or pay the bill and after a dunning note or two, it is no longer worth chasing them.

Analyze your book subject and determine what course might find it useful. The educators are easy to find and direct mail advertising is the most effective method of reaching them. In fact, some publishers find the lists so specialized that they use them to send free examination copies unsolicited.

Mailing list information can be found in your library. See the Standard Rate and Data Service's directories, *An Advertiser's Guide to Scholarly Periodicals* and *Direct Marketing* magazine. Also check the *Yellow Pages* for local list brokers.

Another way to reach the educational market is through book exhibits. With only a title or two, you may like to share a booth with someone else in the same position or turn your book over to a firm which will represent you for a small fee. These shows are listed in *Literary Market Place* and the *Exhibits Directory* published by the Association of American Publishers available in your library.

College buying patterns are affected by their school schedules depending on whether they are on the semester, quarter or early semester system. This may get you into the Christmas jam at the Post Office. The best months to make mailings to colleges are February, April, July and October. Once you make contact with an instructor, add him to your mailing list, he's valuable. Once he has adopted one of your books, some say he is twice as likely to do it again.

PRE-PUBLICATION SALES will bring in some money early and help you pay the printing bill. But it isn't wise to start too soon on the pre-publication publicity for your first book. The first time around is a learning experience and there will be countless delays. You don't want to find yourself spending all your time answering the question: "where is the book?" . With the first book, wait until it is on the press. The next time, adjust and start earlier.

Write up a press release, send in your ads and make a mailing. Offer an early order deal ("to be shipped direct from the printer") to associations and specialty dealers. It is nice to have a pile of orders on the desk when the book comes off the press. But timing is important; these orders must not pour in too early or too late.

If your book is specialized and you are able to find an appropriate mailing list, you should consider a pre-publication offer. Tell them the book is being printed and if they want one hot off the press, to send their money now, that you'll be shipping on a first come, first served basis. Include an early order deal such as "postage free if you order from this ad," "$5 off if you order now," etc. This mailing should be sent to all your friends and acquaintances; many will respond and be pleased that you thought of them. If a prospect is mentioned in the text or the acknowledgments, he is sure to buy one.

SPECIALTY OUTLETS offer many nonfiction publishers with their largest market. For example, a book on mountain climbing may sell better in backpacking shops than bookstores and the size of the store's purchases will be larger. Once you have written a book on a specialized activity, you should know the field well enough that such outlets will immediately come to mind. Citing the large orders and firm continuous market, many writers aim for these outlets and service the book trade only secondarily.

In these specialty shops it is very important to establish, cultivate and maintain a close personal relationship with the management. It is of the utmost importance that they like you and your book so they will promote it at every opportunity. Selling them the first time often requires a personal visit to demonstrate the sales potential of the book. When making a direct mail promotion to these firms, remember their peak selling seasons and the required lead time.

OTHER NON-BOOK RETAIL CHANNELS include gift ships, hardware stores, garden shops, sporting goods stores, etc. Many are establishing book corners to lend prestige to their line. They buy in larger quantities than bookstores and don't expect return privileges. They make more than 40% on most of their stock and if they balk at your smaller mark-up, you may offer to accept returns. Once you have sold a few local stores in person and have a feel for the market, you may wish to pursue distant stores with a mailing.

SELLING TO THE U.S. GOVERNMENT. There are 2,300 libraries in the federal government library system and 80 agencies which purchase books according to *Publishers Weekly*. Most of the libraries come under the Defense Department and have funding problems. Some of the Army's libraries must be approached through central offices while others deal direct. The Office of the Director of the Army Library Program procures hardbound books for Army libraries around the world and paperbacks for distribution in the field. Of the about 60 clothbound titles chosen monthly, some 60% are nonfiction. About 100 paperbound titles are procured each month and distributed in 900 kits; selections are highly recreational. Centralized purchases are made under annual contracts with wholesalers. Navy libraries spend over $3-million each year. The International Communications Agency, formerly the U.S. Information Agency, runs 129 libraries in 110 countries with 6,000 to 25,000 volumes each and devotes about $2-million each year to procurement. They like to see brochures and review copies. The Veterans Administration operates 392 libraries with a budget of more than $2-million. See the listings in the Appendix.

The *U.S. Government Purchasing and Sales Directory* ($4) and *Selling to the Government* ($1.80) are two publications you'll want. They may be purchased at Government bookstores in the major cities or from the Superintendent of Documents, U.S. Government Printing Office, Washington, DC 20402.

Another source of orders is from special groups within the government or military services. For example, a manual on parachute rigging would be of interest to parachute riggers both civilian and military. A mailing to all military parachute lofts might generate some private sales and/or the brochure might be passed on to the procurement office so that a book could be ordered for the library or the loft.

SUBSIDIARY RIGHTS may produce fame and fortune far beyond the regular sales of your book. Essentially, they give someone else permission to reproduce (repackage) your material. Subsidiary rights include book clubs, mass market paperback, film rights, translations, premiums, etc. and they are so important to the big publishers that the rights are auctioned off before the book is printed. See *Literary Market Place* in your library for possibilities.

Some subsidiary rights require only a continuation of the same printing (quality paper back, premiums, etc) but don't let your customer get away with just paying for the additional press time. They should pay for all of your set-up and overhead costs. If you aren't very familiar with negotiating rights, get an attorney who understands the publishing business or a literary agent. The agent will get 10% of whatever he brings in while the lawyer will work for a percentage or a straight fee for checking the contract. Agents are listed in *Literary Market Place*.

Most people feel that selling subsidiary rights helps to sell the original version of the book by generating additional publicity for it. It is also a great morale booster for both the author and the publisher not only for the money but because someone else obviously likes it. Write to likely prospects well in advance of publication and ask if they would like to see photocopies of the manuscript. Then follow with a telephone call. Mail out a lot of inquiries, don't go at them one at a time. There isn't enough time for this luxury.

IRIS was a short-lived monthly rights-information service published by Bowker. It presented books to subsidiary rights buyers all over the world. Starting in January 1979, the new International Rights Information Service was adapted to a classified advertising format in *Publishers Weekly*. It appears in the second issue each month.

"PAPERBACK RIGHTS" usually refer to the production of a "quality" paperback edition after the hardcover has been in the stores for several months. It isn't likely that you published in hardcover only but if you did, you will want to explore the quality paperback market. The distribution program is essentially the same as for hard cover so you

---

"Without subsidiary rights, publishers would operate in the hole" — John Dessauer.

should do it yourself. But if you want someone else to handle the paperback, they'll want a 7-year contract with a right to renew. Royalties range from 6% to 9% with a lower amount until sales reach 10,000 and a higher amount after that. Advances against royalties may be a few to several thousand dollars with half paid on signing the contract and the balance due on publication. It is always wise to get as large an advance as possible as it is good insurance against their losing interest and never going to press. When evaluating their offer, compare the number they plan to print (5-15,000) and the list (cover) price ($4-$10) they intend for the book; they all greatly affect your income.

MASS MARKET PAPERBACKS are those pocket-sized books selling from $1 - $3.50 in the supermarkets. They are different from the quality paperback primarily because of the distribution system. Consequently, you won't be able to break into this market by yourself. Unless you have a very popular book, the mass market firms won't be interested. They like 7-year contracts with renewal options and run 50,000 or more copies. They offer 8% to 10% in royalties but the cover price is low and the scale doesn't slide up until sales reach 150,000 copies. Advances are usually just a few thousand dollars.

SERIALIZATIONS and excerpts by magazines and newspapers may be "first serializations" if before publication or "second serialization" if afterward. Both generate a lot of good publicity. Big publications pay more and the first rights are more valuable than second. The subject matter has to be of great interest to the publication's readers. Serializations help generate sales for the original book. See the discussion in *Writer's Market*.

BOOK CONDENSATIONS in magazines don't normally pay a lot but the publicity they provide will sell more books. They lend further credibility to your self-published work since someone else has "approved" of the material by purchasing it. There are a few important things to consider when you receive a condensation offer, however: obtain a copy of the magazine to make sure it is a quality product, one you will be proud to be associated with. Check their past condensation work and call the publishers of the subject books. Ask if they are happy with the way they were treated, with the quality of the condensation and compare the price they were paid with the one you have been offered. The name and number of the person in charge of subsidiary rights at each publishing house can be found in section one of *Literary Market Place*.

Make sure the condensation includes information where the original book may be purchased complete with price and address. Their work should be a condensation, not a reprint of the two meaty chapters. You can expect them to offer a couple of hundred dollars up to several thousand depending upon the publication. They are responsible for the condensation work. Sell on a non-exclusive basis. They will be first in print but you want to retain the right to sell again to other publications. Always obtain "text approval". They could completely miss your point in making the condensation. Read the draft over carefully and make corrections; your name is on the piece and it will be a major sales tool for your book. You want it to be right.

COLLECTIONS, particularly for school use, often pay small amounts for parts of books.

CO-PUBLISHING is a way for two firms to spread the risk and reward in a new book. Usually one publisher is large and the other small or the two concentrate on different ends of the business such as editorial and distribution.

EXCHANGE TITLE PROMOTION. Mail order customers interested in a certain subject tend to purchase every book which covers the area. Unfortunately many small publishers do not have titles in any depth on any particular topic. When two or more publishers of like material handle each other's books, their customers get a wider range of choices and the publishers get an improved response rate to their advertising. This cross-distribution, formerly common only in other sales channels, is now becoming more familiar in mail order book marketing.

RECORDINGS AND BRAILLE editions are published for the blind.

BOOK CLUBS offer you some money and a great deal of prestige. Since their foundings in the mid-twenties, the Book-of-the-Month-Club (BOMC) and the Literary Guild have been helping their members by selling the best books of the thousands available at lower than normal prices. Now there are more than 170 book clubs, most of which cater to highly specialized groups. Normally, selections are made before the book is printed so that the book club edition costs much less to produce; it only requires more press time. Sometimes, they economize more with cheaper paper, narrower margins, less costly bindings, etc. The usual royalty is 10% of the list price plus any extra production expenses in making the club editions. Smaller clubs and some alternate selections will not require a separate club edition; they just buy from the original run.

    The larger clubs usually want an exclusive; they don't want other clubs to carry it too. Smaller clubs aren't so particular.

    You normally approach book clubs when you have galleys to show them. If they don't respond, write them again after publication and enclose photocopies of your reviews. They have to be convinced it is a desirable book and that is where clippings of reviews can help. Offer your book to the Small Press Book Club (P.O. Box 100-P, Paradise, CA 95969) and look through *Literary Market Place* for other possiblities.

THE INTERNATIONAL MARKET can provide a lot of extra income for several types of books and this may be done in a number of ways. The most common is to fill and mail foreign orders in the same way you fill domestic ones. Sometimes entire editions may be sold to foreign dealers and several big publishers have set up foreign subsidiary companies to distribute their books. Or, the translation rights might be sold to a foreign firm. About 3.5% of the U.S. adult hardcover books are exported along with just over 5% of the adult quality paperbound. But the export figures are 20% for professional books, 14% for university press sales, almost 10% for college texts, 9% for elementary and high school texts and almost 10% for mass market paperback. Almost half of all the exports go to Canada.

    Most of your export sales will come with the daily mail. They will be just like your domestic orders but for the lighter weight paper, strange addresses and pretty stamps. Most of these foreign bookstores will get your address from Bowker's *Books In Print*.

    Postal rates for foreign shipments may be higher or lower than domestic rates depending on which has been raised most recently. There is a 5 kg. (11 lb.) weight limit but if you are shipping more than 22 lbs., you may qualify for "Direct Sacks of Prints" at 36¢/2 lbs. Since it is so inexpensive to export, (the cost is perhaps 15¢ per book for shipping), it makes little sense to print the book abroad unless the press run is huge. Since English is the commercial and aviation language of the world as well as one of the most used tongues in the fields of science and technology, there is a good demand for books in our language. To reach more foreign bookstores and libraries, Bowker maintains a mailing list which may be rented (see the Appendix).

    Many small firms use an export agent. They usually want 55-65% off and then handle all the distribution and debt collection. A list of export agents may be found in *Literary Market Place* in your library. While some of these exporters may ask for large discounts, most of your orders will be for small quantities and you will extend a routine 40%.

TRANSLATIONS offer good possibilities and here you will want to deal with a foreign publisher. If you have a terribly popular book, it should even be translated into "British English" for the commonwealth countries. These foreign publishers will pay you a royalty and take care of everything. Normally you supply the photos and a couple of copies of the book with late changes noted. They translate it, change the measurements to metric and take care of all the printing, distribution, etc. Royalties may be 5-7% for hardcover rights and 3-10% for paperbacks. Some countries impose a tax on exported royalties; Japan, for example, charges 10% of the remitted amount.

When negotiating a contract, consider the number of copies to be printed, the printing schedule, cover price, royalties for both hardbound and paperbound editions, the advance and the government tax, if any. If you are printing in a country with a currency harder than the U.S. dollar, such as Germany or Switzerland, you might ask to get paid in their money and to have it deposited in one of their banks. It should appreciate against the inflating dollar and be worth more to you on your next visit abroad.

FILM RIGHTS will be somewhat unusual for a nonfiction book but it could happen. The usual rate is 15% of the net and this is a very bad deal. Film companies are notorious for their unusual accounting procedures which result in a very small net. Always get a percentage of the gross though it will be considerably smaller. The gross figure is much more objective.

PREMIUMS are big business and there is a lot of room for books. They are products which are given away or sold at a discount to promote business. They may be given away by a store to attract customers or to sales people as prizes for achieving sales goals. Books make especially good premiums as they may be produced with a custom cover and because they are held in higher esteem than some other premium trinkets. In fact, in some areas, regulated industries are prohibited from giving away certain items. For example, in California, banks may not give away custom imprinted Frisbee discs to attract new accounts because they aren't considered to have a sufficient social value. But when packaged with a book on the Frisbee sport, they qualify.

If your book covers a regional topic, try local businesses. Books may be rubber stamped with "Compliments of Tom Dinning Insurance Co." as an example. If you cover a subject with wider appeal such as a book on beer can collecting, contact the beer, aluminum, steel and can companies. They would be ideal corporate gifts or might be worked into a promotion. A tour guide book might be sold to a motel chain. The possibilities are endless. Think of firms which might like to identify with your book or subject.

Premium orders are large, usually 1,000 or more, and the customer may ask for 60% off. Such a discount can be justified for a large order which eliminates the problems of financing, storage and individual shipping. If you can strike some premium sales deals before going to press, you may increase your press run and produce a smaller per-unit cost. Early sales are also a great help in paying that first printing bill. For further ideas, send for a sample copy of *Premium Incentive Business* magazine (1515 Broadway, NYC, NY 10036). If your book is right for the premium market, you'll want to send them a review copy too.

SPONSORED BOOKS are those you are almost commissioned to write. There may be an institution which wants your book printed badly enough to give you a large advance order. For example, if you wrote a book on the Frisbee disc and there were no others on the subject, the Wham-O Manufacturing Company which makes them might want it to be published because the publicity would help their sales. With this sponsorship, they might want some sort of cover credit, such as: "Published in association with Wham-O." This is to your advantage as it would only lend credibility to the book.

Some industries need favorable publicity and find that sponsoring a book is much less expensive than placing full page ads. A book is also much more effective as it appears to be more objective.

NONPROFIT ORGANIZATIONS are always running sales to raise money for their cause. These flea markets, bake sales, etc. promoted by church and civic groups can provide you with an opportunity to move some books, particularly some of your slightly damaged stock. Try approaching some local organizations first to get a feel for the way they operate. If you are successful. consider a mailing to similar groups. Don't forget to tell them of your past good track record and assure them that the unsold books may be returned.

LOCAL CLUBS and local chapters of national organizations raise funds too. If your book is appropriate, you might strike a deal. A gardening book might be sold by a gardening club, for example.

SPECIALTY SHOWS such as sport and boat exhibitions are rarely worthwhile for a small author/publisher. However, you can make sure that your book is carried and offered for sale by someone in the show. Find a booth with related merchandise and offer them some books on consignment. Give them a carton full and an examination copy for the table. They get a piece of the action and you get the exposure while moving books. If you make up a little poster, you won't have to be concerned about their lack of sales concentration on your book.

EDUCATIONAL CAMPAIGNS conducted by special interest groups offer another market for books. These people range from helpful social agencies to business interests promoting their side of an issue. Be careful to remain objective to maintain your credibility. You don't want to become too closely associated with either side. You want the use of their name, you don't want to let them use yours. After all, you will sell your book to anyone and your control over it ends with the sale.

To find organizations with "causes," consult *National Trade & Professional Associations of the U.S. and Canada* and Gale's *Encyclopedia of Associations* available at your library. Write to the managing personnel enclosing your brochure, press release, etc. Tell them why your book would be valuable to them. Hold off on the price until you get a bite. It will depend on the number they want and it could be thousands.

BOOK FAIRS often provide important exposure to your book. The major national U.S. shows are sponsored by:

The American Booksellers Association, 800 Second Avenue, NYC, NY 10017 (often in June and attended primarily by bookstore managers)

The American Library Association, 50 East Huron Street, Chicago, IL 60611 (Midsummer and attended primarily by librarians)

The National Association of College Stores, 528 East Lorain Street, Oberlin, OH 44074. (Usually midspring and attended by college bookstore managers)

The Christian Booksellers Association, 2031 West Cheyenne Road, Colorado Springs, CO 80906. (Midsummer and features general titles as well as religious books).

These national shows are put on for the big firms and tend to be lively reunions for the participants. While you may get some good exposure at them, don't expect to move a lot of books. The best advice is to write to the listed organizations regarding the fairs and then attend a nearby one yourself to assess how you might fit in to your advantage. The big associations also sponsor regional and local book fairs.

International book fairs are held all over the world with the most important being in London, Frankfurt and Montreal. They can give good exposure and may lead to subsidiary rights but obviously aren't worth your own exhibiting effort.

Conventions and conferences of professional, academic and trade associations will present you with a "qualified" audience for your books if you match your subject matter to the show. Educational books do well at educational exhibits and they are especially fun as they provide an opportunity to meet with authors as well as customers. You know the subject matter of your book and the trade shows in your field. For more ideas, consult *National Trade & Professional Associations of the U.S. and Canada Directory* and Gale's *Encyclopedia of Associations* available in your library.

Exhibiting at a book fair is often a great inspirational experience; it will recharge your batteries. You will learn more about the industry, meet some great people, make valuable contacts, sell a few books and, perhaps, even some subsidiary rights. Typically, the show's management provides a space measuring about 8' x 10', a draped table, curtained side and back panels, a sign, carpet, and a chair or two. Check their brochure closely. Take a good supply of books and brochures. Get some book stands or bend-up some bookends to prop up your books for display. Prominently display a price sticker on the cover of the "reading copy" in the display. Plan to sell books and related products. For example, if your book is on jumping rope, sell jump ropes. Check to determine whether you will need a local sellers permit. See the discussion in Chapter 3. Book sales can be made at book fairs but they usually take some selling. Thousands of people will be milling around looking for a place to stop. Greet people as they pass by, make them stop to look at your books. It is a challenge to see if you can sell enough books at the fair to pay your out-of-pocket expenses. Then the contacts you make and the educational experience are gravy.

Many publishers feel that when you have your own exhibit, it doesn't pay to advertise in the program too. Few people actually read them. The same goes for the magazines regularly published by the sponsoring organizations. Advertising there is no better at the time of the fair than any other time of the year.

Shows cost. Booth space at the big American Booksellers Association fair runs $350 to $800. But they also have a small press section at $125. In addition to booth expense, you must consider your personal travel, book shipping, hotels, meals, etc. You can spend $500 but $2,000 is not unusual.

Exhibiting services will put your books on display with those of other publishers very inexpensively and some do a very good job of representing your wares. Write to several of them to compare prices and see which fairs they plan to attend; some offer package deals if you sign up for the whole season. There is a list of exhibiting services in the Appendix.

Some fairs offer a "combined" display area for those publishers who cannot attend. For a small price, your book is placed on a table along with those of several other publishers. The problem is that no one stops by to straighten up the area and before too long it looks like a trash pile. Don't exhibit in a combined display unless the promoter promises to service the area.

Another alternative is to find someone else to add your book to their display. Write to the promoter for a list of exhibitors. Get last year's list if the upcoming one isn't available. Write to those with similar products. Offer to pay them for some space and/or to give them a percentage on all they can sell.

"There's no secret formula. It's simply a good item for which there is a need, at the right price, offered to the right market."

CHAPTER NINE

SELLING YOUR BOOK

REACHING CUSTOMERS THROUGH ADVERTISING

ADVERTISING may be used to create an awareness of your new book and even to stimulate an interest in it. But advertising is expensive and must be approached slowly. Unproductive ads will deplete your bank account fast. It is a cold, hard fact that most advertising doesn't pay. This is because the approach is wrong. So, feel out each of the many areas and test them before you jump in with lots of money.

It is said that advertising will make a good book sell better but it can't turn a poor one into a success. We'll have to assume that more people besides just you see some value in your book.

First we will talk about advertising in general and then we will discuss the details of your brochure, direct mail advertising, classifieds, space ads and radio/T.V. Much of the information is overlapping and may be applied to more than one area of advertising. For example, the coding of addresses in advertisements applies to all, so, it is advisable to read the entire chapter.

The success of your advertising campaign will depend upon the sales potential of your book, whether you contact the right market and whether your ad is effective. You must select your markets and then find the least expensive way to reach them. Target your primary market but don't overlook the secondary ones. Concentrate on one medium of advertising (e.g., direct mail) but don't dismiss the others (e.g., space ads).

In each ad campaign, figure the cost of it "per sale." The cost "per contact" is interesting but it is the cost per sale that tells you if you are winning or losing. Ads placed in magazines to promote bookstore sales must generate sales of five times their cost to be worth your while. For example, a $10 ad must sell $50 worth of books. Ads directing the orders to you (mail order) must produce 2.2 times the cost of the ad, minimum. The difference is because you are also giving the bookstore 40% of the list (cover) price. These figures are quoted by the industry and may vary depending on the original production cost of your book. Keep them in mind as you plan your ad strategy. Don't run unprofitable ads! They waste money and make you work for nothing.

Determining an ad's potential profitability is not the place for wishful thinking. You have to calculate all the possibilities, the types of advertising and the places it might be put and this comparison will help you to choose where to place your money.

Your consumer ads should be concentrated and timed to appear in the few weeks just after the publication date. By concentrating your ads and generating other publicity with tours and reviews, the campaign will appear to be much bigger than it really is.

The people selling advertising talk about the "number of impressions" and "accumulative impact" when they try to get you to spend more on promotion (or try to ex-

"It is cheaper to advertise one book twice than to write a second book."

plain why your ad wasn't successful). A series of good, consistent ads may be of some help as a prospect may remember that he has heard of the book before, but remember that you are selling a $5 or $10 book, not a $5,000 or $10,000 automobile. You have to sell a lot more product to pay for the ad and you can't even justify as much need.

If you are pushing bookstore sales and your book is on a popular subject, space ads may be best while if your subject is normally sold to business, professional and/or educational markets, direct mail should get more of your attention. In fact, many small publishers put most of their effort into direct mail.

Ted Nicholas, author of several money books, describes his advertising system as pyramiding revenue derived from sales. He suggests putting up a small amount of money for advertising, running good space ads (and he tells you how to write them), waiting for the money to come in and then reinvesting it in ever greater amounts of advertising.

If you have a good method, don't deviate. Creativity for creativity's sake is dumb. Whatever worked before will almost certainly work again. All marketing methods must be tested, not just direct mail advertising. Once you find a good system, stick with it.

CREATING AD COPY. You'll need a good basic description of the book that will appeal to the consumer; this material, altered as required, will then be used over and over. Come up with a very few words to describe the book. This becomes its "handle" and might even be the subtitle for the book. This will be expanded for brochures and catalogues while it is directed toward the intended audience. Some small ads will only have space for the handle and a small amount of hard hitting copy. Once this is done, the future copy writing is easier as you aren't starting from scratch each time.

ADVERTISING AGENCIES can be a great help if you aren't particularly interested in plugging your own book or if you plan a lot of promotion. If your account is large enough, or the agency is small enough, there is no charge for most of the service. They get a 15% commission from the magazine or T.V. station. They will prepare the ads, place them, pay for them and may even do some testing. You will still have to do most of the copywriting. All they can do is to put your creativity into correct form. Classified ads are not commissionable, however, and they will charge you extra for artwork and other special services, too. But whether you employ an agency or do the job yourself, it will be valuable to understand what happens in advertising.

Advertising agencies are in business to stay in business just as you are. While they want to do a good job, their primary motivation is to keep the cash flowing in. Keep this in mind when they are trying to sell you more space or time. Don't believe everything you hear or read from advertising people.

YOUR BROCHURE lies at the heart of your promotional campaign and it may be produced long before your book is off the press. It should describe the book, tell about you and answer most of the recipient's potential questions. The basics are the book's measurements, number of pages, type and number of illustrations, binding and price. The contents should be summarized to provide a clear understanding of the book's coverage. Excerpts from reviews will demonstrate that others like your book, too. Follow the proven, standard formats.

It will be stuffed into most of the letters you send out daily to friends, associates and relatives, used with your other pre- and post-publication mailings and sent to those who respond to your ads which invite them to "send for a free descriptive brochure." Yes, your brochure is more important than a business card and has a lot more information.

The best way to answer inquiries is with your brochure. If the writer asks particular questions, the simplest way to answer is by circling the appropriate parts of the mailing. Many booksellers like to return the inquiry letter with the brochure to remind the writer that he asked for it. If you aren't over the postage limit yet, it is nice to stuff in other related information. For example, if the inquiry is about hang gliding, enclose a membership application from the hang gliding association. You will build valuable good will.

Brochures provide you with an opportunity to say nice things about yourself that you can't say in face-to-face selling. It is almost as though someone else wrote the copy. Be direct, clear and give them as much information as possible. Because you will use this brochure for your bookstore and library sales, too, include the ISBNs, LC numbers, etc.

Your local jiffy print shop can give you the best deal on 8½ x 11 paper. If you need more space, they can handle 8½ x 14 and you can fold it four times to fit a standard #10 envelope. If you still need more space, you may have to go to a regular printer for an 11 x 17 sheet, folded down the middle and then into thirds. Every pass through the press costs more money so some people like to use colored paper and sometimes even another color ink. This gives the appearance of a lot of color but it is still a one-color print job. Use good materials and make the brochure slick. If you send out a mimeographed brochure, people will assume you are selling a mimeographed book. Ask the jiffy print shop where you can get some type set. And ask your printer; he just might throw it in free because he is doing your book and has an interest in it.

Some publishers have produced some very nice brochures by printing their ad copy on the back of book cover overruns. This is nice but it isn't cheap. There are the extra trips through the press and the additional mailing weight of the cover stock to be considered.

People like to see what they are buying so a photo of the book should appear in the brochure. You don't have to wait for your book to be printed to take a photograph of it, however. Ask your printer to run the covers while the type is being set on the manuscript. Then make a dummy by wrapping one around another book. Take several photos with different settings and from several angles. Then select the best print and have some 5 x 7's made up. At this point, you won't know exactly how many pages the book will have but you can estimate and then use a description like: "over 180 jam-packed pages."

To make the photo reproduce well, the jiffy printer will have to make a metal plate rather than the usual cheaper plastic ones. It should be saved for the next time you run the brochure.

Brochure designers are available if you don't wish to do the work yourself. But beware of the designers who want to use your brochure to showcase their work. Often they win an award for brochure design while you pay the bill and don't sell books. You are better off roughing it out yourself and taking it to your printer or local graphic artist.

Once the brochures arrive, use them everywhere. Stuff them in every package, letter, press release, mailing, etc. Carry some in the car, leave them at the barbershop, in the seatback pocket on the airplane, at the dentist office, etc. and carry some with you at all times. Pack one in with every book you mail out. The return will be good.

DIRECT MAIL ADVERTISING is one very effective way to contact potential buyers for your book. The mailing usually includes a cover letter, brochure, order form and a reply envelope but it may also direct them to a nearby store. The literature may be sent to your friends and acquaintences, to your list of past customers or you may rent a list from a list company. The list is the heart of a direct mail advertising campaign. Don't confuse this with "mail order" which is a form of distribution. Sales through bookstores would be another way to distribute your book to the ultimate consumer.

> *"Some entrepreneurs say that direct mail compares with a sniper attack whereas display ads compare with a shotgun approach."*

Direct mail advertising is one of the most effective ways of reaching the technical, scientific and medical book market. Direct mail allows you to pinpoint your market. Your message has little or no competition when it reaches the recipient. It provides flexibility in design and format and it allows you to trace and analyze the results through simple address coding.

Most people like to receive mail and one book out of four is sold via direct mail advertising. Most of this volume goes to book clubs but they don't get all the business; there are about a half billion dollars left. Direct mail offers the small publisher an opportunity to sell the customer without competing with the big publishers. Mail provides equal treatment, something you can't get in the bookshops.

People associate books with their authors; they don't remember the publishers. Therefore, you have as much clout as the big firms. What counts is your mailing piece, not your firm name. Since you have written about an area you know, you are more familiar with the people in it than someone's marketing department. You know who they are and why they might buy. No doubt, a significant portion of your sales will be to a specific category of buyers. You have the advantage.

Some of the big publishers make regular elaborate mailings. But be advised that they are mailing millions of pieces and this lowers their per-unit cost of fancy four-color printing and multiple inserts. Further, the books are usually priced very high and are often part of a series. You will have to be much more conservative.

While direct mail advertising is a way to cut out the middlemen and short cut the retailer, it often benefits them due to the "echo" effect. Some people find it easier or faster to drop by a retailer for the product. Since over 75% of libraries deal with wholesalers, the chances are very good that if you make a library mailing, the orders will come to you through Baker & Taylor. Sometimes, publishers even help the potential customers in this direction and, in effect, give him a choice of purchasing by mail or visiting his bookstore. The brochure might say: "Available at your local Walden Bookstore or direct from the publisher." Some publishers imprint circulars for bookstores to be mailed to the bookstore's mailing list. And there are millions of people who live in the sticks and don't have a bookstore handy who are best reached by mail.

ESTIMATING YOUR DIRECT MAIL ADVERTISING COSTS

Use this budget outline to estimate the cost of your proposed promotion.

OPERATION	COST PER 1.000	TOTAL COST
1. Artwork and Creation		
2. Mailing Lists (Rental)		
3. Printing Brochure		
4. Printing Letter		
5. Printing Business Reply Card		
6. Printing Business Reply Envelope		
7. Printing Outer Envelope		
8. Folding Brochure		
9. Folding Letter		
10. Labeling		
11. Inserting		
12. Tie, Bag, Mail		
13. Postage		
14. Postage First Class		
15. Postage Third Class		
16. Total Cost	$_____	$_____
		TOTAL COST

17. Cost of Product _____
18. Fulfillment, Shipping, Postage Cost _____

19. Total Fulfillment, Product Cost Per Order – Line 17 Plus Line 18	$_____
20. Number of Orders Received	_____
21. Total Cost for Orders Received Line 19 Multiply Line 20	_____
22. Total Mailing Promotion Costs Line 16	_____
22A. Overhead – Salaries, Phone, Rent, Etc.	_____
23. Total Cost for Refunds	_____
24. Total Uncollectables/Selling Price	_____
25. Grand Total Mailing Programs Costs Add Lines 21, 22, 22A, 23, 24	_____
26. Number of Inquiries	_____
27. Per Order or Inquiry Costs Line 25 Divided by Line 20 or 26	$_____
28. Cash Received per Order	_____
29. Total Cash Received Line 20 Times Line 28	_____
30. Total Mailing Program Costs Line 25	_____
31. Net Profit for Mailing Program Subtract Line 30 from Line 29	$_____

Use this budget outline to estimate the cost of your proposed promotion.

One must understand the economics to put direct mail advertising of books into perspective. If you tell enough people about your book, a certain percentage will buy it. The challenge is to tell the right ones. A general interest book advertised to a general consumer audience will usually generate a return of 1.5 to 2 percent. In fact, only ten percent will even remember the mailing piece. That is just 15-20 orders per 1,000 pieces mailed. The cost, on the other hand, may be quite high. It all depends upon the price of the list (the more selective ones cost more), the postage, the type and number of inserts and other expenses.

Due to the nature of the pricing of books, it is generally accepted that the return on a direct mail solicitation must be at least 2.2 times the cost. This means you need good literature, a good list and a high-priced book. Highly specialized lists may cost more but they may bring more results. A lot depends on whether the book is highly specialized or of general interest. Normally it costs more to sell books by mail than it does through a store. While your other advertising might cost you 20% of sales, your direct mail effort may run 50%. However, the resulting sales are at retail, 40% isn't being split with the bookseller. And, of course, mail orders come with cheques enclosed; you don't have to wait 60 or 90 days for your money and expend effort to make the collection. 98% of the responses to a mailing will come in within 13 weeks, so you can total your results at that time. But about half the return will come in the first four weeks. Use this period if you need comparative data sooner. One way to increase your return on a mailing is to promote more than one book but don't confuse the customer with a cluttered brochure. Concentrate on those books in a single interest area. Don't bury the gems in garbage. They may not be able to dig out the books they want.

Mailings often outpull space ads in magazines sent to the same people. The magazines use mailings themselves. Where you have obtained a good response in a magazine through a space ad or a review, it is worth renting their mailing list.

Finally, direct mail advertising is no place to be innovative. The margin for error is slim; you can't afford mistakes. Do what everyone else is doing. Advance into direct mail advertising slowly by exercising the less expensive options and then begin to test the more expensive ones. Don't start right off with a fancy color brochure. The big publishers who do, spread their costs with mailings in the millions.

REPETITION is the key to direct mail. Remailing to the same list anytime after 30 days will result in the same response as the first try. You have to hit people at the right time, when they feel a need for your product. Many marketing people feel that a list should be used four times a year and if it fails to draw 2% each time, it is time to change the list. They say that repetitive mailings have a cumulative effect and the message is strengthened.

If you are committed to marketing your book by direct mail, you'll need a continous program, one that you constantly adjust as needed. When a list works, you expand its use. When it fails, you get rid of it.

It is a good idea to remain flexible by continually testing your mailing piece with small changes. Never make two significant changes at once or you won't know which one is responsible for the change in response.

TIME your mail to arrive on a Tuesday, Wednesday or Thursday. A lot of mail arrives on Mondays and the day after holidays and your piece could be lost in the clutter. Friday's mail is often put aside as the recipient is about to leave for the weekend.

The best times of year, according to some experts, are post-Christmas to January, July and August to September. They say that March to April (income tax time?) and May to June are the worst. Others warn against the summer months when people are away and the mail piles up. Early December is bad because the Post Office is jammed and the potential customer is thinking about Christmas. All must be considered in relation to your specialized subject and audience.

FOREIGN mailing lists are available though, generally, they aren't as sophisticated. According to *Publishers Weekly,* the problems in mailing outside the U.S. aren't any greater, they're simply different. With the decline of the dollar and the increase in both the standard of living and purchasing power in many other countries, the potential for book sales is increasingly good. While French has been considered the diplomatic language of the world, English is the aviation and commercial language. English, in fact, is the second language of more people in the world than any other. In Europe, there is a whole new generation who are fluent in English. Leading European business executives consider English language publications their most essential reading matter right behind their local newspapers. Naturally, books in English should be promoted with brochures in English and prices should be quoted in dollars as it is customary to settle international accounts in U.S. currency.

In Germany, direct mail accounts for 30% of the advertising expenditures. Lists in Switzerland are computerized. In the Netherlands, 32.5% of the advertisers use direct mail. Both Italy and France have Post Office problems but direct mail is growing.

The U.S. Post Office doesn't have a perfect record either. Non-first class mail has been known to go straight to the dump. Certainly, due to its classification, it gets much slower service. If you post just a handful of envelopes in each letterbox, they often get sorted and thrown with the first class mail.

Check the postal regulations for foreign mailings. For example, there is a cheap surface mail printed matter rate and you are allowed to seal the envelope if you use a postage meter, permit imprint or precanceled stamps. If you are mailing just a few hundred, it pays to talk to your postmaster about "precans."

In the book industry, direct mail is the most underused marketing technique. It has great potential and is waiting to be properly exploited.

MAILING LISTS make the difference between success and failure in direct mail marketing. The list must target the appropriate group and be up to date. Posting your offer to the wrong person is a waste you cannot afford; the margin is just too slim. You want quality, not quantity. People get new jobs, move, die, lose interest in certain fads and trends, forget hobbies, etc.

The highest quality list is normally your own. It should pull two to ten times better than any you might rent. The people on your list know you and your product, they look to you as an old friend. To your list of past customers, you will want to add more qualified names. These may come from various directories depending on the subject of your book. Some firms have used contests to generate interest and more names while others have sold merchandise at a loss to attract attention. The common way to add to a list is to rent another one, use it and then add the names of those who respond to your own list.

You may begin assembling your own list by going through your Christmas card list. Include all family, friends and acquaintances. Include anyone who might conceivably purchase your book. Code your labels when they buy from you so you won't waste your time sending them more information on the same book.

Also start your commercial lists: bookstores, libraries, magazines, newspapers, radio and T.V. stations.

Keep your lists for your second book so you'll be prepared when it comes time to send out pre-publication announcements.

Lists must be kept up to date if they are to keep up with our mobile society and remain valid. This means keeping it in mind and continually being alert for address changes and returned mail. Periodically, you will want to make a "list cleaner" mailing by using the Post Office Form 3547 "Address Correction Requested" service or asking people for more information about themselves.

Some publishers just clean out the list every couple of years and start over. Even though a name was well qualified as a former customer, if he hasn't responded again in a couple of years, he probably never will.

Should you address your labels to the individual or the company? This depends upon the product and your approach. The question is whether you want the offer to go to the individual or the person in that particular job. People change jobs quite often these days. The Post Office now likes to have the "attention" part of the address on the second, rather than the last, line. For example:

> Promotion in Motion
> Attn: Irwin Zucker
> 9255 Sunset Blvd.
> West Hollywood, CA 90069

If you mail via First Class, the letter will be forwarded, and if it can't be delivered, it will be returned. The problems are that First Class costs more and you won't get a new address to update your file. Third Class isn't forwarded or returned. If your prospect has moved, the letter is discarded. If, however, you mark the envelopes "Forwarding and return postage guaranteed," you can get First Class service and you will only pay the Third Class rate for those which come back. The economics depend on the size of the list, the weight of the pieces, the quality of the list, etc.

There are several ways to keep your list and the most important consideration is its size. If you have just a handful of highly qualified names, you could use a card file. For a thousand or so, use self adhesive address labels. They come 33 to the page in three columns of eleven. Once typed out, they can be reproduced on many of the plain paper photocopy machines. The Avery #5351 labels, for example, are made for this and reproduce cleaner than some of the other label systems. When typing the list, leave the bottom labels blank so you can add new or changed addresses later. To delete a name, simply remove a label from your master. This will work until the list grows very large making it difficult to find the names to be updated or deleted. About once a year, cut the masters apart and sort them in Zip Code order. Preparing the new list this way will help you to find the duplicates. Some people have more than one address or get mail at work addressed different ways. You might be sending two pieces to "Richard Adams, Zeller Mfg. Co." and "Zeller Mfg. Co., Attn: Richard Adams." Once your list grows to the thousands, you will want to investigate the Scriptomatic cards. They are punch card sized and are easily filed individually like 3 x 5 cards. They have a spirit process window which may be typed and the rest of the card may be used for notes such as past buying history and credit information. While the machines are not cheap, local letter shops may have one and their services are quite reasonable. Again, keep the list in Zip Code order. As your list grows, you will want to Zip your mailings to qualify for better postal rates.

A name is not just a name. Lists compiled from directories are just about worthless. You want "qualified" people. These are people who have purchased products similar to yours by mail. It is possible to get specialized mailing lists for just about every human grouping imaginable. Rental lists are "target" or "related" depending upon whether or not they are composed of people for whom your book was written. Target lists may cost more to rent. There are many unusual categories.

Lists and list brokers can be found in *Direct Marketing* magazine, the Standard Rate and Data Service Directories, Klein's Directory and your local Yellow Pages. See the Appendix.

There are two ways to rent a list. One is to arrange for the list you want, forward your stuffed envelopes with a cheque for the postage and the service to the list owner who then addresses and mails them. They may be shipped at your Post Office or his but in either case, you will receive a receipt showing the number that were sent. The other way to rent a list is get it on pressure sensitive labels, Cheshire labels or even on magnetic tape for automatic processing. These rentals are for one time use only and you are obligated not to add them to your file. Copying lists violates the rental agreement, normal business ethics and is against the law. The list owner guards against second usage by sprinkling it with decoy names. Stealing a name from a list will only dilute the quality of your own house list. You are, however, authorized to add a name to your list once you have qualified it, once it has resulted in an order.

Lists go out of date fast. There is a 25% turnover in the addresses of our gypsy-like population each year and it is even higher with younger people. For this reason, many firms like to leave the list maintenance to the expert so they rent the cleanest list possible for every mailing.

Many names appear on several lists as people have more than one interest. It is wise not to use several lists at one mailing unless they are computerized and the duplicates are automatically pulled. When buying more than one list from a broker, ask that it be culled and arranged in ZipCode order.

You don't have to rent the entire list. Why send to all libraries when you are liable to get a better return from those with a higher book acquisition budget. The cost may run $25 to $35 per thousand depending on how difficult it was to compile and its potential market. Highly qualified lists run higher. Unless the list is very small or you are very sure of it, test it first. This is done by renting just part of it and sending your mailing to every "nth" (e.g. tenth) name. Some lists are old or watered down and you want only the best. A minimum sample should be 1,000 names and remember that you are testing the mailing package as well as the list; they both affect the results. Keep working with the small quantities until you are satisfied that you will get a good return if you use the whole list. If a mailing to a sample group produces a 2% response, statistics show that a mailing to the entire list will result in a 1.4% to 2.6% response. Realizing these probability limits will help you to evaluate a list and make the decision whether to take the big plunge. the big plunge.

A lot of things can go wrong with a test. A list can be non-representative or out of date. Or your book could be bad and the word may have circulated between the test and the big mailing. Keep good records; only with them can you effectively evaluate a mailing. Note all your costs. If a test is inconclusive, run another test. Most tests fail; expect it. When one fails, be thankful you didn't mail to the whole list. Then drop it and don't try it again.

SELL YOUR MAILING LIST. Your list may be worth some $25 per thousand names to list-brokers who will sell it to others. If you maintain your mailing list by noting which book (subject area) the customer purchased, it becomes very selective and quite valuable. These are people who have taken the time to sit down, get out the cheque book and mail away for a book. They are very good prospects for similar offers:

See *Direct Mail Lists Rates and Data* and write to a few of the firms listed who seem to maintain similar lists and ask what they are paying. Generally they want lists of 5,000 names minimum.

THE OFFER OR "ORDER FORM," while it usually comes last in the direct mail package, should be written first as it is the cornerstone around which the rest of the mailing is built. The purpose of your mailing may be to solicit an order or to request some descriptive literature and you must guide the recipient to take the specific action you want.

By preparing the order form first, you will assure coordination of all the parts of the mailing and will keep the copy headed in the same direction. Make the offer simple, clear and easy.

Retain this stub for your records

POSITIVE MONEY-BACK GUARANTEE

I understand that if I am not completely satisfied with *The Self-Publishing Manual*, I may return the undamaged book within 10 days for a complete refund of the purchase price.

You may examine *The Self-Publishing Manual* in your home for 10 days. If within that time you decide for some reason – any reason – that you do not wish to keep the book, simply mail it back to me. Your complete purchase price will be promptly refunded.

for Parachuting Publications
P.O. Box 4232-3, Santa Barbara, CA 93103

Please rush me_____copies of *The Self-Publishing Manual* at $9.95 each (California residents please add 60 cents for sales tax).

We pay the postage if you order from this form today.

I understand that if I am not completely satisfied, I may return the book within 10 days for a full refund.

Name_____

Address_____

City_____ State_____ Zip_____

My age is: ☐ 18-24. ☐ 25-35. ☐ 36-50. ☐ 51-60. ☐ over 60

☐ I hope to publish   ☐ I have published

Make cheque payable to:
PARACHUTING PUBLICATIONS

Total $_____   ☐ Enclosed   ☐ Mastercharge   ☐ VISA/Bank Americard

My card number is [ ][ ][ ][ ][ ][ ][ ][ ][ ][ ][ ][ ][ ][ ]

Expiration date_____   Mastercharge inter bank #_____
(4-digit # above name)

Signature_____

PARACHUTING PUBLICATIONS
P.O. Box 4232-3   Santa Barbara, CA 93103 USA   Telephone: (805) 968-7277

Example of an order form.

Many people don't read the whole brochure, they are sold early in the package and turn straight to the order form. If you have more than one title, print a check-off list. Don't ask the customer to write the title in; he may lose interest. If you use the words "I enclosed $_____ for:" you are making it easy for him. If the order form is printed on colored paper, it will be easier to locate.

Make the order form easily detachable or on a separate card. Note the deadline, shipping costs and sales tax, if any. Always include a money back guarantee, an unconditional one. The form should have enough room for the customer to write in his or her name and address; make this area big so you will be able to read the handwriting. If the form is not "business reply" make sure your name and address appear on the front, back or both. The cost of business reply has increased so much that it probably is no longer worth the expense. Pre-addressed envelopes are also expensive but they are probably worth sending to non-business people. Some advertisers like to call their order form a "trial order card." Refer to it in the text of your letter to remind the customer that it is there.

If you are offering air mail delivery for an additional charge, add a box where the customer may make a check mark. Note that "Book Rate" may take three to four weeks while an air shipment will be three to four days.

Check with your bank about offering Master Charge and VISA. They make buying much easier and will bring in some impulse sales, but they increase your paperwork and cost about $15 to set up plus 3 to 4% of your sales.

Code your address, not only on the order form, but on the other literature in the package. Customers don't always use the coupons and you want to know where the order is coming from.

YOUR LETTERHEAD is you. It is a matter of image since your customers and suppliers never see you in the flesh. A nice design costs little more to print than a poor one and

"If you want a response, you have to ask for it" – John Huenefeld.

129

you want to instill trust and confidence. If you wish to appear successful (and this approach will work for you because you are selling a "get rich quick" book) you might like expensive paper and an engraved letterhead. If you use the same list very often, it is a good idea to change your letterhead and package so that the offer doesn't get stale. You don't want the recipient to take one look, recognize it and toss it out unopened. You can give the impression of color by using ink of one color and paper of another and still pay for only one press run. There are a lot of types of paper and you should look through the catalogues at your print shop. The letterhead to promote a carpentry book might be printed on a wood grain paper and you can even add scent. How about cedar?

THE ENVELOPE is often used to arouse the recipient, inviting him to open it by exciting him with some printing on the outside. This is "teaser" copy.

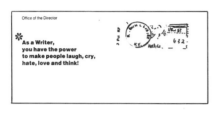

Doesn't this message make you curious?

To get his or her attention, your envelope must stand out from all the rest. Many things affect whether the envelope will be opened, such as color, artwork, size, stock, etc. Ask yourself what your reaction would be to various possibilities. To be cost effective, a minimum print run of 5,000 envelopes is required.

Self-mailers are brochures mailed without envelopes. While less expensive to produce, they usually don't pull as well as offers arriving in envelopes. Self-mailers should have their teaser copy adjacent to the address label.

POSTAGE amounts and forms vary for each class of service and some mailers feel that it affects whether an envelope will be opened or discarded. Some say to use First Class mail and to apply stamps rather than use a postage meter or a postage permit imprint. People like to receive mail, however, and your offer is quite a bit different so you should get good readership no matter how you mail your offer.

If you are going into direct mail advertising in a serious way, investigate "bulk rate"; ask your postmaster for a brochure. Don't use bulk rate, however, whenever time is important.

CIRCULARS are introduced by your cover letter and both pieces work together. Until you get into big mailings with specially designed packages, you may use your regular brochure with a cover letter. In a big mailing, it won't cost any more to print up a specific circular for that mailing and it will bring greater results. Remember that the circular has a photo of the book while the letter does not — and photos sell. Circulars are more likely to be filed for future action whereas letters have a more limited life. So don't send a letter without a circular.

To lay out the circular, start with a blank folded dummy and plot the location of each part of it: the teaser copy, order form, photos, etc. Set it up and then write the copy to fit.

The "AIDA" formula is the oldest and most widely used method of reader motivation. It is designed to lead the recipient to the offer and impel him to take action. "AIDA" stands for: get ATTENTION, arouse INTEREST, stimulate DESIRE, ask for ACTION. It is just as effective today as it has always been.

The circular should have big impelling headlines that give the recipient a chance to see himself in the mailing. He will respond favorably if he identifies subconsciously with the product. Always include a photo of the book so he can see how big and nice it looks. Make the copy easy to read: one thought to a sentence, short words, short paragraphs and don't overdo it. Make the type big and bold and use the layout to lead the reader from start to finish in one logical, flowing sequence. Special emphasis may be given to the more important paragraphs by setting them in italics, bold face or by indenting them. Use subheads. Use all the information necessary and end with an order form. Look over the slick promotions you receive in the mail every day and analyze them.

Most mailings succeed or fail within about ten seconds after they are opened. If they don't catch the recipient's attention in that time, they go into the round file. We are bombarded with hundreds of advertising messages from the mail, billboards, T.V., etc. and we tend to build up a defense toward them.

"Teaser" copy by way of words, photos, etc. is used to suggest a strong and clear relevance to an immediate need. To be effective, the teaser must be directed to the type of people in the specific list. Individuals want to know what the book can do for them, librarians want to know what it can do for their patrons and a bookstore owner wants to know why it will sell (as opposed to why it may be a good book).

The teaser copy may be located on the outside of the envelope or self mailer but it should also be repeated on the inside to help the recipient find the place to start reading and to reassure him that you are going to deliver on your promise. Even if he keeps the contents, he will surely discard the envelope and you don't want to lose the teaser.

Little grabbers can also help. Words like "you" and "new" and "save" and "free" still work. And gimmicks like offering to pay postage "if they order today from this form" invite action, even though it is your policy to ship all retail sales postpaid anyway.

Highlight the important aspects of the book in the rest of the copy. Relate to the reader and use testimonials, which are more objective, if you have them. Keep it brief or the reader will get lost in the copy and give up. He feels his time is valuable so don't insult him by wasting it. Give details on the number of pages, illustrations, chapter titles, etc. Facts, not words, sell books.

If your circular is mixed-up and illogical, what will he think you're capable of doing in a book? Be specific. If yours is a technical manual directed at a select audience, the package doesn't have to be terribly fancy but it should be very detailed.

TESTIMONIALS may be placed in the circular or on a separate sheet. You never know which part of the mailing may catch the eye of the recipient first and these objective endorsements do help. Collect the testimonials from your "happy letters" and use them when writing up your next mailing. Be sure to get permission if you use their full name or enough information so they could be identified.

THE DIRECT MAIL LETTER introduces the circular. It should be interesting and easy to read. As with any personal message, it should be friendly but not insincere or disrespectful. Sincerity is hard to define but insincerity can be spotted instantly. Make sure it is clear and complete by having a friend read it both to himself and aloud. Write as you talk, don't search for big words. The letter may run one to four or even more pages, whatever it takes to make the pitch. Be concise and don't use any more space than necessary. Keep the paragraphs short; five sentences should be the limit. Sentences should be short and simple; ten to twelve words are enough.

Your letter should have a date so it will look like a letter. Use wide margins; the eye is trained to handle narrow newspaper columns. Small margins make a letter look too detailed, too much of a project to read. It is nice to address the recipient such as "Dear Mr. Curtis" but this requires time and some automatic equipment. A "Dear Friend" may

---

"Show how your book solves problems and enhances the stature of the user among his or her contemporaries."

be printed on. Some people like to use a headline to grab attention even though it is much less personal. Important points may be set off from the body of the letter with indented paragraphs, underlining, or italicized type. But don't overdo it or the value becomes diluted. If your audience tends to be older, be sure to use a typewriter with larger pica (10 characters to the inch) type rather than elite with 12 to the inch. If you run the letter in two colors, say black and blue, you may use the blue for your signature and while you're at it, include a personal P.S. Many feel the P.S. is second in importance only to the headline.

If you print on both sides of the letterhead, put "Please turn over" at the bottom. It is surprising how many people never think to turn the paper over. Don't end a sentence at the bottom of a page. Keep the reader "hanging." Carry him over to the next page with some provocative copy.

The "second chance letter" increases sales. It is the one which says: "Don't read this unless you have decided not to order." You get them every day.

Type out your letter and have it reproduced offset at your local jiffy print shop. Don't have it typeset, it won't look like a letter. Don't use a mimeograph, you want quality. Fold the letter printed side out so the recipient doesn't have to open it.

Always include a letter in your direct mail advertising package. There is an old saying: "Let the flyer do the telling and the letter do the selling."

THE GUARANTEE CARD may be separate, part of the brochure or part of the order card but the guarantee itself should be mentioned several times. Some publishers leave their address off the guarantee card to make it more difficult to find (it is on the order card and that was mailed). Some ask for insured Parcel Post which is more expensive than "book rate" and makes the customer go to the Post Office to mail the book back.

A general "satisfaction guaranteed" is fine. Unless your book is worthless, you will experience few returns.

THE ORDER OF INSERTION will be the way you want the recipient to read the material. The most logical way is: cover letter, circular, testimonial sheet, order card and return envelope. And remember, people open envelopes from the back, not the front. In foreign mailings, check the local custom. Do their envelopes close on the top or the side?

If you deal with a mailing house, they will deliver the stuffed and addressed envelopes to the Post Office. They will send you a photocopy of the Post Office receiving form, detailing the quantity delivered, with your bill. Make sure you get copies of both sides of the form. They fill out the front but the Post Office personnel fills out the back. Make sure the numbers are the same.

Whenever you make a large mailing, send a few pieces to yourself in order to time the delivery and to make sure the Post Office has processed them.

Consider a postcard with a photo of you and your book as an inexpensive way to reach prospects. They are not as expensive to print as a full mailing package and they cost less to mail.

In direct mail advertising, you will start out slow and easy at first but it helps to know how the big firms approach this method of selling. They do what they do, the way they do, for a very good reason; it works.

MAGAZINE AND NEWSPAPER ADVERTISING can be broken down into two subgroups: classified and space (display). Unless you are covering a very broad or strictly

> *"It is a good rule to have your name and address on every piece of a mailing package. One piece alone sometimes makes the sale."*

local subject, you probably won't consider newspapers. Their audience is too general and the life of the paper is too short. Most new entrepreneurs start with the cheaper magazine classified and then graduate to space advertising as their business expands and their expertise increases. Space ads cost more but pull better: greater risk, greater potential reward. You get what you pay for. Your problem is that a book is a low-priced item. You have to sell a bunch to make an ad pay.

Bookstores respond to face-to-face approaches by sales people, not ads. Librarians rely on reviews. But space ads can work with proper direction. The last few years have seen a great proliferation of highly specialized magazines which cater to particular groups. The costs are usually lower and the response is ordinarily higher. If your book is on parachuting, you would want a monthly ad in *Parachutist* magazine. If your book is about left-handed people, advertise in their magazine. Since 10-12% of the population are lefties, an ad in any other magazine will be wasted on 88-90% of the readers.

"TIL FORBID" is abbreviated "T.F." and it means you want the ad to run continuously until you tell them to stop. They will bill you upon publication of each edition and may even charge it to your Master Charge or VISA account. Make sure you get your 2% for "cash" (paid in advance) if they bill one of your cards.

TEST YOUR AD in inexpensive publications and compare the response with your total cost. Using the ABC circulation figures and the demographics, consider (but don't rely) what you might get from other similar magazines.

Start with magazines with "short term closing dates," where the lead time between placing your order and its appearance in the magazine is less. In the beginning, you'll want some test numbers as soon as possible. The bigger national magazines may have closing dates three months earlier than their cover date.

If your ad does well in one publication, stick with it. If it bombs, pull it and spend your ad money elsewhere. Don't be overwhelmed by the high price on large ads; they are cheap if they pull in sufficient orders. But don't jump right in. Work your way up to them slowly.

TIME your ads for the best time of year. A how-to book on skiing won't sell well in June. Group your exposures and concentrate on the best periods rather than advertise everywhere. Try a magazine with one ad and wait to check the results. If it is good, try every-other-month. If it still pulls, try monthly. Big ads pull better than small ones and you might do better with a half page in alternate months than a quarter page every month.

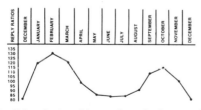

Traditional advertising reply ratios by month.

Time your ads for the prime months unless your book is seasonal. Christmas books should be advertised in October and November editions. Most magazines pre-date their covers; i.e., the March issue may go on the stands early in February. This provides them with more exposure time on the stands. No one wants to buy last month's magazine.

Don't run newspaper ads on any holidays or just before one. Your potential readers will be out of town just like you.

"They all want the same thing – a magic button to push that will make them thinner, more beautiful, richer."

AD FREQUENCY. Some ad people talk of the "number of impressions": they say that you must repeat an ad to make it stick. What they don't say is that their commission is 15% of what they sell you. They want you to advertise as much and as often as possible. Most small publishers will tell you that an ad pulls best the first time out. So if it fails to pay its own way the first time, don't try it again. When the responses taper off, pull out and wait awhile. On the other hand if an ad is working, continue to use it. To quote the master John Caples: "Clients get tired of an ad before the public does." If the ad is pulling well, don't change a thing. One word could make the difference.

ROTATE YOUR ADS between publications. Keep half of them in old magazines where you have been before and half in testing new ones. When one fails to pay its own way, pull out and go elsewhere. Some publishers like to add a new magazine each month while dropping the poorest one no matter how well it has been pulling. Don't just advertise any-where. Some books have wider general interest and, therefore, a greater number of maga-zines in which they might do well.

SELECTING MAGAZINES in which to advertise begins back at the library. Look through the magazine files. In a big city there are hundreds, and this could take days. There are magazines for every possible group and subject. Make a list of the magazine names and addresses. Next, consult any or all of the following references: Standard Rate and Data, Ulrich's and Ayer's. Request them from your reference librarian. They list every magazine by subject along with circulation figures and other information. Send for the Chicago Advertising Agency's *Ad Guide*, listed in the Appendix.

PARACHUTING PUBLICATIONS.
Books By Dan Poynter
POST OFFICE BOX 4232
SANTA BARBARA, CA 93103 USA
Telephone: (805) 968-7277

Date

⌐

L

Your magazine is being considered as an advertising medium for some of our books.

Please forward your media package to include an ABC statement of cir-culation, your readership demographics, a recent sample copy and an advertising rate card.

Our current brochure is enclosed for your inspection. Would you like us to send you review copies of any of our titles?

Please place us on file to be notified of future rate or policy changes.

Sincerely,

Example of a media package request letter.

134

Make up a form letter and mail one off to every magazine which shows potential. Just type it up on your letterhead and photocopy a number of them. It is then a simple matter to fill in the address, date and signature before slipping it into a #10 windowed envelope.

To consider a magazine for your advertising, you not only need prices and circulation information, you want to look over the magazine to decide if it is the place for you, what location is best, and whether you should go for space or classified. Also look for book review sections and, if the magazine is appropriate, send off a review copy.

The circulation figures come in a pink folder marked "Audit Bureau of Circulation" (ABC). Don't confuse the ABC's "circulation" figures with the ad rep's "readership" number. He is talking about "pass on" or the number of people who may see the publication and this number may be estimated to be three or four times higher than the circulation figure. What you want are the actual circulation figures so you may compare the rates in similar magazines.

Also check the ratio of newsstand sales to subscriptions. Those who go to the trouble of purchasing the magazine might read it more thoroughly. They may also be new, fresh names for your mailing list.

The little magazines with small classified sections can be very good and they are often underpriced. The editors probably haven't given much thought to this section lately. They often use larger type and there is less competition in each section.

Advertise first in those magazines where your book reviews pulled well. They wouldn't have reviewed the book it they didn't feel it fit the interests of their readership. Look at the ads in the rest of the magazine and you'll get a good idea of their readership profile. Check the demographics in the media packet.

Be careful of newspapers with circulations below 100,000. Their cost per reader is usually too high. "Free circulation"(throwaway)shopping news type papers don't pull well.

Once you begin to advertise, other publications will respond with ad rate material. These low circulation publications are rarely worth your while.

CLASSIFIED ADS are normally run to generate a mailing list rather than to move a product but there are many exceptions. The experts feel that classifieds must be limited to items with a price of $2 or less. To ask more, they recommend a "display classified" (words and photo, and often in a box but located in the classified section). They reason that it is not possible to describe the product sufficiently in a couple of lines of type to justify the higher amount. Recent inflation may have moved this $2 figure higher to, say, $4 and/or books may be an exception. If your subject is a hot one, people will send even $10 just to get more information.

Many classifieds for expensive items simply offer a brochure with more details or a choice of the product or a brochure. This establishes a very good mailing list almost guaranteeing a higher than average response rate to a direct mail campaign. Interestingly enough, many advertising people feel that classifieds reach different people than space ads so they take out both in the same edition.

It is a good idea to charge something for your "information kit" as some people suffer from "freebee-itis" and will send for anything offered without charge. They waste your time and money while cluttering up your mailing list.

The above discussion is terribly discouraging to someone with a single book to offer but many authors are marketing their books through classified successfully. It takes a lot of sales to justify a 15 word, $75 ad in *Popular Science* and they must be making money or they wouldn't be there more than a couple of months. One secret is placing your book in the best classification. Don't advertise in the "book" section. If it is a hang gliding book, stick it under "aviation." These people are air-minded and want to fly, they would

135

never think to look for a book. But they'll soon find that a book will bring them the information they seek. If you were the consumer, where would you look? You can test your locations by advertising in two different sections in the same edition. Be wary when comparing ads appearing in different issues, however. Traditionally, classifieds pull better in some months than in others.

If your classified isn't pulling as well as it once did, it could be due to the season, a saturated market or competition from other ads near it. Don't hesitate to stop an ad that isn't paying its own way. Advertise only in the best months. Books sell best in February through April because people are confined to their homes by the weather. They are planning the Summer's activities. A few months later they are outdoors and don't have time for books. If the market seems saturated, try running the ad every other month for awhile. If you have competition from other advertisers, see if you can't word a better offer. Repetition seems to work in classifieds, especially in some rural publications. It takes several months to become "established" so that the readers become used to seeing your ad.

Always code your address and then keep accurate records of the response by month. Plot your own chart; it will be a great help in your ad planning next year. Knowing your response to each ad and knowing your costs will help you to determine whether you should continue to advertise in that magazine.

Many ad writers prefer a street address to a P.O. Box. See the discussion in Chapter three.

It is generally agreed that you should use your personal or company name rather than an abbreviation such as initials. People like to know who they are dealing with.

If the magazine makes an error in your ad, don't be afraid to ask for a credit. Make a photocopy of the ad and your ad insertion letter and, depending on the severity of the difference, request a refund, another ad or a partial credit on a new ad. Quite often they are very quick to volunteer a free ad in a future edition.

Some magazines will send you a copy of the issue featuring your ad while others will send "tear sheets" of the page only. Keep them in a filing folder along with all your correspondence to the magazine.

DRAFTING YOUR CLASSIFIED AD. Remember that people respond to classifieds and order by mail for three reasons: convenience (no driving, parking or crowds), novelty (can't find it locally) and price. Since your book probably isn't in the local bookstore and because you aren't giving it away, your best case is novelty. Think about this as you draft your ad. Your message must be brief because you are paying for each word but it must be sufficiently descriptive to encourage the reader to buy. You have to write the winning classified.

In many magazines it costs just a little more for bold face or all caps and you should use these in your first few words. Be specific by offering a recognizable product or a benefit. For example, if your book is on coin collecting, start the ad with "COINS" or "MAKE MONEY collecting coins." Now that you have their attention, develop your concept. Stress uniqueness and personal benefits. Be brief, every word costs, but be complete. Tell the reader what you have and why he should want it. Don't use large, flowery, technical or cute words. Stick to the small words which are easy to grasp; those which are easy to understand. Close with the price and your address. Avoid using verbs, articles and unnecessary adjectives; they cost while adding little. If a word doesn't make a direct point, don't use it, don't waste your money. Remember that eight-word copy will sell better than 800 word copy if you can make a case in eight words. Benson Barrett has used his winner for years without change: *"Make money writing short paragraphs at home."* Seven beautiful, well-chosen words.

If you want the reader to send for more information because you can't make your pitch in a few words, use the word: "details" rather than "free information." Then follow up with a powerful sales letter.

You will pay by the word in some ads and by the line in others. In some you may like to use "ppd" and in others the ad will cost no more and will look bigger if you use "postpaid." If you are paying by the line, you may wish to add some words to fill out the last one. Unused white space is called a "widow." If you abbreviate your address, try it out on your postman first; you want to get every cheque.

Before mailing off the ad, try it out on a friend or relative to make sure it is understandable and interesting.

You can make big money from small classified ads. While you may take in only a few dollars on one ad, you may take in fifty times as much with fifty ads.

SPACE ADVERTISING consists of a regular word and picture message. It gets its name because what you are buying is "space." You may put most anything you want into it.

Space advertising in newspapers and magazines may both sell books and build your mailing list. But it is very expensive and may not be hitting the right audience. Prices for a full page may range from $100 for a local paper to $30,000 in Playboy; in either case you will have to move a lot of books to pay for the ad. While space ads might give the best rate PER EXPOSURE, they don't necessarily provide the best rate PER RESPONSE. The big publishers take out book list announcement ads in publications such as *Publishers Weekly, Choice, ALA Booklist* and *Library Journal* mainly because all this clutter is an industry custom; it's sort of a birth rite. Display ads are often placed only to prove to the author that they are supporting his title. It takes a lot of repetitive advertising like this to generate any response and it may not be cost effective. One industry rule of thumb is that for every 100 exposures, 1% will remember they saw the ad and .01 to .12% will respond. Most won't even notice the ad.

So the big publishers may be placing those big space ads because they are too big to adjust or for other specific reasons. They may be supporting their bookstores trying to direct traffic there, they may be investing to build up a special mailing list or they may be after "door openers" for their salesmen. Whatever, their motives, the chances are slim that the same type of space advertising will work for you.

Space ad size may be sold by the part of a page: ½, ¼, 1/8, 1/16, etc. Or, it may be sold by the "column inch": ½", 1", 2", etc. by one column wide. Often, it is sold by the "line." There are 14 lines to the inch and the width would be that of a column. One inch is often the minimum. Check the width of the columns, by the way. Some magazines run three while others run four to the page.

The size of your ad should be as big as you can justify through past testing. The larger the ad, the more stable you look. Small firms can't afford full page ads.

ADVERTORIALS are large ads made to look like a regular article. *Reader's Digest* always has a couple. The only way to tell they aren't articles is by the word "advertisement" at the top or bottom of the page. They are very effective as many people start reading them without realizing what they are.

Most magazines are printed offset today so they can accept ads pasted up just as your book was. Many will accept your rough copy and will lay out your ad for a small charge. However, you may wish to have it done by your local graphic artist so you'll know what you're getting.

> *"The ad worked because it attracted the right audience . . . because it aroused curiosity and because it offered a reward"* — John Caples.

THE POSITION of your ad in magazines should be on the outside of a right-hand page in the first third of the issue. The bigger the ad you buy, the more leverage you'll have regarding position. It is best to be the only ad on the page and a full page ad insures it. Vertical half pages seem to pull better than horizontal half pages. You can expect 60% of your response within 30 days after the magazine reaches its readers.

In newspapers, your ad should be positioned above the fold, on a right-hand page and in the correct section. Don't run it in the "mail order section." If your book isn't appropriate to the financial page, sports pages, etc., try the TV page, the best read of all. The next best place is the general news section, up front. If you place your ad in the TV section of the Sunday paper, put it toward the back so it will have a longer life. You can figure on 60% of your responses the first week and they drop off fast after that.

MAIL ORDER RATES are offered by most magazines and they may be half the price of the regular rates. Always ask and make sure you get the right rate card; they issue more than one. Just call the space rep listed on the card and ask. Most of them are authorized to make deals, so it never hurts to ask for a better price on the assumption that you are small, just starting out and that if the ad pulls, you will be back for more.

Place the ad through your own advertising agency and deduct the 15% commission. Take 2% for cash if you pay in advance and try to put it on a credit card so it won't be billed until the ad appears. If they extend credit, pay in ten days and take the 2%. Most important: make sure you get the "mail order" rate card and then don't be afraid to haggle with the ad rep. Try asking for your first "trial" ad at the twelve time rate.

REMNANT SPACE occurs when advertisers purchase certain regional areas in a national publication. Picking up the rest on a fill-in basis can result in considerable savings. The magazine has to fill it with something. It never hurts to ask.

BULK BUYERS are people who purchase a large amount of ad space at greater discounts. They use some of it to move their own products and they sell off the rest of the space. You probably won't be dealing with these people for a while.

ANOTHER COUPON may be on the back side of your ad and clipping it will destroy your message. Always specify that your ad is not to "back up" a coupon.

FAVORS FROM EDITORS come to advertisers who ask for them. Try for some editorial coverage by sending in press releases, book review copies, and articles by yourself which reference your book. The smaller the magazine, the more they can wheel and deal.

PREPARING YOUR AD has to be done carefully and properly. You must capture and hold the reader's attention; then you must sell him your book. Read the ads others have used. If they have appeared for several months, they either work or the advertiser has more money than he knows what to do with. This is particularly true of a mail order ad where the results are measurable in a short time. Study the work of other copy writers to get into the ad writing mood.

Consider your audience and aim your ad only at those who will be interested in your book. Don't try to be cute or funny; you want people to take you seriously enough to send you their money.

HEADLINES make ads work. They must stop your prospect as he pages through the magazine, arouse his curiosity and persuade him to start reading the ad. It will be in large bold face type and may be the title of your book. The best headlines give news or appeal to one's self interest. Use provocative words such as "secrets of . . . reveals." The headline must stop the prospect with a believable promise.

SUBHEADS amplify the headline and may run above or below in smaller type. They get more specific but are usually more intriguing and do more selling. They whet the appetite for the text of the ad.

A PHOTOGRAPH of the book is a requirement. Sure, all books look the same but a photo is some proof that the book exists. The reader wants to be assured he isn't buying a few mimeographed sheets. It helps the prospect to focus on something; help him to know what you are selling. Photos cost a little more but they are worth a lot more.

THE BODY COPY is where you tell the major features of the book. Select three or four objective facts and work on them. The body copy should take as long as it is necessary to tell the story. Keep it conversational as if you were leveling with a friend about something that has you enthusiastic. You have to excite him too, so much that he'll want to act. The copy should be clear, simple, direct and logical. Make it personal, appeal to his self interest and tie him to it. Tell a compelling, dramatic but credible story using simple vivid language. Repeat the important points. List the special features and advantages of the book; a list of chapter titles might be the best way.

Overwrite your text and trim it back. Facts are interesting and they sell. Put your best benefit first. If you save it until last, he may never read far enough to see it. Avoid humor; this is a serious sales deal. Use simple words your whole audience can understand. Demonstrate why your book is unique, useful, timely. Don't be afraid to use the proven words: "you," "new," "free" and "save." Some other good ones are: benefit, comfort, economy, effective, lasting, practical, service, thrifty, truth, money, help, discover, proven, guarantee, how-to, safety, love and results.

Victor Schwab used the title of Dale Carnegie's famous book *How To Win Friends And Influence People* as an ad headline. Using the old formula: a failure to success story followed by the promise that the same can happen to the reader, the book caught on. It sold 100,000 copies by mail and generated over $5 million in bookstore sales.

A time limit, at the top of the ad or set off in bold type, will stimulate action.

TESTIMONIALS are the subjective, emotional part of your ad and they come next. Show what people are saying about your book. Of course, it helps to have them from people who are recognized in the field covered by the book. Many copy writers like to put the testimonials in a box to the side of the body copy.

SOME AUTHOR BACKGROUND information will lend a bit of credibility to the book. Concentrate on only those parts of your background that affect the book. Include a photo of yourself and if this is a success type book, you should be at play or if it's about law you should be in court or in a library.

THE GUARANTEE is particularly important in a mail order book ad. Offer a full refund within ten days if not satisfied. Of course, the book must be returned in good resaleable condition. Naturally the customer could read and even photocopy the pages he wants to retain and then return it, but this rarely happens.

THE COUPON is your contract with the purchaser and it must be large enough so that you will be able to read the name and address when filled in. You might like to precede it with a line saying: "At your bookstore or direct from:." It doesn't hurt to have people

---

"If you use a FREE offer, be sure there are no strings attached. Folks get mightly fed up with "free" offers that cost them money."

ask for it in the store. Always code your ad so you know where the order is coming from. You might like to offer an early order bonus or say at least: "We pay the postage when you order from this ad." Normally, you would pay the postage anyway.

COLOR sells better than black and white, some say 70% better. It also costs a lot more. Once you work your way up to full page ads you can start thinking about color. If your black and white ad pulls well, color may attract more readers to it. If your black and white ad bombs, color won't help it.

ADVERTISING REPS have a single motivation: to make money by selling space. Don't let him oversell you. Make a friend of him and make him hustle and he'll bring you the deals.

RADIO AND TELEVISION advertising has great potential in book marketing and the big publishers have tried it sparingly only in the last few years. While everyone seems to agree that T.V. can move books, the expense is so great that it usually isn't recommended unless you have an ad budget totaling $100,000. To succeed, you need the right book and the right approach. There just aren't enough book buyers to support such an inexpensive product.

Small author/publishers should test the medium by trying for a free talk show and measuring the results before venturing any ad money. If the book is regional, you might be successful in a local broadcast.

When buying radio and T.V. time, ask for the "local" rate, it is much lower than the "general" or "national" rate.

CO-OP MAILING is offered by a number of companies which combine your brochure with other related solicitations and mail them to a selected list in a single envelope. The postage savings can be considerable. Each firm operates differently and uses different lists, so you should write to them all and compare their deals.

PIGGYBACK PROMOTION consists of adding information on additional books to your regular promotional work. While not a major part of your promotional effort, this element is worth constant consideration as it leads to bonus sales; it moves more books at little additional cost or effort.

Add brochures and flyers to your outgoing mail. Postage is priced by the even ounce (or half ounce for foreign air mail) so use it to the limit by filling up each envelope. Calibrate your postage scale easily with nine new pennies. Add the pennies and set the scale on one ounce. This is much more accurate than setting an empty scale at zero.

Filling up the monthly statement envelopes may have less value. Some of these people are "slow pay" and it is questionable whether you want to encourage any more of their business. Secondly, the statements go to the business office not to the buyers. So unless you have an office procedures type book, the brochure may never get to the right person. Some accounts are with small firms where one person handles everything; here a stuffer will get to the right one.

Exchanging brochures with other firms works well. This operates on the theory that once you have sold a customer your book, you have nothing more to offer. But you and another small author/publisher with a similar book can pat each other on the back and give each other a hand by each stuffing the other's brochure. It is like exchanging mailing lists except that it is easier and cheaper (no licking, postage or envelopes). When a brochure arrives in a mailing from another publisher, it is an implied endorsement of your book.

Dustbooks (P.O. Box 100-P, Paradise, CA 95969) will pay you $3.40 for each copy of their *International Directory of Little Magazines and Small Presses* which is sold via their piggyback stuffer.

Bookstores are sometimes receptive to stuffing your brochures in their outgoing mail. They'll want their address on the flyers and, if you are printing up thousands for many stores, they may agree to use a rubber stamp. To make a rubber stamp imprint look nice, it must be clean and used firmly, often slowly. So you might offer to do it. When your printer is running your brochures, have him run a batch for you with your address and then opaque out the address and run the rest blank.

Direct mail advertising is the most obvious place to piggyback. You want to be sure the extras don't detract from and dilute the main offer. Many do this by simply including a brief backlist of other books rather than another fancy brochure. If you are offering a lot of books, all in your own line or jointly with other firms, they will get more individual attention if they are offered on separate slips of paper. You can get a #10 envelope, four sheets of paper, a stamp and a label under the one ounce limit, and more if you are going for the two-ounce third class. Be careful, staples and stamps add to the weight, too. But you can get twelve or thirteen 3 5/8 x 8½ slips into the envelope. They provide the recipient with an easy reading/sorting format. He is more likely to look over each offer when it is presented separately than to inspect a page with several offers jumbled together. To get the maximum out of your postage, weigh up several stuffed envelopes at the same time. Ten should be just barely under 10 ounces on the scale, for example. That's cutting it close!

Your brochure and other promotional materials should be stuffed into every package you ship out. Your customers are your best bet for repeat business. The Post Office limits this activity to "incidental announcements" when using Book Rate and this means a few flyers, not heavy catalogues. Again, you might strike a deal with another publisher to stuff each other's brochures.

Dust jackets on hardcover books and the inside covers on paperbacks may also be used for mentioning other books, but they are not as favored a location as the last few pages of the last signature. Printing the inside of paperback covers with ads requires another press run and looks "cheap," terribly commercial. Customers are buying a book, not a magazine. Bookstores won't be too happy if you direct customers to mail order purchases.

Now that you have read *HANG GLIDING*, pick up a copy of *KITING* and learn even more about these aviation sports.

KITING is devoted to tow launching and covers flying, materials, design and construction of towed hang gliders in great detail. Over 100 pages and 150 illustrations.

See your nearest dealer, or send $3.95 to:

Parachuting Publications
P.O. Box 4232-P
Santa Barbara, CA 93103
(Californians add .24¢ sales tax)
202

Use the blank pages in the back of your book to announce other titles.

Blank end papers may also be used to announce your other titles. Book copy and signatures rarely come out even, there are usually a few blank pages at the end. These pages may be put to work rather than wasted. This principle is so common in Germany that the last section of many books looks like a catalogue. When the book is being pasted up, be prepared to add some additional promotional copy to fill up the last signature. This will also add to your mailing list since it will bring in sales from those who have purchased books before, not directly from you, but from bookstores and other indirect outlets. Check the postal regulations about the number of these "incidental announcements of other books" you may include before being excluded from the use of "Book Rate."

"Pass along" approaches work well in large organizations such as libraries and schools, particularly when you aren't sure who you should be contacting or if more than one person is involved in the decision-making process. Just send two or three pieces of the same brochure (consider postage again) and ask the recipient to pass the others on to someone else.

Envelopes can be used for piggybacking by printing ads on the outside. Some firms use their envelopes to promote "hot" forthcoming books with an exciting blurb. Then they use these envelopes for all their mail. When you grow big enough for a postage meter, you can order your message on an imprint slug. Photo stamps may be added to your envelopes and look especially nice on the lower

Photo stamps are a good promotional tool.

left or right face or on the mid-back like a seal. Just take a photograph of your book and have some sheets of photo stamps made. Generally, they are available in two sizes: ¾" x 1" and 1" x 1½" at $3 per sheet. Write Photo Stamp Co., 173-P North 9th Street, Brooklyn, NY 11211.

Remember that the piggyback principle is an "add on" to other promotion only. While it will generate more business from existing customers, it will not bring in new clients. Every time you make a contact with a potential customer, you want to show him everything you have to offer. Chances are, at least one will appeal to him. But remember that stuffers cost money and must not be wasted. Send them only when there is a chance of an order.

CO-OP ADVERTISING is a popular way the big publishers direct sales to bookstores with local space ads. Typically, the publisher pays 75% of the ad cost and the bookstore pays 25%. If the store is a regular advertiser in the local papers, they usually get a slightly better rate. The procedure is to have the store place the ads but the tear sheets and bills go to the publisher. Then the publisher credits the store with 75% of the bill toward book purchases. In other words, you may pay your 75% in books but if they don't sell, the books will be returned so this doesn't make the deal any better. To justify co-op advertising you have to anticipate that the store will move a lot of books. And, while the stores may be the major outlet for the big publisher, it may be a minor one for a small firm which concentrates on mail order sales.

The Federal Trade Commission (FTC) regulations insist that any deal offered to one dealer must be made available to all. A small publisher who tests co-op ads with one store could find himself in great financial difficulty being obligated to advertise for everyone else.

Some wholesalers won't handle a small press book unless the publisher is willing to take out a space ad in their catalogue. This may be little more than a disguised bonus discount and each request must be considered on its own merits. For example, the charge for inclusion may be $250. If they agree to order $5,000 worth of books at 50% and normally you would give 55% for this large quantity, then the $250 can be justified as it is 5% of $5,000. It all works out the same to you. Sometimes these are first-time only charges to get you into the system and to test your book. Also, some offer to give one-line listings to the rest of your books if you will pay for display space for one of them.

Many small firms feel that co-op advertising is just too complicated and too time-consuming and they routinely answer all inquiries in the negative. They save time, money and stay away from the FTC.

AD PARTICIPATION may be worked to benefit both you and another firm with a similar book or product. It allows you greater flexibility while your participant gets a sure bet. You place your own ads and then supply him with a mailing list of those who responded but at a higher per-name price. This is not just another random mailing list. These are people who have sent for a related product lately. For example, if you are routinely offering a hang gliding book in general magazine ads, you are attracting customers from outside the sport and you are selling them on the activity with your book. A list of these prime prospects would be very valuable to a hang glider manufacturer and he should be willing to spend 50¢ a name for them. It is a good deal for him because he doesn't spend time on this part of his advertising program and he pays only for results. It is a good deal for you because it allows you to advertise in more places and to continue with marginal return ads. Some marginal sales are better than no sales.

BE YOUR OWN AD AGENCY and save over 15% on your space ads. Advertising firms make their money through the 15% commission they get on all the space they write for a magazine or newspaper. Normally this applies only to space ads, not to classifieds. And if you place your own ads, you can get even more. For example:

Cost of ad	$100.00
Ad commission (15%)	−15.00
Cash with order (2%)	− 1.70
Total ad cost	$ 83.30

Being a new account, they probably won't extend credit anyway, so simply write up your ad insertion order like the above and take the 2% deduction for cash and enclose your cheque. It is very unlikely that they will reject your terms.

Check to see if the magazine offers Master Charge or VISA. By charging your advertising, you won't be billed until the magazine appears. This can give you use of your money between then and when you placed the ad order.

To establish credit with the magazines, place some continuous running "til forbid" orders. Pay in advance deducting the 15% and the 2%. If they accept Master Charge or VISA, you will be charged each month. After a few months, write the head of the credit department and enclose a financial statement and some credit references. You can pick up forms at your bank. Say you intend to advertise more and ask to be extended "open account status."

As the writer/publisher of your book, you are in a much better position to write ad copy for it than a copy writer who isn't familiar with the product. You will write better and work harder. Remember that ad agencies get 15% of the ad space they sell you; they want "more," not "better." You will be more alert to special deals and package prices than they.

When wearing your other hat as an ad agency, you'll be in a better po-

INSERTION ORDER

A.M. FURMAN ASSOCIATES
527 Madison Avenue
New York City, NY 10022
(212) 421-3707

Example of an advertising insertion order.

sition to promote the author and the publisher. All this "hype" sounds better coming from a more objective, outside source.

To establish your own ad agency, there will be a small investment necessary to give the appearance of a completely separate entity. You will need a different firm name, letterhead, telephone, cheque book, etc., make sure that all are signed by people outside of your publishing company. Many publications such as *The National Enquirer* will not allow commissions to "in house" ad agencies. Some will even spend quite a bit of time trying to match up telephone numbers, signatures, etc.

"PER INQUIRY" ads require no investment and are a good way for you to try out new advertising media. Many smaller newspapers, magazines, radio and T.V. stations will run your ad for a share of the results. The orders are sent to them with the cheques made out to you, thus giving you both a check on the other. Their cut is usually 33% to 50% of the order, about what you would give any retailer. The reason they do this is to fill unused space or time, making blank areas generate some income.

Normally you have to prepare the ad. This means nice "camera ready" artwork for newspapers and magazines or tapes for radio and T.V. A one minute videotape may run $100 and about $25 for each duplicate. Many authors (and other entrepreneurs) prefer to do their own shows to hiring an actor at $50 or more. An author is very much a part of his book and the personal touch can go a long way.

The best approach is to write the station, paper, etc. describing your book and asking if they accept Per Inquiry advertising. They want sure deals so if you have done this before, recite your good track record.

If you have already tested a medium and experienced a good return, it would not be worth your while to offer them a P.I. deal. It is better to pay for your ads and get all the money than to go P.I. and take only part.

Even free advertising is wasted if it fails to generate business; it is a waste of your time and energy. Ads still must be placed properly and carefully.

POINT-OF-PURCHASE SALES AIDS include bookmarks, dumps, posters, etc. Posters can be very useful in specialty shops and booths but there just isn't any room for them in a bookstore. Free bookmarks with advertising are used 30 to 38% of the time by bookstores. Dumps are special shipping cartons/display units which are used by 38 to 40% of the stores depending on the available floor space. Many larger stores suggest and request them. Some clever publishers have designed small dumps with directions for detecting counterfeit bills on the back. This assures premium display space on the counter near the cash register.

CATALOGUES, whether for books or related specialty goods, offer a prime market to publishers. Some catalogues list general interest books, some concentrate on a line of special titles (for example, business and finance) while others may carry a line of merchandise and a section on related books.

Special merchandise catalogues are those featuring a line of merchandise but which devote a page or two to related books. Since you are already in the field (having written about it), you probably know who they are.

For more, go through the ads in related field magazines. After you send for a few, you will find yourself on the mailing lists for most of them.

Also while scanning the magazines, look for book clubs; you'll find that many are operated by the magazines themselves. Contact the buyer.

A brochure may get you into a catalogue sooner. For example, if you have a book on sport parachuting, the mail order parachute supply firms will want to carry it. However, your publication dates rarely coincide with their catalogue deadlines. If you supply them with a brochure which they may insert into all catalogues and outgoing mail and packages, they will be offering your book immediately. Again, of course, they will want their name imprinted on the brochure. This may be used in certain cases as a sneaky sales tool. Sometimes you can't convince a firm to handle your book. But if you take them a bunch of free brochures and convince them to stuff them, the orders will come in. Soon they will become convinced of its sales potential and forced to add it to their line.

YOUR CATALOGUE is probably a long way off. After you've published ten books, you'll need a catalogue just to maintain organization. It is a good reference and a public relations tool. With just a few books, a much cheaper brochure is all you'll need. Few bookstores and other buyers refer to catalogues anymore; it is easier to consult *Books In Print.* They look nice and make you look good but the expense is difficult to justify.

Flyers on individual books will usually out pull a catalogue which is too big and takes too much time to read through. Catalogues are successful for professional associations and where they concentrate on books in a particular field. A list of general interest books just won't be read; it is too much trouble to seek the nuggets.

The big publishers separate their catalogues into two distinct sections: the new titles and the "backlist." The catalogue may be titled "Books for Spring" and will feature all the current offerings up front. Last season's titles which are still available will be in the less prominent backlist in back.

If you want to publish a catalogue but have only a few titles, you might consider carrying related titles from other publishers.

COMMISSION SALESMEN offer to do for the smaller publisher what the sales force does for the larger ones. Their job is to call on bookstores to brief the buyers on new titles, straighten up the stock, take orders and otherwise service the account.

Commission reps get 10% of the amount of the sales to retailers and 5% of the sales to wholesalers and they'll ask for more. The first thing they'll want, though, is a protected territory, an exclusive. Since most bookstore sales are made because of consumer demand in response to outside promotion, the only value in the rep is that he tries to get your book on the shelf. However, he gets his 10% even if he stays home and doesn't visit the store. The rep has many books and too little time in the bookstores. He will push only the sure-fire sellers in order to maintain credibility with the book buyer. All these sales reps really want is an exclusive territory to expand their sources of income. If you want to better understand what a commisssion rep can do for you, visit a bookstore yourself and give it a try. Compared to direct mail, reps are quite a luxury; many publishers don't feel they are worthwhile.

When you get a telephone call from a sales rep, don't be snowed by his offer for "world distribution rights." Tell him you don't give exclusive territories explaining that if you had given an exclusive to someone last week, you couldn't consider his offer. Don't make any deals over the telephone, you are under too much pressure. Always ask for the offer in writing. Then you'll have several days to evaluate it.

If you are still interested in locating commission salespeople, there is a good list in *Literary Market Place* and also check the classified ads in *Publishers Weekly.*

TELEPHONE SELLING may be used to complement your other promotion. It should be used aggressively on both incoming as well as outgoing calls to stimulate business. Time is money and travel takes a lot of time. While the important accounts almost have to be sold in a face-to-face presentation, there are others which may be handled by telephone. And with the telephone, those important accounts may not have to be visited so often. This is particularly important to the small author/publisher who is pushing a single title. Many buyers appreciate a call instead of a visit as it uses less of their valuable time.

Plan your call. What is your objective? What do you plan to accomplish? If you want to make a sale, get organized.

A written script is the best way to start. Write it up the same way you would an ad by starting with the most important point to get their attention. In calls to the trade, emphasize how well the book is selling and invite them to get in on the action. Offer to send a review copy, tell them about your return policy, get it all in there. Say: "Shouldn't I put you down for ten copies at 40%, fully returnable?" Then practice your delivery until it becomes smooth and natural. You don't want to stay on the line longer than necessary to get what you want.

Make a written record of every call incoming and outgoing. Keep a pad near the telephone and write down who, the date and what. Keep these slips on file. Before calling an account, pull their file and review your past contacts. This will make the contact more personal.

Always call the same person. Look them up when making a visit or touring a book show. If you establish your credibility and treat them right on your first book, they'll probably take the second one sight unseen.

Important book reviewers should be contacted by telephone after you send the complimentary copy. A good opening line is "have you received the book?" They are more apt to review books by authors they know and the telephone is an easy way to reach them.

Subsidiary rights, remainder offers, etc., may be negotiated over the telephone but always ask to get their offer in writing. This delay of a few days will provide you with some breathing room to think it over and, perhaps, even to find a better deal.

When customers call to order one title, use this opportunity and *their* telephone money for an add-on; tell them about other related titles which are new and they might want.

Check your telephone directory for the rates for both intrastate and interstate calls. Clip out the charts and stick them on the wall next to the telephone. A 7:30 am call from California is much cheaper than one made a half hour later and it reaches New York at an ideal 10:30 a.m. East coast publishers can use the reverse by calling the west coast after 5 p.m. when the rates drop again.

Many large firms have toll-free 800 numbers. To find whether the company you are calling has one, simply dial: (800) 555-1212 and give the operator the company name and address. There is no charge for the directory assistance call and it never hurts to ask.

Used properly, the telephone can be a great sales tool without greatly increasing the communications bill. It is much cheaper and easier than travel.

IF YOUR BOOK DOESN'T SELL it is probably your fault and due to poor packaging (cover, etc.) or less than outstanding promotion. Don't worry about unsold books. Just let them sit and write another. When you do connect and produce a bestseller, your old books will become rediscovered gold. With a new package and new hype, they will move too.

REMAINDERS are overstock books which are sold off at reduced prices. The big publishers are only interested in books while they are maintaining a certain level of sales. When the demand drops to the point where the books fail to pay for their storage costs,

---

"Good judgement comes from experience, and experience — well, that comes from poor judgement."

out they go. Your situation is different because you are storing the books at home, have a lower overhead, like the prestige of having a current book and can get by on the occasional sales. Initially, each book in your brochure adds to your size. You will have to have a number of titles before you will be interested in dropping any. In fact, since you have the plates, you can always run off another 1,000 copies. There is no reason to go out of print. If it is a good how-to book and you have kept it up-to-date with revisions at each printing, it should continue to sell.

John Huenefeld offers this rule of thumb for determining when to dump a title: Multiply the quantity on hand by the list price. Then divide by 20 to get 5% of the list price value of the stock. Now compare this 5% figure with the net sales for the last 12 months. If the sales were not greater than this 5% figure, it's time to call the truck.

You might be able to move the books more profitably with a sale via your own mailing list at, say, 50% off. Try the big chains, over 65% of them purchase remainder stock.

Remaindering is big business. A lot of big firms are in it; many wholesalers carry remainders and they may account for 1/3 of a bookstore's gross. Some books see their sales pick up once remaindered. The new price and marketing effort has turned books completely around. They have sold out and have gone back on the press.

Notify your wholesalers before remaindering a book and offer to take their stock back. They are needed customers and too valuable to upset and lose. You might start by offering them a special buy on the books for, say, 60 to 70% off.

Lists of remainder dealers may be found in *Publishers Weekly, Literary Market Place* and *American Book Trade Directory,* all at your library. Write to a number of them indicating the quantity, list price, title, hardbound or paperback, condition, location and whether they are prepackaged and if so, in what increments. Enclose a copy of the book and your sales materials. Establish a closing date and announce that you will accept the best offer for any quantity. Shipping is FOB your warehouse, terms are net 30 days and the books are not returnable. Once you have selected the highest bidder, call him and make sure you have a deal. You aren't making enough to ship the books two ways.

Your offers may be between 5 and 10% but don't be surprised at hearing 10¢ each. Since your name is on the book, it is worth your while to get it out to the field and onto peoples' shelves, rather than to throw them in the dumpster. Even at 10¢, they are still "sold." Most remainder dealers will want 1,000 to 5,000 books, minimum, and they want your entire stock so as to have an exclusive. Some will take your slightly damaged stock — those scratched copies returned by bookstores. Hopefully, you won't have to deal in remainders.

CHAPTER TEN

DISTRIBUTION

GETTING YOUR BOOK TO MARKET

Distribution consists of invoicing, inventory storage, packaging and shipping, or "fulfillment." It involves opening the mail, sorting it, typing the invoices, wrapping the books, affixing the shipping label, applying postage to the package, making the trip to the Post Office and maintaining a record of the sale. Inventory management includes stock monitoring so you'll know when to order another printing.

"MAIL ORDER" businesses refer to those which deal with their customers at a distance, without face-to-face selling. The product may not be delivered by the Post Office; a large shipment might go by truck. Mail order is particularly appropriate for the distribution of books. In fact, over half of the business and professional books are shipped directly from the publisher to the final consumer.

The Maxwell Sroge company reports that $779-million worth of books were sold via mail order in 1975. Of course, most were through book clubs but not all. Sroge says the boom largely reflects the growing number of working wives. They find shopping from home more convenient and, with two incomes, they can afford it.

It should be noted that some books are designed to be marketed primarily by mail; the Association of American Publishers calls these "Mail Order Publications." Other books are aimed at other markets but may also have a small portion marketed through mail order. Many bookstores ship books and are, therefore, dealing through mail order. Incidentally if you see a book you like and are willing to order three or more, find the address of the publisher in *Books in Print*. Then simply order direct taking your 40% discount.

Smaller publishers are attracted to mail order selling because it is easier than getting into bookstores. They ship to wholesalers and stores but they don't spend the money on visiting them. In fact, there are many stories about books which have done poorly in the stores which when properly promoted sold well through mail order.

Mail order buyers probably don't frequent bookstores and it is likely they don't even think of themselves as book buyers. They are probably more interested in the subject than in reading. If they go to a store looking for a book on a particular subject and can't find one, they consult the subject index of *Books in Print*. Then, finding a suitable title, they take the information home to do it themselves rather than ask the store to special order it. In a *Publishers Weekly* article on Bantam it was noted that geographically mail orders line up proportionately with population figures. Most orders come from the most populated states, California and New York, not from the states with fewer bookstores. Mail order purchasing is a habit. Many people prefer to buy informational books this way. Once they begin, they buy everything they can find on the subject.

> *"Books on money-making, self-improvement, weight-reduction and recipes are staple mail order sellers."*

Mail order selling offers you the opportunity to run a high volume, worldwide business without a large cash investment. You can easily compete with larger companies. All you need is a better ad or mailing piece. All you see are the sales, you never experience a "turn-down" like a regular salesperson. You deal with friends who keep coming back. The business continues to run even when you take a few days off. You are only limited by the quality of your advertising copy and the amount of money you are willing to invest. Dealing direct with the customer, you eliminate all the middlemen. You can operate an international business out of your mail box. Mail order is probably the best way to get started in book distribution.

THE FEDERAL TRADE COMMISSION (FTC) has some strict new rules for mail order operations. You must ship an order within 30 days unless you have clearly stated another date in your offer. If you cannot ship within the 30 day period, you must inform the customer of the delay, quote a new shipping date and offer to return their money if requested. If you miss the second announced date, you must automatically refund the money to all customers except those who have given explicit instructions to you to keep it. See the FTC pamphlets listed in the Appendix.

Orders should be shipped as soon as possible after receipt and there is no reason why they cannot go out the next day. This involves a trip to the Post Office once each day to pick up the mail and to deliver the wrapped books from orders received the previous day. The sooner the orders are processed, the sooner the money will be deposited; the best incentive for speedy fulfillment.

Customers want their book as soon as possible. A few who are not familiar with mail order will even write two days later looking for their package, but this is rare. When business is slow, Post Office runs may be made every other day, say Monday, Wednesday and Friday. For efficiency, it may even be stretched to once a week. And if you must be away from the business, you will find that only one or two inquiries will be received if you fail to ship up to 30 days. But, remember, the Federal Trade Commission (FTC) says you must send an explanatory postcard if you can't ship within 30 days.

Once your business grows to where you have numerous titles and several employees, you'll require a more elaborate fulfillment system but initially you'll do it all yourself so you can keep it simple. One way is to streamline the workload to avoid any duplication of effort. For example, typing up an invoice and then typing a separate label is a waste of time and money (cost of label, etc.). A number of pieces of information must be recorded to process an order. Through the use of carbon copies, all may be done at the single initial invoice typing. This "one-writing" also avoids transposition errors in figures and addresses.

To enable you to visualize the distribution system, the fulfillment process will be discussed in sequence.

Open the mail and check the contents but do not take the orders and cheques out of their envelopes. Sort them into piles according to whether they are individual retail sales, book dealers (stores or distributors), libraries or special accounts such as associations, sport centers, etc.

INDIVIDUAL ORDERS from retail customers who are sending cash or cheque with their order (CWO) are best handled with a 33-part address label with pressure sensitive adhesive (e.g., Avery Label #5351). Make a carbon copy using carbon paper and ordinary typing or mimeo paper.

Type the date in the first label in the upper left hand corner. Then, going down the column as you pull each order out if its individual envelope, type the customer's name and address. On the last line, type the cheque number, the amount of the cheque without a decimal ($9.95 becomes 995), your code for the book being shipped and any special shipping instructions, if applicable.

A "one-write" system for individual orders.

The label might look like this:

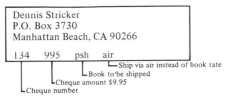

The labels are easy to affix to the shipping bags. The carbon copy is your permanent record for tax and other management (planning) purposes. This system is much faster, simpler and cheaper than using individual invoices for each order.

Cheques rarely bounce, and it isn't worth the record keeping and loss of customer goodwill to delay shipments until the cheque clears the bank. When one is returned, scan the label carbon to find the date it was shipped and to identify the name with the cheque number. Send off a short direct letter requesting the customer to send you another cheque plus bank charges, if any. Enclose a photocopy of the returned cheque and the bank notice that came with it. Perhaps half of these "paper hangers" will make the bad cheque good.

Save the envelopes with their orders. At the end of each month, total up the responses to each address code and record them on a spread sheet (see Chapter seven). Save the envelopes. Then if a book is returned by the Post Office as undeliverable, check the label carbon to determine which month it went out and then go through the envelopes to find the original order. The book may have been sent to the address on the cheque rather than the one on the envelope, numbers may have been transposed, etc. Keep the envelopes for at least six months.

If you have another need for this individual order information (perhaps you are selling the mailing list), make another carbon or photocopy your file copy.

When a retail order arrives without a cheque, make a note of it on the envelope. Then send a brochure with a note requesting money in the correct amount. Occasionally, you'll get a letter back saying that cheque was sent with the original order. But you'll have your note on that envelope. Make a photocopy of it and request that he check to see if you cashed the cheque "he sent." This will make your point.

Small improper payments (high or low) aren't worth haggling over. Just ship the book. When they send too much, ship the book by air; they'll be happy you used their money this way. If not quite enough, it isn't worth trying to collect the difference.

As you grow, you may investigate credit card sales, accepting orders via toll-free (800) telephone numbers, etc. But initially, Postal and regular telephone communication will be sufficient. Remember that you are dealing with a low-priced product. Credit card sales mean more paperwork. Toll-free numbers probably won't increase your business enough to justify their expense.

Occasionally a customer will write complaining that he hasn't received his book. Check back through the label carbons to make sure you received the order, that the book was sent and when. Then write him stating the date it was shipped and that it was sent via slower but cheaper "book rate" which often takes some 30 days in the U.S. and 90 days to foreign addresses. Rarely does the Post Office lose books. Tell him if the book does not arrive in a couple weeks more "to return this letter and you'll ship out another book." When you ship it, write it up on an invoice and note on it that if he receives two books to "refuse delivery" of the second one. This way the Post Office will return it to you with only postage due. If he accepts it, he'll never get around to sending it back and you are out a book. If he has already received a book the chances are very good he'll refuse delivery of a second one.

Refunds should be handled promptly. "The customer is always right" or, at least, he must be treated as though he is. A cheerful, fast refund will let him know he can trust you and there is a good chance he'll be back.

Complaints should be answered promptly. Even if the book has probably arrived by the time you get the complaint, you should answer. The customer will be waiting for it and you must maintain credibility.

DEALER ORDERS from commercial customers and those who must be billed are best handled with a multiple copy, carboned invoice. Initially, when your business is slow and you have to keep stationery investments small, you may use standard invoice forms with your address rubber stamped on them. Next you may wish to order a more attractive imprinted standard invoice form. And finally, you will graduate to your own custom designed invoice.

Invoices should be typed to insure clarity but, unfortunately, most standard invoices are not laid out for typewriter use; they require you to tab and index all over them to insert the necessary information. To be conducive to typewriter usage, all the most often needed information should be on the left hand margin. So a single typing takes care of everything.

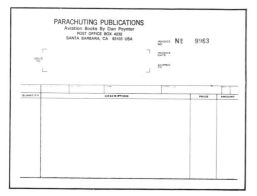

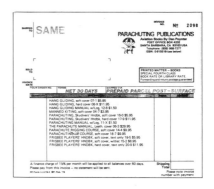

Example of a standard invoice form. It requires a lot of tabbing with the typewriter.

Example of a custom designed invoice form. The common information such as "shipped to." the terms and "shipped via" are light so they may be overtyped if the information is different.

All your commercial mail should focus on an individual. This is more effective than simply addressing a letter to a company. The people in the mail room may misdirect it if you haven't included a specific person in the address.

Don't forget the customer's purchase order (P.O.) number; they want it on all invoices, packages, etc. Make sure you are sending the invoices and packages to the correct addresses; they may be different and they are particularly hard to find on military and government purchase orders. Some purchase orders have three to five different addresses on them.

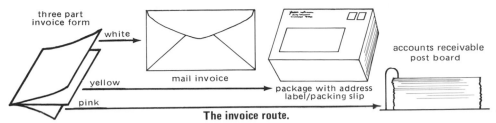

The invoice route.

Send the first (white invoice) copy via first class mail by simply folding and slipping it into a windowed #10 envelope. Include your brochure and other promotional information. The yellow second copy goes to your shipping area and the third (pink record) copy is stapled to the purchase order, hole punched and placed on your accounts receivable post board in invoice number order.

If you have another need for all this information, you may use a four-piece invoice. Occasionally, orders will be received with requests for "four copies of the original invoice." But suppliers often just send one with the thought that if the purchaser really needs more copies, he can use his own photocopy machine. Most customers only require one.

Invoices may be purchased with or without sequenced numbers. Some companies like to add their own invoice numbers and work a code into them. On the other hand, others like the prenumbered forms as typing in numbers only takes valuable time.

When you have only one title and business is new, you won't mind typing out the full name of the book. When you graduate to several titles, you may like to use a code or abbreviation along with a list of all your books. For example, initials for the title might be followed with the suffix of the ISBN, such as "PSH 160." But make certain these codes are uniform and appear everywhere: in your brochures, in the stock room and your ads.

The sales tax will have to be added onto the invoice on those retail sales made within your state. See the discussion in Chapter three. The sales tax is on the merchandise only, not the shipping charges.

The bottom of the invoice may be used for any other pertinent information or even nice personal notes. Most publishers use a common code of abbreviations to cover the most frequent problems: "TOS" (temporarily out of stock), "OP" (out of print), "TOP" (temporarily out of print), "OS" (out of stock), "NOT" (not our title), "NYP" (not yet published), etc. On those titles you can't ship right away, state an estimated shipping date or suggest an alternative title.

COMPLIMENTARY COPIES will be sent to certain reviewers, teachers who wish to inspect them for course texts and subsidiary rights buyers. They should be written up on an invoice and marked "no charge." This not only gives you a record of the freebees, helping you to keep track of the inventory, it is also more formal and lets them know they are receiving something of value. You will have to decide on an individual basis who deserves a complimentary copy and who does not; it is a question of balancing the inexpensive publicity against the ripoff artist. Of course, many of your aquaintances will expect a special "friendship discount" (free) too and here you must draw the line. If they are really your friends, they'll purchase the book. After all, you don't ask them to work free for you. It is common practice to use slightly damaged books in these complimentary shipments. This saves you money as they have little other value to you. See the discussion on book reviews in Chapter seven.

BOOK STORAGE may become quite a problem. If your floor won't support a water bed, don't haul in a ton of books. The people downstairs won't like them any better than the water. The best place is in the garage along with the shipping table. This way, the books may be off-loaded in the driveway and stacked in the garage, wrapped as needed and placed back in the car for the Post Office run. All these operations will be with a minimum of carrying. Hauling them down steep steps into a cellar only to be wrapped and hauled back up gets old very soon and makes no sense at all. This is heavy work.

Store the books all in one place for the best inventory control. If you have them scattered around your place, at the printer's, with friends, etc. some will disappear and you'll never know how many you have. If you don't have a garage or spare room, try renting warehouse space. Mini warehouses are quite common now, check the Yellow Pages.

Tell the printer you want the finished books packed in plastic bags and sealed in cardboard cartons. They'll weigh around 55 lbs. (25kg) per carton making them easier to stack and move. The plastic bags will keep the books clean, dust free and they won't rub on the carton.

Books must be kept in a cool, dry, dust-free place. Dampness may curl the pages, make them stick together and rust wire stitches (staples). It may be wise to stack the cartons on pallets so air can circulate under them. Sunlight will fade and yellow paper. Dust will scratch the covers and dirty the edges. Fire is always a problem and insuring the inventory in a non-commercial (hence non-fire-rated) area may be impossible. Better to invest in a smoke alarm than a sprinkler system which will only damage the books further.

If your books are damaged, slow or fast, you are out of business. They must be protected and this means starting by leaving them in their protective cartons and bags and opening only one carton at a time as needed.

INVENTORY CONTROL is easiest if all the books are stored in one place as they can be checked instantly, visually. The rate of sales may be easily monitored and compared with the time normally required to reprint the title. If you quickly count the books on hand monthly, you'll be able to plot a good sales chart. This is the easiest way to get the information; it is faster than going through the invoices. These figures will be a great help in your planning next year. Reorders must be scheduled so the reprints will arrive just before exhausting the previous supply. Having to report a delay in filling an order costs in paperwork, and time is money. Decisions to reprint will be determined by rate of sale, stock level, seasonal sales expectations (outdoor books sell better in the spring), the time required to print and, in some states, the date of the inventory tax. For example, in California, every commercial operation pays a stiff tax on all stocks held in the state on 1 March. Consequently, no one orders stock in February and most stores run big sales. Nevada doesn't have such a tax and many large retailers have established huge distribution centers in Reno and Las Vegas.

If your state has an inventory tax, you can avoid most of the bite by careful ordering or by having your printing done in another state. Then, keeping an eye on the tax date, have the printer ship in a pallet of books as needed.

As noted above, the books should be bagged, boxed and sealed. Then they may be palletized and banded and shipped to you as a unit. This keeps them from shifting in the cartons which scratches the covers.

New titles may be shipped direct from the printer to your wholesale accounts. If you maintain well documented records, there is no reason to expend the time and money to route them through you.

Dun & Bradstreet reports that 9.5 percent of all business failures are due to excessive inventory. Keep it under control.

THE SHIPPING AREA is where you do the picking, packing and posting. It should be arranged so as to require as little motion as possible; books, bags, cartons, etc. must all be within easy reach. Store hardcover and paperback of the same titles next to each other to make them easier to locate. Position the faster selling books closer to the shipping table.

PACKING involves the placing of the books in a protective wrapper so that your customer receives the clean, unmutilated goods he is paying for. Small wire stitched (stapled) paperbacks may be safely shipped in a heavy kraft envelope; make sure the size is correct. Hard cover and multi-signature paperbacks require a padded bag. Standard padded bags are heavy (postage consideration), dirty and can only be stapled closed. The plastic bubble Mail Lite bag, on the other hand, is clean, light and waterproof when heat sealed. They cost more but you'll save on postage. A standard 6 x 9 hardcover book measures a half inch wider and longer and is a quarter inch thicker than its paperback edition. Both fit the #1 Mail Lite bag when they have less than 200 pages. Mail Lite bags may be stapled closed and they must be stapled for foreign shipments where sealing is prohibited. Get the heavy hand grip type stapler. The bags may also be heat sealed; the sealing machines come in several sizes. Write to Sealed Air Corporation, 19-01-P State Highway 208, Fair Lawn, NJ 07410 for the name of the nearest Mail Lite dealer and for their promotional deal on heat sealers. Your return address and other postal information may be printed on the bags though they require quite a large order; initially you'll use a couple of rubber stamps.

Multiple book orders, up to three books, may be shipped in larger bags. Greater quantities should be boxed. Check the Yellow Pages for a nearby office supply store and purchase standard 6 x 9 cartons of various depths which ordinarily come 25 to the bundle. While there, pick up some plastic bags. It's incredible how much protection they provide to the books in the carton. If you'll standardize all your books, you'll minimize the carton and bag sizes you require. Incidentally, some states do not charge sales tax on shipping supplies, probably to encourage exports. Check on this with your office supply store.

To seal the cartons, the least expensive way is with 3" non-reinforced brown paper tape. The reinforced tape is strong but it's also dirty and hard to cut with inexpensive tape dispensers. The fancy tape machines cost over $100 — quite a shock — so look around for a used one. You'll need ½" reinforced glass strapping tape for large cartons, so you should also use it on the small ones. Don't bother with twine. It takes too long to put on and it falls off. You'll also need some cellophane tape to seal the packing list/label envelope.

The machinery will include tape dispensers, knife, stapler or heat sealer and a 0-50 lbs. scale. Packages heavier than 50 lbs. don't protect their contents well and should not be used.

Single orders may be prepackaged and stacked to wait for a label. Done in front of the T.V. set, the time passes quickly. Don't overlook this opportunity to generate more sales. Always stuff in your brochure and consider inserting them for others. If it is a hang gliding book, gather goodwill by inserting a membership application for the hang gliding association. Or, make a deal with another publisher whereby you stuff his brochures in your book and he stuffs yours in his.

Once the bag is stuffed or the carton is wrapped, it is time to apply the commercial yellow packing list/shipping label. This copy of the invoice is simply folded in half and inserted into a large, pressure sensitive adhesive backed clear envelope and placed on the bag or carton. If any other special insert is required, it should come with the packing slip and be included with it now. Now the person receiving the shipment will have exactly the same information as the person receiving the bill. Occasionally, the one receiving the bill will not want the one receiving the books to know the prices and terms. In this case, simply use scissors to clip off this information. When the "ship to" address is not the same as the invoiced address, cross out the latter and circle the former with a felt tip pen.

Example of a wrapped carton with a different "ship to" address.

Even if you have the shipping bags custom printed, you'll need some rubber stamps for the cartons.

EDUCATIONAL MATERIALS
Special Fourth Class
BOOK RATE
Forwarding and return
postage guaranteed.

AIR MAIL
SPECIAL HANDLING

FIRST CLASS MAIL

PARACHUTING PUBLICATIONS
POST OFFICE BOX 4232
SANTA BARBARA, CA 93103 USA

PRINTED MATTER · BOOKS
Forwarding and return
postage guaranteed

THIRD CLASS MAIL

SHIPPING. Most books are shipped with the Post Office at the special fourth class "Book Rate." To qualify, books must have at least 24 pages of which 22 are printed, contain no advertising and be permanently bound. Book rate is much cheaper than regular Parcel Post and there isn't any zoning. The same rate applies to any destination with a Zip code (all states, territories, possessions, APOs and FPOs). Those packages going to libraries get unbelievably low rates and there is even a special deal for manuscripts though many authors prefer insured air mail for their work.

United Parcel Service (UPS) gives excellent service including daily pickup (for $2 per week) but the prices are only competitive with book rate for nearby deliveries and there is more paperwork involved. By way of comparison, at 1979 rates, a one pound parcel shipped coast to coast would cost the following:

POST OFFICE
    Book rate (surface): 59¢
    Library rate (surface): 17¢
    Parcel post (surface): $2.22
    Priority mail (air): $2.25
UNITED PARCEL SERVICE (estimated due to fuel surcharges)
    Brown label (surface): $1.24
    Blue Label (air): $1.73

| | BOOK RATE | | LIBRARY RATE |
LBS	US	FOREIGN	(US)
1	.59	.59	.17
2	.81	.81	.23
3	1.03	1.25	.29
4	1.25	1.25	.35
5	1.47	1.69	.41
6	1.69	1.69	.47
7	1.91	2.02	.53
8	2.04	2.02	.58
9	2.17	2.52	.63
10	2.30	2.52	.68
			& 5¢/lb.

There is a slightly better special rate for Latin America which you should investigate if you find yourself shipping a lot of orders south.

These are the 1979 rates. Make up a new postal chart when they change.

Make up a postal chart and you will save yourself a lot of repetitive figuring.

chart continued on next page . . .

LBS	BOOK RATE US	FOREIGN	LBS	BOOK RATE US	FOREIGN
11	2.43	3.02	31	5.03	
12	2.56	(11 lb. limit)	32	5.16	50¢/ea.
13	2.69		33	5.29	2 lbs.
14	2.82		34	5.42	
15	2.95		35	5.55	Direct
16	3.08		36	5.68	sacks
17	3.21		37	5.81	of
18	3.34		38	5.94	prints.
19	3.47		39	6.07	
20	3.60		40	6.20	
21	3.73		41	6.33	(see
22	3.86	Direct	42	6.46	postal
23	3.99	sack	43	6.59	manual
24	4.12	of	44	6.72	224.9)
25	4.25	prints	45	6.85	
26	4.38	to	46	6.98	
27	4.51	60 lbs.	47	7.11	
28	4.64	Canada,	48	7.24	
29	4.77	66 lbs.	49	7.37	
30	4.90	rest	50	7.50	

(Over 50 lb. cartons become unmanagable and this is the limit for UPS.)

Obtain both the domestic and international rate booklets from the Post Office and make up postage charts for both the invoicing and wrapping areas.

International parcels of books are limited to 5 kg (11 lbs.). Larger shipments must be broken down to 5 kg increments or wrapped in a large carton weighing over 22 lbs., inserted into a mail sack and shipped as "direct sack of prints." Visit your Post Office for details and some sacks. As long as the carton is plainly marked and it is obvious the contents are books, no customs forms are required. But international shipments must not be sealed. All this means is that once all wrapped up, the paper tape on the two top sides should be slit. Now, technically, the carton isn't "sealed."

POSTAGE METERS are nice but they cost extra time and money. It takes time to have them reloaded at the Post Office, there is no discount on postage and they must be rented from the meter company. The only good reason to have a postage meter is when your firm has grown and you are afraid some employees might be walking off with stamps. You can never stop them from running a few personal letters through the machine but this is better than pinching a couple of one dollar stamps every day.

Weighed and stamped, you can drop the packages off at the loading dock at the rear of the Post Office. Just drop them into a wheeled bin. There is no need to wait in line.

It isn't worth the effort to insure books. The Post Office very rarely loses one and insuring only involves more cost and paperwork.

PROCESSING RETURNS is not the best part of the book business. When a book comes back, make out a receiving slip. This doesn't have to be a fancy form, a note on a scratch pad will do but you will need a written record. Note the date received, the sender and the condition of the books. Determine whether any damage was caused in mailing or before shipping by the condition of the package.

Bookstore shipments almost always arrive damaged because they just won't pack the books correctly. They'll dump them in a carton without a protective plastic bag or cushioning material so the books rattle around and become scuffed and bent. On receipt, the good books should be returned to the shelves and the bad set aside in their box pending settling up with the dealer. Damaged books may be used as review copies, offered to acquaintances as "selected seconds" and donated to institutions.

When an individual retail order is returned by the Post Office marked "undeliverable," check the original order to verify the address. If it is wrong, slip the whole book and bag into another larger bag so the addressee will see what happened and what took so long. If it is correct, put the order and book aside and wait for his anxious letter or call.

Books lost or damaged in the mails should be replaced by the shipper. There won't be many and the cost is small compared to the value of a happy customer.

JOINT REPRESENTATION is the result when a large publisher accepts a smaller one with like titles. Commonly, the big firm takes over all the marketing, distribution and billing functions as well. But the cost can be high, 20% or more of the net sale. Like the commission salesmen, the firm gets credit for all the sales no matter who generates them. Not only does the arrangement cost more than doing it yourself, you never learn the ropes. You become more dependent than ever. Since your efforts are creating the demand, most of the business will come your way with or without the middleman. Unless you simply haven't the time or the will to do your own marketing and fulfillment, joint representation is not a good choice.

MORE ON FULFILLMENT. If you are unable to spend the time picking, packing and posting, lack the necessary space, or would rather concentrate on writing or marketing, there are commercial fulfillment organizations which can do the job. Typically, they may charge 50¢ per order for packaging while you supply the postage and all packing materials. Additionally, they may charge $5 per month per skid of books for storage. Fulfillment firms advertise in the classified in *Publishers Weekly* and a large listing can be found in *Literary Market Place*; consult your library.

As your business grows, you may consider hiring someone to do the shipping, hiring someone to work part time out of their own home or dealing with a self-employed independent contractor. The independent contractor is usually better motivated providing better service and you avoid payroll taxes. Unless you already have other employees, hire a business not an individual for your shipping. Check the Yellow Pages and ask your printer about these independent contractors.

Whichever fulfillment choice you make, continually calculate the cost. As you grow, the figures will change and you may deem it wise to alter your procedure.

APPENDIX
YOUR BOOK'S CALENDAR

One of the biggest pitfalls in small publishing is the lack of sufficient planning, especially the first time around. You don't want to tie up funds by purchasing materials too soon and you don't want to miss out on some important publicity because you missed a filing date.

This checklist will help to keep you on track. Follow this schedule for your first book. On your second, you will want to move some items up while skipping some others.

NOW

1. Send for five copyright forms. See Chapter five.
2. Subscribe to *Writer's Digest*. See the Appendix.
3. Join COSMEP. See the Appendix.
4. Review the Appendix. Send for the books, magazines, brochures and catalogues which interest you. Join those associations which can help you.
5. Order some office supplies such as letterhead stationery and envelopes. See Chapter three and the Appendix.
6. Write to Bowker for ABI information and forms. See Chapter five.

WHILE WRITING YOUR BOOK

1. Review Chapter two.
2. Write the CIP Office for *"Information for Participating Publishers"* and some "Publisher Response" forms. Fill out a form and send it in 30 days before you deliver the manuscript to the printer.
3. Send to Bowker for ISBN information. See Chapter five.

WHEN YOUR MANUSCRIPT IS NEARLY COMPLETE

1. Send Request For Quotations to printers. See Chapter four.
2. Send to Bowker for an ISBN log book sheet. See Chapter five.
3. Design the book covers.
4. Fill out the ABI form. See Chapter five.
5. Send a photocopy of your ABI form to Baker & Taylor Co., Academic Library Services Selection Department, P.O. Box 4500, Somerville, NJ 08876.

WHEN THE MANUSCRIPT IS READY TO BE DELIVERED TO THE PRINTER

1. Set the publication date. It will be at least five months in the future. See Chapter seven.
2. Assign ISBN's, See Chapter five.
3. Prepare a news release. See Chapter seven.
4. Contact book clubs. See Chapter eight.

WHILE THE BOOK IS BEING PRINTED (composition, layout, printing and binding)

1. Write the CIP Office for your CIP data and LCCC number. See Chapter five.
2. Maintain a good proofreading schedule. Don't hold your printer back.
3. Write Contemporary Authors for information. See Chapter five.
4. Prepare mailing lists. See Chapter nine.
5. Order shipping supplies and the rest of your office supplies. See Chapter ten and the Appendix.
6. Send photocopies of the boards to magazines. See "pre-publication reviews" in Chapter seven.
7. Prepare ads for specialty magazines. See Chapter nine.
8. Prepare news release. See Chapter seven.
9. Prepare brochure. See Chapter nine.
10. Send inquiry to reviewers. See Chapter seven.
11. Mail pre-publication offer. See Chapter eight.
12. Print book review slips and order rubber stamp. See Chapter seven.
13. Pursue subsidiary rights. See Chapter eight.
14. Apply for a resale permit and, if applicable, a business license. See Chapter three.
15. Write to Book Publishers of the United States and Canada for an application form. See Chapter five.
16. Write to Publishers' International Directory for an application form. See Chapter five.
17. Write to the International Directory of Little Magazines and Small Presses for an application form. See Chapter five.
18. Order reply postcards. See Chapter seven.
19. Set up storage and shipping areas. See Chapter ten.

WHEN BOOKS ARRIVE (3+ months prior to the official publication date)

1. Make promotional mailing. See "Copyrights, listings and early reviews" in Chapter seven.
2. Photograph book and order prints.
3. Print brochure. See chapter nine.
4. Pursue dealer sales. You want the books to be in the stores when all the promotion hits on the publication date.
5. Draft magazine articles. See Chapter seven.
6. File Copyright. See Chapter five.
7. Pursue book reviews. See "Book reviews" in Chapter seven.
8. Pursue promotional possibilities per Chapter eight.
9. Send copy to CIP Office. See page 70.

PUBLICATION DATE

Ninety percent of your initial promotional effort will be done before your official publication date. Your consumer advertising should be concentrated in the first few weeks after the publication date.

1. Pursue consumer-oriented promotion such as autograph parties, talk shows, author tours, etc. See Chapter seven.
2. Outline your continuing promotional program.

APPENDIX

RESOURCES

BOOKS

Most of the reference books may be found in your local library. In addition, there are many good books on writing, publishing, printing, marketing, distribution, etc. A few are listed here. Check the card file in your library and visit a nearby bookstore. Write to the publishers for latest price and delivery information.

Be advised that the R.R. Bowker Co. is a large firm with numerous functions, products and services. While they have several offices, most of them are at the same New York address. Each office should be treated separately.

Brochures on books of interest to writers and publishers are available from:

The Writer, Inc.
8-P Arlington Street
Boston, MA 02116

R.R. Bowker Co.
P.O. Box 1807-P
Ann Arbor, MI 48106

Writer's Digest Books
9933-P Alliance Road
Cincinnati, OH 45242

REFERENCE BOOKS AND DIRECTORIES

AB Bookman's Yearbook
P.O. Box AB
Clifton, NJ 07015

AD Guide — An Advertiser's Guide to Scholarly Periodicals
American University Press Services
One Park Avenue
NYC, NY 10016
Lists editors of specialized journals.

American Book Trade Directory
R.R. Bowker Co.
P.O. Box 1807
Ann Arbor, MI 48106
Lists booksellers, book clubs, etc

American Library Association
Membership Directory
50 East Huron Street
Chicago, IL 60611
Lists the names and addresses of 31,000 members.

American Library Directory
R.R. Bowker Co.
P.O. Box 1807
Ann Arbor, MI 48106
Lists 30,000 U.S. and Canadian libraries.

American Publishers Directory
K. G. Saur Publishing, Inc.
175 Fifth Avenue
NYC, NY 10010

Ayer Directory of Publications
210 West Washington Square
Philadelphia, PA 19106
Publication circulation, rates, etc

Book Buyers Handbook
American Booksellers Assn.
122 East 42nd St.
NYC, NY 10017

Book Publishers of the United States and Canada
Gale Research Co.
Book Tower
Detroit, MI 48226

Books in Print
R.R. Bowker Co.
P.O. Box 1807
Ann Arbor, MI 48106
Lists all books currently available by title and author. Annual.

Subject Guide to Books in Print.
R.R. Bowker Co.
P.O. Box 1807
Ann Arbor, MI 48106
Lists all books currently available by subject. Annual. Non-fiction.

Subject Guide to Forthcoming Books
R.R. Bowker Co.
P.O. Box 67
Whitinsville, MA 01588
A preview. Bimonthly. Non-fic.

Paperbound Books in Print.
R.R. Bowker Co.
P.O. Box 1807
Ann Arbor, MI 48106
Lists all softcover books currently available by subject, title and author as well as addresses of publishers.

Broadcasting Yearbook
1735 DeSales St. NW
Washington, DC 20036

Contemporary Authors
Gale Research Co.
Book Tower
Detroit, MI 48226
Lists biographical information on authors.

The Dewey Decimal Classification and Relative Index
Forest Press, Inc.
85 Watervliet Avenue
Albany, NY 12206

Direct Marketing Market Place
R. R. Bowker Co.
P.O. Box 1807
Ann Arbor, MI 48106

Directory of College Stores
B. Klein Publications
P.O. Box 8503
Coral Springs, FL 33065

Directory of Mailing List Houses
B. Klein Publications
P.O. Box 8503
Coral Springs, FL 33065

Directory of Private Presses and Letterpress Printers and Publishers
Press of Arden Park
861 Los Molinos Way
Sacramento, CA 95825

Directory of Small Magazine/Press Editors and Publishers
Dustbooks
P.O. Box 100-P
Paradise, CA 95969

Directory of Syndicated Features
Editor and Publisher
575 Lexington Ave.
NYC, NY 10022

Educational Directory
One Park Avenue
NYC, NY 10016

161

Encyclopedia of Associations
Gale Research Co.
Book Tower
Detroit, MI 48226
Lists over 13,000 national
organizations.

Exhibits Directory
Association of American
Publishers
One Park Avenue
NYC, NY 10016
Lists book fairs and exhibits.

The Foundation Directory
Columbia University Press
562 West 113th St.
NYC, NY 10025

The Foundation Grants Index
Columbia University Press
562 West 113th St.
NYC, NY 10025

The Free Stock Photography
Directory
Infosource Business Publications
1600-P Lehigh Parkway East
Allentown, PA 18103

Guide to American Directories
B. Klein Publications
P.O. Box 8503
Coral Springs, FL 33065
When you run out of leads, use
this list of all the other
directories.

Information Market Place
R. R. Bowker Co.
P.O. Box 1807
Ann Arbor, MI 48106

International Books In Print
K. G. Saur Publishing, Inc.
175 Fifth Avenue
NYC, NY 10010

International Book Trade Direc-
tory
R.R. Bowker Co.
P.O. Box 1807
Ann Arbor, MI 48106
Lists 30,000 booksellers in 170
countries which handle U.S.
publications.

International Directory
of Booksellers
K. G. Saur Publishing, Inc.
175 Fifth Avenue
NYC, NY 10010

International Directory of Little
Magazines and Small Presses
P.O. Box 100-P
Paradise, CA 95969
A comprehensive listing of small
publishers.

International Literary Market
Place
R.R. Bowker Co.
P.O. Box 1807
Ann Arbor, MI 48106
Lists publishers, agents, sup-
pliers, etc. in 160 countries
outside the U.S. and Canada.

International Publishers,
Imprints, Agents and Distri-
butors Directory
R. R. Bowker Co.
P.O. Box 1807
Ann Arbor, MI 48106

International Yearbook
Editor and Publisher
575 Lexington Ave.
NYC, NY 10022
Lists newspaper personnel, ad
agencies, etc.

Literary Market Place
R.R. Bowker Co.
P.O. Box 1807
Ann Arbor, MI 48106
Very important. Lists agents,
artists, associations, book clubs,
reviewers, exporters, magazines,
newspapers, news services, radio
& T.V., and many other services.
Annual.

Magazines for Libraries
R.R. Bowker Co.
P.O. Box 1807
Ann Arbor, MI 48106
Lists 6,500 magazines of interest
from over 60,000 available.

Mail Order Business Directory
B. Klein Publications
P.O. Box 8503
Coral Springs, FL 33065
Lists 5,900 mail order and cata-
logue houses.

Market Guide
Editor & Publisher
575 Lexington Ave.
NYC, NY 10022

Media Personnel Directory
Gale Research Co.
Book Tower
Detroit, MI 48226

National Union Catalogue
Library of Congress
(available in your local library)

National Trade and Professional
Associations of the U.S. and
Canada
Columbia Books, Inc.
734 15th St. NW #601
Washington, DC 20005
A directory of organizations.

Publishers Of The United States:
A Directory
R. R. Bowker Co.
P.O. Box 1807
Ann Arbor, MI 48106

Publishers' Trade List Annual
R.R. Bowker Co.
P.O. Box 1807
Ann Arbor, MI 48106
A compilation of publishers'
catalogues.

Small Press Record
Of Books In Print
Dustbooks
P.O. Box 100-P
Paradise, CA 95969

Standard Rate & Data Service
5201 Old Orchard Road
Skokie, IL 60076
A series of directories covering
all types of advertising media
and mailing lists.

Translation And Translators:
An International Directory And
Guide
R. R. Bowker Co.
P.O. Box 1807
Ann Arbor, MI 48106

Ulrich's International Periodi-
cals Directory
R.R. Bowker Co.
P.O. Box 1807
Ann Arbor, MI 48106
61,000 Periodicals listed.

Vinebrook Documents
P.O. Box UP
Bedford, MA 01730
Huenefeld's forms for publisher
planning, control, etc.

World Guide To Libraries
K.G. Saur Publishing, Inc.
175 Fifth Avenue
NYC, NY 10010

Working Press of the Nation
National Research Bureau
424 North Third Street
Burlington, IA 52601
Lists newspapers, magazines,
T.V./radio, feature writers and
internal publications. Includes
(old) Gebbie House Magazine
Directory.

Writer's Handbook
The Writer, Inc.
8 Arlington Street
Boston, MA 02116
Lists over 2,000 places to sell
manuscripts, etc. Annual.

Writer's Market
Writer's Digest
9933 Alliance Road
Cincinnati, OH 45242
Lists over 5,000 paying markets
for writing, etc.

Writer's Digest also publishes
market directories for photographers, artists, song writers
and craft workers.

The Writer's Resource Guide
Writer's Digest Books
9933 Alliance Road
Cincinnati, OH 45242

Writer's Yearbook
Writer's Digest
9933 Alliance Road
Cincinnati, OH 45242
Information on writing, mar-
kets, etc.

BOOKS ON WRITING, PRINTING, PUBLISHING, MARKETING, DISTRIBUTION, ETC.

Publisher addresses may be found in *Books in Print*. Order through your bookstore or from the publisher. Write to the publishers for descriptive brochures.

Allen, Herb. *The Bread Game.* Explains how to get grants.
Allen, L. & D. *Printing with the Hand Press.*
Aronson, Charles. *The Writer Publisher.*
Assoc. Am. Univ. Presses. *One Book/Five Ways.*
Balkin, Richard. *A Writer's Guide to Book Publishing.*
Barnes, J. E. *How to Make Money Writing & Selling Simple Information.*
Bjorkman, David. *Write, Publish & Sell It Yourself.*
Blackey. *Publicizing Your Self-Published Book.*
Bohne, Harold and Van Ierssel, Harry. *Publishing: The Creative Business.*
Bowker. *The Business of Publishing.*
Brown, Steve. *The Writer's Guide to Self-Publishing.*
Burke, Clifford. *Printing It.*
Cain, Michael Scott. *The Co-op Publishing Handbook.*
Caples, John. *Tested Advertising Methods.*
Chesman, Joan & Andrea. *Guide to Women's Publishing.*
Copyright Office. *General Guide to the Copyright Act of 1976.*
Crawford, Tad. *The Writer's Legal Guide.*
D'Aquila, Thomas. *How to Sell Information by Mail Successfully.*
Dessauer, John. *Book Publishing: What It Is, What It Does.*
Dible, Donald M. *How to Write, Publish, and Market Your Own Book.*
Dible, Donald. *Up Your Own Organization.*
Doyle, Thomas F. Jr. *How to Write a Book About Your Specialty.*
Evans, Nancy and Appelbaum, Judith. *How to Get Happily Published.*
Friday, Bill. *Successful Management for 1 to 10 Employee Businesses.*
Gadney, Alan. *Contests, Festivals & Grants.*
Geisler, Ross & Tejeda. *How to Make a Book.*
Goodman, Joseph. *How to Publish, Promote and Sell Your Book.*
Graham, Walter. *Complete Guide to Pasteup.* Book and Learning Systems Division, 401 North Broad
    St., Philadelphia, PA 19108.
Grannis, Chandler B. *What Happens in Book Publishing.*
Greenfield, Howard. *Books: From Writer to Reader.*
Gross, Edmund J. *Penny-Pinching Postal Pointers for Everyone.*
Gross, Edmund J. *101 Ways to Save Money on All Your Printing.*
Gross, Edmund J. *Copy Stimulators.*
Gross, Edmund J. *How to Do Your Own Pasteup for Printing.*
Kingsport Press. *Glossary of Book Manufacturing Terms.*
Hawes, Gene R. *To Advance Knowledge: A Handbook on American University Press Publishing.*

Henderson, Bill. *The Publish-It-Yourself Handbook.*
Hill, M. & Cochran, W. *Into Print.*
Huenefeld, John. *The Huenefeld Guide to Book Publishing.*
Johnston, Donald. *Copyright Handbook.*
Kamoroff, Bernard, CPA. *Small Time Operator.* How to start a small business, keep records and stay out of trouble.
Lee, Marshall. *Bookmaking: The Illustrated Guide to Design and Production.*
McLarn, Jack Clinton. *Writing Part-Time for Fun and Money.*
Melcher, D. & Larrick, N. *Printing and Promotion Handbook.*
Mueller, L.W. *How to Publish Your Own Book.*
Nemeyer, Carol. *Scholarly Reprint Publishing in the United States.*
Nicholas, Ted. *How to Self-Publish and Make It a Best Seller.*
Nicholson, Margaret. *A Practical Style Guide for Authors and Editors.*
O'Brien, William. *How to Make Your Fortune out of Classified Ads.*
O'Brien, Richard. *Publicity. How to Get It.*
Olsen, Udia. *Preparing the Manuscript.*
Owens, Bill. *Publish Your Photo Book.*
Perrin & Ebbit. *Writer's Guide and Index to English.*
Peters, Jean. *The Bookman's Glossary.*
Poynter, Dan. *The Self-Publishing Manual.* How to write, print and sell your own book.
Rice, Stanley. *Book Design: Systematic Aspects.*
Rice, Stanley. *Book Design: Text Format Models.*
Ross, Marilyn & Tom. *The Encyclopedia of Self-Publishing.*
Shaffer, Susan E. *Guide to Book Publishing Courses.*
Sheehan, John G. *The Self-Publishing Boom.*
Sheldon, Harvey. *Publish, Promote & Profit with Your Own Book.*
Shinn, Duane. *How to Publish Your Own Book, Song (etc.).*
Simon, Julian. *How to Start and Operate a Mail Order Business.*
Stern, Al. *Mail Order Dealer's Advertising Rate Manual.*
Stern, Al. *How Mail Order Fortunes Are Made.*
Stone, Bob. *Successful Direct Marketing Methods.*
Stricker, Dennis J. *Write Yourself Rich.* P.O. Box 3730-P, Manhattan Beach, CA 90266.
Strunk, Frank C. *Making Money in a Small Business of Your Own.*
Strunk, W. & White, E.B. *The Elements of Style.*
Tebbel, John. *Opportunities In Publishing Careers.*
Thompson. *How to Be Your Own Publisher and Get Your Book into Print.*
Uhlan, Edward. *The Rogue of Publishers' Row.* Defends vanity publishing.
University of Chicago Press. *A Manual of Style.*
Venolia, Jan. *Write Right! A Desk Drawer Digest of Punctuation, Grammar & Style.*
Watson. *Hand Bookbinding.*
Weber, Olga S. *Literary and Library Prizes.*
Weckesser, Ernest. *Dollars in Your Mailbox.*
West, Celeste and Wheat, Valerie. *The Passionate Perils of Publishing.*
Weiner, Richard. *Syndicated Columnists.*
Wilbur, L. Perry. *How to Write Books That Sell.*
Wilson, Adrain. *The Design of Books.*
Zinsser, William. *On Writing Well, an Informal Guide to Writing Nonfiction.*

And you will want Roget's Thesaurus, Bartlett's Familiar Quotations, a good dictionary and a ZIP Code directory.

MAGAZINES FOR AUTHOR-PUBLISHERS
Write for a sample copy and current subscription rates.

AB Bookman's Weekly	Abraxas Magazine	Advertising Age
P.O. Box AB	2322 Rugby Row	740 Rush Street
Clifton, NJ 07015	Madison, WI 53705	Chicago, IL 60611

Amer. Book Publishing Record
R.R. Bowker Co.
P.O. Box 67
Whitinsville, MA 01588

The American Book Review
P.O. Box 188
New York City, NY 10003

American Bookseller
122 East 42nd Street
New York City, N.Y. 10017

American Libraries
50 East Huron Street
Chicago, IL 60611

Azimuth
P.O. Box 842
Iowa City, IA 52240

Book Production Industry
P.O. Box 429
Westport, CT 06880

Booklist
50 East Huron Street
Chicago, IL 60611

Broadcasting Magazine
1735 DeSales Street NW
Washington, DC 20036

Canadian Author & Bookman
P.O. Box 120
Niagara-On-The-Lake, Ont.
LOS IJO
Canada

Choice
100-P Riverview Cen.
Middletown, CT 06457

The College Store Journal
528 East Lorain Street
Oberlin, OH 44074

Direct Marketing Magazine
Hoke Communications, Inc.
224 Seventh Street
Garden City, NY 11530

Directions Magazine
Baker & Taylor
1515 Broadway
New York City, N.Y. 10036

Editor & Publisher
575 Lexington Avenue,
New York City, NY 10022

Forecast Magazine
Baker & Taylor
1515 Broadway
New York City, NY 10036

Graphic Arts Monthly
666 Fifth Avenue
New York City, NY 10019

The Horn Book Magazine
Park Square Bldg.
31 St. James Street
Boston, MA 02116
Books for children and young
adults.

Incentive Marketing
Hartman Communications, Inc.
633 Third Avenue
New York City, NY 10017

The Independent
156 Pleasant Street
Arlington, MA 02174

Introduction to Mail Order
1008-P Dawn Street
Bakersfield, CA 93307

Kirkus Reviews
200 Park Avenue South
New York City, NY 10003

Learning Today
P O. Box 956
Norman, OK 73070

Library-College Omnibus
P.O. Box 956
Norman, OK 73070

Library Journal
R.R. Bowker Co.
P.O. Box 67
Whitinsville, MA 01588

The Library Scene
88 Needham Street
Newton Highlands, MA 02161

NewsArt
Attn: Harry Smith
5 Beekman Street
New York City, NY 10038

Potentials In Marketing
A Lakewood Pulication
731 Hennepin Avenue
Minneapolis, MN 55403

Printing Impressions
401 North Broad Street
Philadelphia, PA 19108

Public Library Quarterly
Haworth Press
149 Fifth Avenue
New York City, NY 10010

Publishers Weekly
R.R. Bowker Co.
P.O. Box 67
Whitinsville, MA 01588
Western Correspondent:
Patricia Holt
2566 Washington Street #1-P
San Francisco, CA 94115
This is the magazine of the pub-
lishing inductry.

San Francisco Review of Books
1111-P Kearny St.
San Francisco, CA 94133

School Library Journal
R.R. Bowker Co.
P.O. Box 67
Whitinsville, MA 01588

Select Press Review
Bridge Street
Milford, NH 03055

Small Press Review
P.O. Box 100-P
Paradise, CA 95969
Len Fulton's magazine for
authors and small publishers.

Stony Hills
P.O. Box 715
Newburyport, MA 01950

Weekly Record
R.R. Bowker Co.
P.O. Box 67
Whitinsville, MA 01588

West Coast Review of Books
Rapport Publishing Co.
9420-D Activity Road
San Diego, CA 92126

West Coast Writer's Conspiracy
P.O. Box 3041
Seal Beach, CA 90740

The Writer
8 Arlington Street
Boston, MA 02116

Writer's Digest
9933 Alliance Road
Cincinnati, OH 45242
Inspirational reading for writers.

Zip
North American Bldg.
401 North Broad St.
Philadelphia, PA 19108

NEWSLETTERS FOR AUTHORS AND PUBLISHERS
Write for a sample copy and current subscription rates.

BP Express
Butterick Publishing
708-P Third Avenue
NYC, NY 10017

Classified Ad Letter
Joseph A. Zodl
303 Main Street
Little Ferry, NJ 07643

Copley Mail Order Advisor
P.O. Box 405-P
Prudential Centre
Boston, MA 02199

Graphic Communications World
P.O. Box 12000
Lake Park, FL 33403

The Huenefeld Report
P.O. Box UP
Bedford, MA 01730

Jessyca Russell Gaver's Newsletter
6546 Montezuma Road #21
San Diego, CA 92115
Two editions: one for writers
and one for publishers.

JGS Self-Publishing Report
P.O. Box 525-P
Merrifield, VA 22116

Literary Monitor
Attn: Gary Lagier
1070-P Noriega #7
Sunnyvale, CA 94086

LJ-SLJ Hotline
R.R. Bowker Co.
P.O. Box 67
Whitinsville, MA 01588

Memo To Mailers (free)
P.O. Box 1
Linwood, NJ 08221

Output Mode
P.O. Box 1275-P
San Luis Obispo, CA 93406

P.E.N. American Center Newsletter
47 Fifth Avenue
New York City, NY 10003

Self-Publishing for Profit Newsletter
Jim Wildman
3328-P Indian Mesa Drive
Thousand Oaks, CA 91360

Selling To Libraries
50-P East Huron Street
Chicago, IL 60611

Success in Self-Publishing
P.O. Box 12201-P
El Cajon, CA 92022

Towers Club USA Newsletter
Jerry Buchanan
P.O. Box 2038-P
Vancouver, WA 98668

Up-To-Date On The Arts
And Humanities (free)
Congressman Fred Richmond
House Of Representatives
Washington, DC 20515

Writer's Newsletter
110 Morgan Hall
Indiana University
Bloomington, IN 47401

PAMPHLETS OF INTEREST TO AUTHORS AND PUBLISHERS

Federal Trade Commission
Washington, DC 20580
1. Shopping By Mail? You're
   Protected!
2. FTC Buyer's Guide No. 2
3. Consumer Alert — The Vanity
   Press News release dated 19
   July 1959
4. Vanity Press Findings.
   Dockets 7005 and 7489

Popular Mechanics
224 West 57th Street
New York City, NY 10019
1. Profits from Classified Ads.
   $1.00

Superintendent of Documents
U.S. Government Printing
Office
Washington, DC 20402
1. Domestic Mail Manual,
   $17.00
2. Postal Bulletin
3. International Mail
4. U.S. Government Purchasing
   and Sales Directory, $4.00
5. Selling to the Military, $1.80

P.E.N. American Center
47 Fifth Avenue
New York City, NY 10003
1. Grants and Awards Available
   to American Writers. $2.25

Literature Program
Nat'l Endowment for the Arts
2401 E Street NW
Washington, DC 20506
1. Assistance, fellowships and
   residencies for writers.

Poets & Writers, Inc.
201 West 54th Street
New York City, NY 10019
1. Awards List. $2.50
2. The Sponsors List. $2.50
3. Literary Agents: A Complete
   Guide. $2.50

Departments of the Army and
Air Force
Hqs. Army and Air Force Exchange Service
Dallas, TX 75222
1. Contract Terms and Condi-
   tions (AAFES Form 4200-
   13/19)

Bank of America
Small Business Reporter, "Mail
Order Enterprises."
P.O. Box 37000, Dept. 3120,
San Francisco, CA 94137
$1.00

Chicago Advertising Agency
Ad Guide
28 East Jackson Blvd.
Chicago, IL 60604
$1.00

The Copyright Office
Office of Public Affairs
Library of Congress
Washington, DC 20559
1. General Guide to the
   Copyright Act of 1976

Writer's Digest Books
9933-P Alliance Road
Cincinnati, OH 45242
1. Getting Started in
   Writing
2. Jobs & Opportunities
   For Writers

PROFESSIONAL ORGANIZATIONS

Write for an application and inquire about benefits and dues. Many associations publish a magazine or newsletter.

American Booksellers Association
122 East 42nd Street
New York City, NY 10017

American Library Association
50 East Huron Street
Chicago, IL 60611

The Association of American
Publishers, Inc.
One Park Avenue
New York City, NY 10016

The Association of American
University Presses
One Park Avenue
New York City NY 10016

The Authors Guild
234 West 44th Street
New York City, NY 10036

Aviation&Space Writers Association
Cliffwood Road
Chester, NJ 07930

Book Publicists Of Southern
California
9255 Sunset Blvd. #625-P
West Hollywood, CA 90069

Bookbuilders of Southern
California
5225 Wilshire Blvd. #316-P
Los Angeles, CA 90036

Bookbuilders West
9-P First St.
San Francisco, CA 94105

Children's Book Council
64 University Place
NYC, NY 10003

The Christian Booksellers Assn.
P.O. Box 200
Colorado Springs, Co 80901

COSMEP (Committee of Small
Magazine Editors and Publishers)
P.O. Box 703-P
San Francisco, CA 94101
This is the international association of independent publishers

COSMEP East
255-P Humphrey Street
Marblehead, MA 01945

COSMEP South
P.O. Box 19332-P
Washington, DC 20036

International Book Printers Assn.
1730 North Lynn Street
Arlington VA 22209

The National Assn. of College
Stores
528 East Lorain Street
Oberlin, OH 44074

The National Writers Club
1450 South Havana # 620-P
Aurora, CO 80012

New England Small Press Assn.
45-P Hillcrest Place
Amherst, MA 01002

P.E.N.
156 Fifth Avenue
New York City, NY 10010

Poets & Writers, Inc.
201 West 54th Street
New York City, NY 10019

Progressive Booksellers Assn.
1896-P North High St.
Columbus, OH 43201

Special Libraries Assn.
235 Park Avenue South
NYC, NY 10003

Western Book Publishers Assn.
P.O. Box 558-P
Corte Madera, CA 94925

Women Writers West
2067-P Linda Flora Drive
Los Angeles, CA 90024

The Woman's Salon
Attn: Sallie Finch Reynolds
24 Bay Avenue
Sea Cliff, NY 11579

The Word Guild
119 North Auburn Street
Cambridge, MA 02138

For a list of writers' associations,
see *Writer's Market*.

BOOK WHOLESALERS

For a complete list, see the *American Book Trade Directory* and *Literary Market Place* available in your local library.

The Baker & Taylor Co.
Attn: Maureen Gordon
6 Kirby Avenue
Somerville, NJ 08876

Ballen Booksellers Int'l.
66 Austin Blvd.
Commack, NY 11725

Banner World Distributors
13415 Ventura Blvd.
Sherman Oaks, CA 91423

Blackwell North America
10300 S.W. Allen Blvd.
Beaverton, OR 97005

Bookazine Co.
Attn: William Epstein
303 West 10th Street
New York City, NY 10017

The Book Bus
Visual Studies Workshop
31-P Prince Street
Rochester, NY 14607

Bookpeople, Inc.
Attn: Davide Atchoux
2940 Seventh Street
Berkeley, CA 94710

Bro-Dart, Inc.
1690 Memorial Avenue
Williamsport, PA 17701

Carrier Pigeon
75 Kneeland St. #309-P
Boston, MA 02111

"There are many objects of great value to man which cannot be attained by unconnected individuals, but must be attained if at all, by association." — Daniel Webster.

Coutts Library Service
736-738 Cayuga Street
Lewiston, NY 14092

Dimondstein Book Co.
Attn: Sandy Dreiser
38 Portman Road
New Rochelle, NY 10801

The Distributors
702 South Michigan
South Bend, IN 46601

Eastern Book Co.
131 Middle Street
Portland, ME 04112

Emery-Pratt Co.
1966 West Main Street
Owosso, MI 48867

Ingram Book Co.
Attn: Susanna DePalma
347 Reedwood Drive
Nashville, TN 37217

International Service Co.
333 Fourth Ave.
Indialantic, FL 32903

Key Book Service
425 Asylum Street
Bridgeport, CT 06610

Pacific Pipeline
P.O. Box 3711-P
Seattle, WA 98124

Publishers Group/West
Attn: Charlie Winton
5855-P Beaudry St.
Emeryville, CA 94608

Small Press Book Service
Bridge Street
Milford, NH 03055

The Touchstone Press
Attn: Oral Bullard
P.O. Box 81-P
Beaverton, OR 97005

United Book Service
1310 San Fernando Road
Los Angeles, CA 90065

CHAIN BOOKSTORES

For a complete list, see *Literary Market Place* and *The American Book Trade Directory* in your local public library. Direct your letter to the "small press buyer" or the "paperback buyer."

B. Dalton/Pickwick
Attn: Jerry Rogart, Small Press Buyer
9340 James Avenue
Minneapolis, MN 55431

Walden Book Co.
Attn: Tom Paynter
201 High Ridge Rd.
Stamford, CT 06904

U.S. GOVERNMENT PROCUREMENT OFFICES.

See the "Selling to the Government" discussion in Chapter eight.

The Adjutant General, Department of the Army
Attn: DAAG-REL
Washington, DC 20314

Acquisitions Librarian
Chief of Naval Education and Training Support
General Library Services Branch
N32
Pensacola, FL 32509

Acquisitions Librarian
Air Force Libraries Section
AFPMPPB-3
USAF Military Personal Center
Randolph Air Force Base,
TX 78148

Veteran's Administration Library
810 Vermont Ave., NW
Room 976
Washington, DC 20420

International Communications Agency
Attn: Acquisitions Librarian
1750 Pennsylvania Avenue
Washington, DC 20547
or: Paul Steere
ECA/FL
International Communications Agency
1717 H Street #756
Washington, DC 20006

Army and Air Force Exchange
Procurement Office
Attn: Acquisitions Librarian
The Pentagon, Room 5E479
Washington, DC 20310

Co. Comm., Navy Resale Systems
Office
Third & 29th Streets
Brooklyn, NY 11232

U.S. Coast Guard
Code G, FER-1/72
Washington, DC 20590

U.S. Marine Corps
Headquarters. Marine Corps
LFE
Washington, DC 20380

For the addresses of other government offices, call the local office of your congressperson. Look up the name in your telephone directory.

EXPORTERS

For a complete list, see *Literary Market Place* in your local public library. See the discussion of international markets in Chapter eight.

ADCO Int'l Co.
80-00 Cooper Ave #3
Glendale, NY 11227

Kaiman & Polon Inc.
456 Sylvan Avenue
Englewood Cliffs, NJ 07632

Worldwide Media Service, Inc.
386 Park Avenue South
New York City, NY 10016

Feffer & Simon, Inc.
100 Park Avenue
New York City, NY 10016

REVIEWERS

For a complete list of book reviewers and book review syndicates, see *Literary Market Place* in your local public library. The "Media" section in *Publishers Weekly* lists a couple of new reviewers almost every week. Also see the discussion and listings in Chapter seven. Here are just a few.

American Library Assn.
Attn: Carol Felsenthal
50 East Huron Street
Chicago, IL 60611

Best-In-Books
Attn: Forest Wallace Cato
205 Moonshadow Court
Roswell, GA 30075

George A. Crago
300 North 70th Street
Harrisburg, PA 17111

The DeKalb Book Review
Community Services Office
College Of Continuing Education
Northern Illinois University
DeKalb, IL 60115

Jan Frazer
P.O. Box 368-P
Naples, FL 33939

Burton Frye
P.O. Box 2505
Myrtle Beach, SC 29577

The Independent
156 Pleasant Street
Arlington, MA 02174

Los Angeles Times
Attn: Art Seidenbaum
Book Review Editor
Times Mirror Square
Los Angeles, CA 90053

The Madison Review Of Books
1121 University Avenue
Madison, WI 53715

New York Post
Attn: Harriet Van Horne
11 East 68th Street
New York City, NY 10021

Albert F. Nussbaum
P.O. Box 546-P
Los Angeles, CA 90028

Patrician Productions
WGCH
250 West 57th Street
NYC, NY 10019

San Francisco Examiner
Attn: Mickey Friedman
Scene Department
P.O. Box 31000
San Francisco, CA 94119

Washington Post
Attn: Brigitte Weeks
Book Review Editor
1150 15th Street NW
Washington, DC 20005

WIM Publications
P.O. Box 5037
Inglewood, CA 90310

GRAPHICS AND PRINTING SUPPLIES

A.H. Gaebel, Inc.
P.O. Box 5-P
East Syracuse, NY 13057
Catalogue

Forward Graphics
7031-P University Avenue
Des Moines, IA 50311
Clip Art

Graphics Master
Dean Lem Associates
P.O. Box 46086
Los Angeles, CA 90046
Graphics kit

Hartco Products Co.
226 West Pearl Street
West Jefferson, OH 43162
Graphic supplies catalogue

Letraset USA
40 Eisenhower Place
Paramus, NJ 07652
Press type

Midwest Publishers Supply Co.
4640 North Olcott Avenue
Chicago, IL 60656
Catalogue

The Printers Shopper
111-P Press Lane
Chula Vista, CA 92010
Clip art and supplies.

Volk Corporation
1401 North Main Street
Pleasantville, NJ 08232
Clip art.

Zipatone, Inc.
150 Fencl Lane
Hillside, IL 60162
Press type

BOOK PRINTERS

Here are a few of the printers who specialize in books. For more, see the advertisements in *Writer's Digest* Magazine.

Adams Press
30 West Washington St.
Chicago, IL 60602

Arcata Book Group
P.O. Box 191-P
Kingsport, TN 37662

Automation Printing
P.O. Box 12201-P
El Cajon, CA 92022

George Banta Co.
Menasha, WI 54952

Braun-Brumfield
100-P North Staebler Rd.
Ann Arbor, MI 48106

Bookcrafters, Inc.
P.O. Box 892
Fredricksburg, VA 22401

California Syllabus
1494-P MacArthur Blvd.
Oakland, CA 94602

Champion Printing Co.
P.O. Box 148-P
Ross, OH 45061

Delta Lithograph Co.
14731-P Califa St.
Van Nuys, CA 91401

R.R. Donnelly & Sons
2223 Martin Luther King Dr.
Chicago, IL 60616

Edwards Bros, Inc.
2500 South State Street.
Ann Arbor, MI 48104

Harlo Press
16721 Hamilton Ave.
Detroit, MI 48203

Lithocrafters, Inc.
P.O. Box 370
Chelsea, MI 48118

Lorell Press
Attn: Merrill Rosenberg
Industrial Park
Avon, MA 02322

Maverick Publications
P.O. Box 243-P
Bend, OR 97701

Mosaic Press (Miniature Books)
358-P Oliver Rd.
Cincinnati, OH 45215

McNaughton & Gunn, Inc.
P.O. Box M-2060-P
Ann Arbor, MI 48106

Triton Press
13850 Big Basin Way
Boulder Creek, CA 95006

OFFICE SUPPLIES

To obtain the business forms described in this book, order from the following firms:

The Drawing Board
P.O. Box 505
Dallas, TX 75221
Memo letters ML 5-N72

Grayarc
822 Third Avenue
Brooklyn, NY 11232
Invoices and clear packing slip
envelopes.

Business Envelope Manufacturers
900 Grand Blvd.
Deer Park, NY 11729
Envelopes.

MAILING LISTS

For mailing list brokers and mailing services, see the Yellow Pages of your local telephone directory. Brokers may also be found listed in *Direct Marketing* Magazine and *Literary Market Place*. See the discussion in Chapter nine.

R.R. Bowker Co.
Attn: Sal Vicidomini
1180 Avenue of the Americas
New York City, NY 10036
Bookstores, libraries, etc.
broken down many ways.

Service
P.O. Box 29214-P, Presidio
San Francisco, CA 94129
The COSMEP list of bookstores
and libraries.

Market Data Retrieval
Ketchem Place
Westport, CT 06880
Lists of elementary and high
school teachers, broken down
many ways.

Curriculum Information Center
Ross Bldg.
1726 Champa Street
Denver, CO 80202
Elementary and high school
teachers broken down many
ways.

College Marketing Group
6 Winchester Terrace
Winchester, MA 01890
College faculty broken down
many ways.

The Educational Directory
One Park Avenue
New York City, NY 10016
College faculty broken down
many ways.

American Library Assn.
50 East Huron Street
Chicago, IL 60611
Libraries and booksellers.

Hugo Dunhill Mailing Lists
630 Third Avenue
New York City, NY 10017

Ed Burnett Consultants
2 Park Avenue
New York City, NY 10016

If you don't mind hand addressing, go to your library and look up Bowker's *American Library Directory* which lists libraries and the *American Book Trade Directory* which lists bookstores.

For lists outside the book field, consult *Direct Mail Lists Rates and Data,* published by Standard Rate and Data Service available in your library. Another source is Bulletin No. 29 published and available from the Small Business Administration.

BOOK FAIR EXHIBITING SERVICES

If you can't attend the fair yourself, you might like to hire an exhibiting service to represent you. For a complete list, consult *Literary Market Place*. See the discussion in Chapter nine.

Books On Exhibit
North Bedford Road
Mount Kisko, NY 10549

College Marketing Group
6 Winchester Terrace
Winchester, MA 01890

The Combined Book Exhibit
12 Saw Mill Road
Hawthorne, NY 10532

The Conference Book Service
P.O. Box 298
Alexandria, VA 22314

COSMEP Exhibit Service
P.O. Box 703-P
San Francisco, CA 94101

EBSCO Subscription Services
P.O. Box 1943
Birmingham, AL 35201

Independent Publishers
Services
431 Belvedere St.
San Francisco, CA 94117

New England Small Press Assn.
Traveling Exhibit
45-P Hillcrest Place
Amherst, MA 01002

Publishers' Exposition Displays
235 Park Avenue South
New York City, NY 10003

COURSES, CONFERENCES AND SEMINARS

There are many educational programs of interest to authors and publishers. For conferences, see the list published in *Writer's Market*. Many courses are listed in the Calendar section of *Publishers Weekly* and *The Guide to Book Publishing Courses* by Susan Shaffer. Write to the addresses listed below for brochures.

Copy Concepts
Marilyn & Tom Ross
P.O. Box 9512-P
San Diego, CA 92109

Du Vall Seminars
920-P West Grand River
Williamston, MI 48895

Huenefeld Seminars
P.O. Box UP
Bedford, MA 01730

Lachlan P. MacDonald
P.O. Box 1275-P
San Luis Obispo, CA 93406

School of Graphic Art Pasteup
Walter B. Graham
1612-P California Street
Omaha, NE 68102
Workshop and home study
course.

Self-Publishing for Profit
Seminar/Workshop
Jim Wildman & Dennis Stricker
P.O. Box 4154-P
Westlake Village, CA 91359

Stanford Conference on Book
Publishing
Stanford Alumni Assn.
Bowman Alumni House
Stanford, CA 94305

CO-OP PUBLISHING HOUSES

See the discussion in Chapter one.

Alice James Books
138 Mt. Auburn Street
Cambridge, MA 02138

Assembling Press
Box 1967
Brooklyn, NY 11202

Berkeley Poets' Cooperative
P.O. Box 459
Berkeley, California 94701

Capra Press
631 State St.
Santa Barbara, CA 93101

Fiction Collective
English Dept.
Brooklyn College
Brooklyn, NY 11210

Inwood Press Collective
128 Post Ave.
New York City, NY 10034

Minnesota Writers' Cooperative
P.O. Box 211
Bloomington, IN 47401

US-1 Poets Cooperative
21 Lake Drive
Roosevelt, NJ 08555

INDEX

Also consult the Table of Contents.

Also consult the Table of Contents.

AFTERWORD

This manual is the result of many years in the publishing, marketing and mail order businesses. It is as thorough and complete as I know how to make it. Every attempt has been made to cover every possible aspect of writing, publishing and marketing your own books: self-publishing.

"We learn by doing" and your first book will be your hardest. "We learn by our mistakes" and, hopefully, through the use of this book yours will be small ones. I hope you will learn the entire business by doing everything yourself before you begin to "farm out" some of the work. It will provide you with a better understanding of publishing. I hope it introduces and guides you to a richer, more rewarding life.

The first step, the next one, is up to you. I hope you'll take it. As you write, publish and market, refer to this manual. As you learn the business, make notes in it. Let me know where it may be improved. When you do get that first book into print, please send me a copy — autographed, of course.

Dan Poynter

The revised, third edition of *The Self-Publishing Manual* is due off the press in 1980. By ordering now, you will receive it as soon as it becomes available.

☐ I want to be notified as soon as the book is ready.

☐ I want the book as soon as possible. Here is $9.95 ($10.55 in California) for a postpaid copy.

☐ Please add my name to the Self-Publishing Grapevine by circulating my address to people in publishing.

Name of firm:_____

Contact person: _____

Address: _____

_____ZIP:_____

Send to:
Parachuting Publications
Attn: Dan Poynter
P.O. Box 4232-P
Santa Barbara, CA 93103 USA